REXFORD G. TUGWELL

REXFORD G. TUGWELL

A BIOGRAPHY

Michael V. Namorato

New York
Westport, Connecticut
London

Library of Congress Cataloging-in-Publication Data

Namorato, Michael V.
 Rexford G. Tugwell: a biography / Michael V. Namorato.
  p. cm.
 Bibliography: p.
 Includes index.
 ISBN 0-275-92961-2 (alk. paper)
 1. Tugwell, Rexford G. (Rexford Guy) 1891-   . 2. Economists—
United States—Biography. 3. Political scientists—United States—
Biography. I. Title.
HB119.T83N35   1988
330'.092'4—dc19
[B]   88-2397

Library of Congress Catalog Card Number: 88-2397

ISBN: 0-275-92961-2

First published in 1988

Praeger Publishers, One Madison Avenue, New York, NY 10010
A division of Greenwood Press, Inc.

Printed in the United States of America

The paper used in this book complies with the
Permanent Paper Standard issued by the National
Information Standards Organization (Z39.48-1984).

10 9 8 7 6 5 4 3 2 1

To
Mom and Dad
Cono, Ray, Pamie, Carmine,
and
Karen Ann, Michael John, and Rachel Marie

Contents

Preface

It was in 1972 that I seriously began working on Rexford Tugwell as a subject for research. In the time since then, I like to believe that I have come to know him. Along the way, many people helped me in that learning process, starting with Rexford Tugwell, who patiently answered the questions of an inquiring graduate student, and Mrs. Tugwell, who graciously assisted this author. It would be almost impossible to single out everyone who offered advice at one time or another. I hope that a general "thank you" will suffice for those left unnamed. To the others, though, special acknowledgment is hereby given.

Undoubtedly, the most important individual to be noted is the late Dr. Madison Kuhn. Often, people don't tell those closest to them just how much they have helped. I am afraid that this is particularly true in this author's case. Through his knowledge of American history, his understanding of people, and his patience with an impatient graduate student, Dr. Kuhn taught me what history really is, as well as what a commitment a historian must make if he or she is to contribute anything of substance. For that and much more, I will always be grateful.

During the research stages of this project, I came into contact with a number of individuals who assisted me in a variety of ways. I would like to express my gratitude to them for their kindness, patience, and guidance, especially to Mr. William Emerson and his staff (particularly Ms. Elizabeth Denier and Mr. Paul McLaughlin) at the Franklin D. Roosevelt Library, to the staff and personnel at the Library of Congress and the National Archives, to Ms. Elizabeth Mason at the Columbia Oral History Project, to Dr. Donald McDonald at the Center for the Study of Democratic Institutions, and to the staff and personnel at the libraries of Michigan State University and the University of Mississippi.

Special acknowledgment is expressed to the Special Research Fund, Department of History, University of Mississippi and to the Franklin

D. Roosevelt Four Freedoms Foundation for providing invaluable assistance at critical junctures in this project.

It is a privilege to work with scholars who give their time and expertise to others. This author was particularly fortunate in having Profs. Frank Freidel and Winthrop Jordan read his manuscript and express their suggestions for improving it. There is no question that the final product is far better as a result. Along these lines, a special note of thanks is in order for Mark Gelfand, who generously provided this author with copies of his work on the New York City Planning Commission.

Once a research project reaches the writing stage, support staff become indispensable. Thanks are publicly expressed to Ms. Fredonia Hairston, who helped this author type chapters into the computer, print out the copies, and then redo what the author did wrong in the first place.

Similarly, my gratitude is given to Dan Eades, Editor at Praeger Publishers, for his kind assistance in the initial stages of publication. Thanks are also due to Lauren Pera at Praeger who took my scribbles and made them into a readable book.

Finally, no listing of acknowledgments would be complete without expressing my sincere affection and appreciation for the people to whom this book is dedicated. Both my mother and my father did not live to see the project's completion. Without them, the biography would have remained an idea only.

As this manuscript goes to press, the recent death of my oldest brother, Cono, weighs heavily on my mind. So often he helped me throughout my life as well as serving as an inspiration. My deepest regret is that I never told him these things when I had the chance. Even now, though, I know he understands. Similarly, special heartfelt thanks are expressed to my sisters, Ray and Pamie, and my brother Carmine, for all the times they helped their baby brother. And, finally, affectionate gratitude is expressed to Karen, Mikie, and Rachel, who made this study a rewarding and positive experience. As always, they were there.

REXFORD G. TUGWELL

Introduction

[Rexford G. Tugwell] (was) a man of angel's wit and singular learning; I know not his fellow. For where is the man of that gentleness, lowliness, and affability? And as time requireth, a man of marvellous mirth and pastimes; and sometimes of as sad a gravity; a man for all seasons.

> James Bartlett, *Familiar Quotations*, edited by Emily
> M. Beck (Boston: Little, Brown, 1980), 155.

Although Robert Whittinton wrote the above passage on Sir Thomas More for a group of schoolboys studying Latin, it is equally appropriate for Rexford G. Tugwell. In many ways, he was a man of wit and singular learning who could be gentle and affable. While it is difficult to say much about his mirth and pastimes, there is no question that he was indeed "as sad a gravity," especially when he considered mankind and its future after 1945. But, most of all, the one statement that particularly suits Tugwell is the last—a man for all seasons. If nothing else, Tugwell was that. He was many things for many different people. Given his prolific writings, his activist personality, and his outspokenness, people could find in him whatever they might be looking for. Indeed, that often happened during his lifetime and after. Even a survey of his contemporary press, his colleagues' opinions, and later scholarly judgments demonstrates just how much Tugwell was something for everyone.

If there is any one way to describe Tugwell's press reception, especially in the New Deal years, it is to say that it was colorful. He was assaulted by opposition from the left and the right. From Mark Sullivan's columns in the *New York Herald Tribune* to the *Saturday Evening Post*, Tugwell was painted as the New Deal subversive revolutionary who secretly planned to destroy American capitalism.[1] He was the Columbia professor who frightened conservatives and liberals alike.[2] His critics, moreover, motivated by their patriotism, tried desperately to convince the public that "Rex the Red," "Tugwell, Rex," or "Rex, the Sweetheart of the Regimenters" was dangerous.[3] With a self-confidence that frequently was arrogance and an outspokenness that was unbridled, Tugwell tried in vain to placate the press. Even after he announced his resignation from the Resettlement Administration, his critics refused to call a cease-fire.[4]

There were, of course, some Tugwell supporters in the press corps. Ernest K. Lindley, for example, considered Tugwell "the philosopher, the sociologist, and the prophet of the Roosevelt Revolution, as well as one of its boldest practitioners." Despite Tugwell's trip to Russia and his unguarded talk, Lindley argued that Tugwell-phobia was absurd because Tugwell was not a dangerous radical but, rather, a practical liberal who was trying to reform America.[5] Drew Pearson and Robert Allen agreed, arguing that Tugwell's "radicalism ends with his belief that every man should have a home and a garden."[6] Unfortunately, not everyone adhered to this view. When Tugwell submitted his resignation in 1936, the *New Republic* editorialized that Roosevelt had thrown him to the wolves, thus ending the controversial government career of a controversial man.[7] Actually, that career did not end then. By 1938, Tugwell was again in government service, first as chairman of the New York City Planning Commission and then, in 1941, as governor of Puerto Rico. The radical stereotype cast of the early 1930s remained to affect what his contemporaries and later historians said of him.

Contemporary opinion of Tugwell followed along these lines. People were influenced not only by Tugwell's press but also by their own opinions of the New Deal and their personal relationships with Tugwell. J. Franklin Carter, the anonymous New Deal sympathizer, openly confessed his biases in the preface to *The New Dealers*. An associate and friend of most of his subjects, he believed his opinions were accurate and trustworthy.[8] If any New Dealer was misunderstood, Carter believed, it was Tugwell. Labeled a Bolshevik, a radical, and a clever revolutionary, he was genuinely a conservative "who would save the profit system and private ownership of property by adapting them to the technical conditions of the power age." Tugwell was not a utopian of the socialist stripe or a dogmatic laissez-fairist. He was as much a collectivist as "J.P. Morgan is a collectivist." The reason he was seen as such was because he was too honest and incapable of keeping his ideas to himself.[9] In short, Carter concluded, Tugwell was politically naive and, as a result, paid the price of being labeled a radical.

Writing years later, one of the original Brains Trusters took a somewhat different view than Carter's. Raymond Moley, disenchanted New Dealer who in 1935 confessedly turned conservative, saw Tugwell in terms of his own political philosophy and view of the New Deal. To him, Tugwell was a statist and a planner who always supported Roosevelt.[10] In *The First New Deal*, Moley writes that Tugwell's economic thinking "closely resembled that of the British socialists who as time went on submerged their socialism under the guise of national planning."[11] Tugwell, moreover, was impractical and "ignorant of politics." Although he stimulated people "like a cocktail," his ideas were consistently dangerous and alien to the American way.[12]

Other New Dealers were not as politically motivated in their views on Tugwell as Moley was. Samuel I. Rosenman, for example, believed Tugwell was a planner and a capable individual within the Roosevelt administration.[13] Felix Frankfurter, on the other hand, thought differently. To him, Tugwell was outspoken and a pain in the neck.[14] Frankfurter preferred Cohen, Corcoran, or Lilienthal within the New Deal; they were his protégés and links with Roosevelt, particularly in the Second New Deal. One of those protégés, David E. Lilienthal, had links with Tugwell.

As TVA director, Lilienthal was a practitioner of planning in the piecemeal, regional sense. It was only natural for him to seek Tugwell's support for his programs. Support, however, was not what he received. Tugwell opposed TVA piecemeal planning because, Lilienthal believed, he "never quite understood it; was temperamentally unable to really sympathize with it."[15] Not surprisingly, Tugwell the national planner could not understand Lilienthal the regional planner or the entire Brandeisian program of the Second New Deal. The Lilienthals and Brandeisians, in turn, did not understand or accept Tugwell.

There were, however, New Dealers who understood Tugwell and even liked him, such as Harold Ickes and Jerome Frank. "Honest Harold," outspoken and irascible, considered Tugwell a "man of real vision and ability."[16] Like Carter, Ickes believed that Tugwell was continually under attack because he did not guard himself carefully in what he said and did. He was not a radical but a reformer who, like Ickes, possessed a truly progressive social vision of America's future. Saddened by Tugwell's resignation in 1936, Ickes wanted him to have another chance—so much so that he was instrumental in Tugwell's appointment as governor of Puerto Rico in 1941.[17] Ickes liked Tugwell and identified with him.

Jerome Frank also felt that way. In his opinion, Tugwell was decisive, self-reliant, and the Harry Hopkins of 1932-1933.[18] He was a reformer who understood the changes in American capitalism and who tried to do something about it. Unfortunately, no one, not even in the Department of Agriculture, would let him.

Whether they agreed or disagreed with Frank, these contemporaries of Tugwell had one thing in common—they were all influenced by what the news media had said of him. Their own general positions on the New Deal and their personal relationships with Tugwell also affected them, but in such a way that they either defended or attacked the stereotype that had been established. In the long run, these contemporary opinions affected what later historians would say about Tugwell.

Generally, when discussing Tugwell, historians have continued to utilize the stereotype either offensively or defensively. Tugwell is consistently seen as a planner; some scholars consider him a radical, while others do not. Tugwell's popularity increased almost in proportion to the decline of Roosevelt's, particularly with the New Left historians of the 1960s. This was not always the case, though.

According to Barton Bernstein, the liberal scholars of the 1950s and 1960s—Arthur M. Schlesinger, Jr., Frank Freidel, William Leuchtenburg, and James M. Burns—"wrote from a liberal democratic consensus viewpoint."[19] Generally favorable to the New Deal, they argued that Roosevelt had replenished democracy, rescued the federal government "from the clutches of big business," and redistributed political power within the American system.[20] Their disagreements centered on the degree of the New Deal's success and Roosevelt's responsibility for it. They also disagreed somewhat in their portrayals of Tugwell.

Freidel, Burns, and Leuchtenburg believed that Tugwell was a radical planner who advocated the "drastic overhauling of the economic system."[21] Schlesinger, on the other hand, modified that view somewhat. In his thinking, Tugwell remained staunch in his progressivism. Always a consistent planner with well-defined programs, Tugwell demonstrated the fundamental conflict between "the theorist and the activist," one being radical and the other realistic. He was audacious and shocking, but not so radical.[22] He was essentially a practical planner whose "occasional cockiness or condescension of manner" got him into trouble and eventually caused his downfall.[23] Tugwell, in his planning proposals, offered an alternative to Roosevelt —but an unacceptable one as long as Tugwell was the one doing the offering. In the 1960s, New Left historians such as Howard Zinn and Paul Conkin changed this view.

Unlike the so-called liberals of the 1950s and 1960s, New Left historians were quite critical of Roosevelt and the New Deal. They generally agreed that Roosevelt was too conservative to institute the radical measures necessary to have made America more democratic, that the New Deal failed to help the underprivileged groups in American society, and that Roosevelt simply restored the undemocratic capitalistic structure that had existed before 1929. They also agreed that Tugwell knew what had to be done, since he was the only true radical in the New Deal. He was a "bold advocate of national planning" that was designed to help the lower-income groups.[24] An embittered reformer, he also pointed the way to recovery and a new America, but Roosevelt was too conservative in his philosophy and experimentalism to heed his advice. In Tugwell's proposals, "there were faint echoes of technocracy, a hint of the corporate state, and a near arrogant contempt for such traditional values as competition, small economic units, and fee simple property" that caused Roosevelt to ignore his designs for America. It was Roosevelt's fault, not Tugwell's, for not employing planning on a grand scale. Roosevelt, not Tugwell, failed to achieve a better American society.[25] The alternative was there, but Roosevelt refused it.

What these New Left historians were saying, in effect, was that they preferred the "radical" Tugwell to the "conservative" Roosevelt. In so doing, they exaggerated many of Tugwell's ideas as well as the pervasiveness of his programs. Writing more as a reaction to what they believed previous scholars had said, they offered nothing new in understanding either the New Deal or Rexford Tugwell.

In at least one respect, this was also true of Ellis Hawley's study of the New Deal. Using categories and labels more in tune with his theoretical framework than with the reality of the 1930s, Hawley described Tugwell in terms of the "typical" intellectual planner. Without actually analyzing much of Tugwell's writings, he portrayed him as one who favored strong government supervision of the planning function out of a distrust for businessmen.[26]

Of all the scholarly studies done, the one that addressed Tugwell the New Dealer directly and in considerable detail was that by Bernard Sternsher. In Sternsher's opinion, Tugwell was neither a socialist nor a communist, but a democrat who "criticized the capitalistic system not because he wanted to destroy it . . . but because he wished to improve it." His proposals were in the pragmatic-idealistic American tradition.[27] Tugwell's critics, however—including Alva Johnston, Frank Kent, David Lawrence, Mark Sullivan, and Blair Bolles—deliberately created a distorted image of him.[28] They believed Tugwell was the clever revolutionary in the New Deal who was seeking to overthrow the American system, and therefore they felt compelled to warn the American public about him. Despite their false accusations, Tugwell was forced to resign in 1936 and to go through life with the image of a radical. As for his planning and collective proposals, Sternsher argued that there was "no apparatus available in the 1930s for executing a collectivistic scheme in the general interest," and Tugwell knew it. Such a scheme required popular acceptance, careful preplanning, and competent personnel, none of which was available at that time.[29] Time would make them operational, but time was one ingredient lacking in Tugwell's program. Tugwell the planner, in other words, was an idea man with limited influence.

Interestingly, that limited influence has led to an examination of Tugwell's intellectual roots and heritage. According to Steven Kesselman, Tugwell perceived "stasis" in the world. He rejected ideology, was utilitarian, had a "pragmatic morality," functioned without ideals, and had a "pluralistic" intellectual structure.[30] Unquestionably, as a man for all seasons, Tugwell could fit even this description, regardless of whether he ever spoke or thought in such terms.

Could Tugwell be all these things that press reporters, contemporaries, and historians have said he was? It's highly doubtful. Nevertheless, what this brief survey does indicate is that Tugwell was many things to many different people. People saw in him what they wanted to see. Historians found in him what they wanted to find. Yet, in all this, Tugwell himself was lost. Who he was, what he was striving for, and what he actually did—all of this is tied to the individual's own predilections.

In the pages that follow, Rexford Tugwell is presented as a unique, complex individual. He was the type of person who learned about life, the world, and people by his reading, by his life experiences, and by the people he came into contact with. In many ways, this explained his rather "anti-formal" education attitude. Instead of what he called "department store" education, he wanted students to be taught to look at and think about the future, and to do so by studying alternatives. He was a paradoxical individual, in that there was always a tension in him between the hardheaded realist and the romantic. Nowhere is this seen more clearly than in his views on the simple life and the small farm.

From a more personal viewpoint, this biography will show that Tugwell was a man who "wrote out loud" instead of talking out loud. To a large degree, this explains his massive output of writings. In writing out loud, Tugwell demonstrated over and over how much he evolved in his thinking. He was always probing an issue, a topic, a problem—trying to understand and deal with it better. Thus, to cite one article or book and say this is what Tugwell said on this or that issue/topic is to miss the point—his evolutionary thinking process. It will be seen that as a person, he was strong-willed and self-confident, many times too outspoken and possessing a self-confidence that more often than not crossed the border into arrogance.

Yet, underneath that exterior, was a man who truly cared about others, who had a deep love of people, life, nature, and its abundance. Tugwell wanted everyone to share in America's abundance, and he found it abominable that an economic philosophy and system refused to allow that. As a result, he was often frustrated, and in those moments of frustration, his so-called radicalism appeared. He was never a revolutionary, but always an evolutionary. He wanted order in society through planning and accountability on everyone's part, from the economist to the businessman to the politician. For him, accountability meant public service and, as this biography will show, he always sought to serve others. In the New Deal, New York, Puerto Rico, and finally in academe after 1946, this need to help others persistently prevailed.

In his public service roles, moreover, Tugwell's record was more impressive than he has been given credit for. He was not only loyal to Roosevelt but also a good administrator in the New Deal and beyond. In the pages that follow, there is presented a different Tugwell than has been seen before. It is a Tugwell speaking for himself through his writings and his papers, from his boyhood days to the end of his long life. Also, it is an active Tugwell who used his official positions in the New Deal, New York, Puerto Rico, and academe to accomplish what he believed in. The Tugwell who follows is not one who "cerebrated" but one who acted. And it is on the basis of what he believed, said, and did that he should be evaluated and assessed.

NOTES

1. Bernard Sternsher, *Rexford Tugwell and the New Deal* (New Brunswick, N.J.: Rutgers University Press, 1964), 337-56. Sternsher's discussion is excellent, especially in identifying Tugwell's critics and the fallacies in their attacks on him. See also T. W. Koch, telegram to Franklin D. Roosevelt, February 21, 1935; H.

T. Collord to Roosevelt, December 17, 1935; Frederick Sullen to Roosevelt, October 10, 1933—all in Franklin D. Roosevelt papers, FDR Library, official file 1-Misc.—for examples of popular and business reactions to Tugwell.

2. "We Shall Make America Over," *Saturday Evening Post*, October 29, 1938, in Raymond Clapper papers, Library of Congress, box 107; Alva Johnston, "Tugwell, the President's Idea Man," *Saturday Evening Post*, August 1, 1936, p. 9.

3. Blair Bolles, "The Sweetheart of the Regimenters: Dr. Tugwell Makes America Over," *American Mercury* 39 (September 1936): 77-86, is an excellent example of Tugwell's hostile reception by the press.

4. Paul W. Ward, "The End of Tugwell," *The Nation* 143 (November 28, 1936): 617-18.

5. Ernest K. Lindley, "War on the Brains Trust," *Scribner's Magazine* 94 (November 1933); *The Roosevelt Revolution: First Phase* (New York: Viking Press, 1933), 304-14; *Half Way with Roosevelt* (New York: Viking Press, 1936), 42.

6. "The Daily Washington Merry-Go-Round," n.d., in Henry A. Wallace papers, Library of Congress, scrapbooks, reel 41.

7. "Tugwell to the Wolves," *New Republic* 85 (December 25, 1936): 186-87.

8. J. Franklin Carter, *The New Dealers* (New York: Simon and Schuster, 1934), preface. Carter published the study as being written by an "unofficial observer."

9. Ibid., pp. 85-91.

10. Raymond Moley, correspondence with author, July 21, 1972.

11. Raymond Moley, *The First New Deal* (New York: Harcourt, Brace, and World, 1966), 356.

12. Ibid., pp. 356-58; Raymond Moley, *After Seven Years* (New York: Harper and Brothers, 1939), 15. James Farley, *Jim Farley's Story: The Roosevelt Years* (New York: McGraw-Hill, 1948), indirectly indicates his agreement with Moley by his actions in the 1936 campaign. Farley was instrumental in having Tugwell kept silent and out of the campaign.

13. Samuel I. Rosenman, correspondence with author, September 28, 1972; Samuel I. Rosenman, *Working with Roosevelt* (New York: Harper and Brothers, 1952), 145-46. Ironically, Rosenman doubted Moley's influence in the First New Deal. See Samuel I. Rosenman to Rexford Tugwell, January 16, 1969, Samuel I. Rosenman papers, FDR Library, box 31.

14. Felix Frankfurter to Louis Brandeis, February 9, 1934; Philip Kurland to Frankfurter, November 11, 1953; Frankfurter to Kurland, November 13, 1953—all in Felix Frankfurter papers, Library of Congress, boxes 29 and 72.

15. David E. Lilienthal, *The Journals of David E. Lilienthal: The TVA Years, 1939-1945* (New York: Harper and Row, 1964), 14-16, 480.

16. Harold Ickes, *The Secret Diary of Harold Ickes: The First Thousand Days, 1933-1936* (New York: Simon and Schuster, 1953), 241, 474-75.

17. Harold Ickes, *The Secret Diary of Harold Ickes: The Lowering Clouds, 1938-1941* (New York: Simon and Schuster, 1954), 6; Harold Ickes to Franklin

D. Roosevelt, July 28, 1941, Franklin D. Roosevelt papers, FDR Library, official file 6-S.

18. Jerome Frank, "The Memoir of Jerome Frank," pp. 25, 29-34, 143, Oral History Research Office, Columbia University. Lindsey Rogers agreed with Ickes and Frank. See Lindsey Rogers, "The Memoir of Lindsey Rogers," p. 90, Oral History Research Office, Columbia University.

19. Barton Bernstein, "The New Deal: The Conservative Achievements of Liberal Reform," in Barton J. Bernstein, ed., *Towards a New Past: Dissenting Essays in American History* (New York: Vintage Books, 1967), 264.

20. Ibid.

21. Frank Freidel, *Franklin D. Roosevelt: The Triumph* (Boston, Little, Brown, 1956), 263, 265, 351, 353; James M. Burns, *Roosevelt: The Lion and the Fox* (New York: Harcourt, Brace, and World, 1956), 177, 188, 193, 153-54, 372; William Leuchtenburg, *Franklin D. Roosevelt and the New Deal* (New York: Harper and Row, 1963), 35, 68-69, 75-76, 84, 85. 197-98, 248. Quote is from Freidel, p. 263.

22. Arthur M. Schlesinger, Jr., *Crisis of the Old Order* (Boston: Houghton Mifflin, 1956), 196ff., 400.

23. Arthur Schlesinger, Jr., *Coming of the New Deal* (Boston: Houghton Mifflin, 1958), 351, 360-361.

24. Howard Zinn, ed., *New Deal Thought* (New York: Bobbs-Merrill, 1966), xxii.

25. Paul Conkin, *The New Deal* (New York: Thomas Y. Crowell, 1967), 32, 39.

26. Ellis Hawley, *The New Deal and the Problem of Monopoly* (Princeton: Princeton University Press, 1966), 45-46, 401-02.

27. Sternsher, *Rexford Tugwell and the New Deal*, p. 400.

28. Ibid., pp. 337-56.

29. Ibid., pp. 400ff.

30. Steven Kesselman, *The Modernization of American Reform: Structures and Perceptions* (New York: Garland, 1979), 420-23.

1

Early Years: 1891–1911

The elation that followed the dropping of the bomb on Hiroshima, followed closely by the second one dropped on Nagasaki, tailed off into decades of guilty rationalization by all those who had been involved in the decision to use them. Americans have not absolved themselves of the guilt they assumed on those days. So long as any of that generation are alive, they never will.

Rexford Tugwell, *The Light of Other Days*, p. 11

In these opening sentences of *The Light of Other Days*, one of his autobiographies, Rexford Tugwell discusses the dropping of the atomic bomb on Hiroshima and Nagasaki. He goes on to refer to it as "the ultimate crime" with no possible expiation"—"this final sin." In another of his autobiographies, *A Chronicle of Jeopardy*, he refers to it as the "villain" of his chronicle. In other books and articles he wrote after 1945, this theme appeared over and over again. It may seem strange at first that a man who had accomplished as much as he had—who had served in the heyday of the New Deal, chaired the New York City Planning Commission, had been governor of Puerto Rico, and, after 1946, had returned to academe and published prolifically until his death in 1979—should expend so much of his energies and writing talents on this one subject. He wrote literally hundreds of pages on Hiroshima and what it represented. Yet, to anyone who knew him, what may appear strange on first sight was quite natural. To Rexford Tugwell, the dropping of the atomic bomb was his responsibility and the responsibility of his generation. It was his generation that researched, financed, developed, and used it. The bomb was the dividing point between civilization and ruin. Its destructiveness encompassed more than the leveling of a city, for it destroyed a life-style, value system, and set of beliefs that Tugwell had grown up with, lived, and contributed to.[1]

Rexford Guy Tugwell was born on July 10, 1891, in Sinclairville, New York, a small upstate village. His parents, Charles Tugwell and Dessie Rexford, were an unusual couple. Many years later, their son would describe their relationship as "exemplary a couple as any boy could have had for parents."[2] His mother, who had been born in Michigan, moved to Ellington, New York, after her father died, and lived with Tugwell's aunt and uncle in No God Hollow. After completing high school in Sinclairville, she taught in nearby Chautauqua until her marriage in 1899. "An earnest housewife," as her son later described her, she was also quite an individualist. An artistic person, she wrote verses often, read avidly, and generally appreciated the finer aspects of life.[3] She frequently wrote papers for women's meetings, participated in social activities, and was a lively talker and a nature buff. She was moody, humorous, and overprotective of her only son. She so influenced Tugwell that, years later, he admitted that he was more his mother's than his father's child.[4] She was in many ways responsible for Tugwell's desire to write, as well as for his later concern for conservation of America's natural resources. But young boys are usually influenced by their fathers, too, and Tugwell was no exception.

Charles Tugwell was a businessman in every sense. Practical and ambitious, he began his career as a junior partner in his father's cattle business. His entrepreneurial talent led him into canning, orchard farming, banking, and other enterprises. In almost every endeavor before 1929, he was successful, providing his family with a comfortable and financially secure existence. A compassionate and understanding man, he was close to his only son, especially after his two other sons died in early childhood. As a young boy, Tugwell spent time with his father as he visited farmers in Sinclairville and surrounding areas for his business. Charles taught his son how to judge cattle and handle horses. He also advised him frequently as the boy grew older.[5]

Charles's influence, moreover, extended to another area. He provided his son with a model of the businessman and the free enterprise system that Tugwell would later vigorously assault. Like most businessmen of his time, his son believed his father held values that were outmoded in the modern industrialized economy. Charles believed in paternalism toward labor and an iron law of wages, much to the dismay of his son.[6] He emphasized the role of the small businessman in an economy designed to help the big businessman. He also suspected the government's intentions when only the government could have provided him with the economic stability and security he wanted. In short, his value system as a businessman belonged to a free enterprise system that Rexford wanted to change, not overthrow. Tugwell believed that his father became confused and broken in spirit in old age, a not uncommon occurrence among his fellow businessmen.[7] This, of course, came after the 1929 debacle.

Young Tugwell had a "singularly-fortunate childhood." An only child until his sister was born, he was free to develop his interests and enjoy his surroundings. Many years later, Tugwell looked back and admitted that he "was spoiled—whatever that means."[8] As a young boy, he went fishing and hunting, skating and sledding, and played baseball, although not as much as he wanted, since he was frequently ill with colds, croup, and asthma.[9] To compensate for this, he learned to read at an early age. From dime novels to classical literature, he immersed himself in a world of books, eventually nurturing an ambition to write. Though disjointed and unplanned, his reading was impressive, ranging from William Dean Howells to Buffalo Bill. He was aided in this endeavor by his mother's involvement in Chautauqua, which served as a center of learning in the latter part of the nineteenth century. There, young Tugwell could hear some of the most important leaders of education, politics, economics, theology, and other disciplines teach, lecture, and exchange ideas. Tugwell the man, on looking back at these years, felt that Chautauqua made him "more respectful of learning, more disposed to serious study, less inclined to accept dogmas, and more aware of the wide world."[10]

His academic performance, however, did not reflect this. Tugwell did the minimum amount of work necessary to pass his examinations, except in subjects, such as history and English, that interested him. Bored with formal education, he believed that his life experiences and his environment were more instructive. Although he liked his teachers, young Tugwell felt that school days were too filled with routine, recitations, and too brief recesses. He preferred his reading and life experiences, such as his family's trip to Colorado in 1902, taken for his health. This trip had a lifetime impact, or at least that is what he later remembered.[11] It was on this trip, for example, that Tugwell saw his first black man. Years later, on the other hand, he felt that his schooling in Sinclairville had contributed to his developing "slovenly habits even in my best subjects" while allowing him to shirk subjects, such as math and physical science, that he didn't like.[12]

Nor was that all that Sinclairville did. If his generation was responsible for Hiroshima, Tugwell argued that Sinclairville was the first to be accountable in his life. There, the people were "more like the past than the future." There "existed peace, security, and permanence . . . and no one ever went hungry or was cold."[13] Lingering in a state fast becoming obsolete, Sinclairville was a interesting, secure place for a young boy to grow up. It provided its residents with a simple life based on neighborliness, hard work, and individual initiative. Politics and government were distant realities, even though the community was strongly Republican in its political preferences and desire for law and order.[14] In the 1890s, everything seemed bright. "All was movement, change, progress." Any turmoil occurring within the United States, such as the Pullman strike and populism, either passed Sinclairville by or was only slightly noticed. Sinclairville, in short, provided a satisfying life, yet it "was no preparation for the future." The ideals it upheld, the values it treasured, the economics it emphasized—all were dangerously anachronistic in the modern industrial system. It failed to change, to adjust when change was necessary, and, in the end, it contributed to the tragedies of the twentieth century.[15]

Tugwell's characterization of Sinclairville as providing a satisfying life, yet one that was no preparation for the future, was a paradox that remained in his thinking throughout his life: He argued for and defended the industrial process while brooding over the passing of the simple, rural life that Sinclairville had offered. In a similar manner, he would strive hard to modernize the American agricultural system, even eliminating the small farmer, while simultaneously lauding the beauty of the farm.[16] There was a tension in him between practical, hardheaded economics and more sentimental, romantic idealism. Not surprisingly, the tension was never relieved.

While Sinclairville provided young Tugwell with a satisfying environment in which to grow up, it did not provide his father with a bright future. Realizing that the small village was declining and that other business opportunities were in the offing, Charles Tugwell moved his family to Wilson, New York, about 100 miles from Sinclairville. There he established his fruit and vegetable canning business. He did so well with it that he became "moderately wealthy" and a "leading citizen," even helping to organize, and then serving as president of, Wilson's first bank.[17]

By the time the family moved to Wilson in 1904, Rexford was 13 years old. It was in Wilson that he got firsthand experience in business, assisting his father in the canning factory and eventually serving as his field man. The Tugwells, by then, had become a family of means, but Rexford and his father had started drifting apart. As his father's field man, Tugwell saw what it meant to run a business and to deal with a labor force. He felt that his father treated his workers, mostly Italian immigrants, unfairly by refusing to "pay his workers more than the least he could hire them for." Charles Tugwell did not see any connection, moreover, between his company's financial condition and the wages he paid. In fact, he believed that his workers should be grateful for the jobs he provided them. This attitude did not sit well with his son. Years later, Rexford admitted that it was then he began "questioning" the business system and developing an unwillingness to accept the living conditions it provided for its workers.[18]

While these early intimations of his later philosophy appeared, they did not overwhelm him. As early as age 11, he had begun a "secret life" of writing, and he nurtured it in Wilson. Always keeping it to himself except for a few select English teachers, he worked at his writing diligently, even though he didn't know anyone who had ever made a career of it.[19] Once again, however, his performance in school belied his budding creativity. Doing the minimum amount of work necessary, except in English, he got through the Wilson school system, just barely passing his state Regents exams. Though his schoolwork received small effort, his reading did not, for he continued to absorb everything from fiction to poetry to biography to romances. He was particularly fond of H. G. Wells and his commentaries on the future of mankind. At 17, he read more politically motivated materials, such as James Bryce's *American Commonwealth*, Upton Sinclair's *The Jungle*, and Edward Bellamy's *Looking Backward*.[20]

The effects of such reading were seen as Tugwell's attitudes began to form and evolve. With his asthma worsening and keeping him out of athletics, his reading and writing became more serious. He found an outlet for his writing in the *Niagara Falls Gazette*. For nearly a year, during the off season in the canning factory, he wrote the local news section for Wilson, New York. Years later, Tugwell was certain that it was experiences like these, along with working in his father's factory and his reading, that truly educated him, not the Wilson schools. Nevertheless, toward the end of his long life, Tugwell still recalled how "unreasonably" he loved Wilson, New York.

In January 1909, Tugwell decided to leave Wilson and go to a military academy in Virginia. He chose it, convinced his parents that he wanted it, and went there. His military career, however, was quite short-lived, lasting only two weeks. In assessing his brief stint at the academy, Tugwell later believed that there was a combination of reasons for his leaving. The military atmosphere of the school, its location in the South, the unfamiliar town, "clownish student customs," and "tobacco-spitting instructors" all facilitated his return home. On his arrival, he told his parents that he had decided to go to Masten Park High School in Buffalo. He would board there and return home on weekends. This decision, and his parent's acquiescence, demonstrated that Tugwell made his own choices, even at 17.[21]

Masten Park had a wide variety of subjects, well-prepared teachers, and a serious-minded principal, Dr. Frank W. Fosdick. Its student population of 1000 was a totally new environment for Tugwell. Still, his performance remained the same. He passed exams, didn't do much work, and at one point was told by Dr. Fosdick that he was wasting his time in school. While this warning scared Tugwell, it didn't devastate him. He worked enough at his subjects to pass and overcome the crisis.[22]

For Tugwell, high school was a place to meet people, explore one's environment, and enjoy life. With his father's financial backing and understanding, he did just that, frequenting the theater, going on dates, visiting saloons, and surveying Buffalo. Enjoying the good life, though, had other results as well. It was during his high school years that certain themes and ideas began to form. Tugwell's emphasis in later years on the use of biological terminology and analogies, for example, stemmed from his biology course with Marion Gemmel.[23] At the Wharton School, Simon Nelson Patten reinforced what Ms. Gemmel had begun. It was also at this time that he noted that the purpose of the social sciences and the use of government were to improve mankind and life in general. Studying economics under Mr. Jay Stagg at Masten High strongly influenced his decision to choose economics as a profession. And, finally, living in Buffalo, "an ugly city, getting uglier every year," reinforced his growing concerns about the American free enterprise system and its lack of order or systematic planning.[24]

This is not to say that Tugwell the reformer was flourishing at Masten High. Rather, it shows that he was thinking of these things at the ripe age of 17 and that the evolutionary process in his thinking, characteristic of his life, was well under way. At 17 he saw himself as a writer, not a reformer. Later, that perception would gradually change. In line with his writing desires, he got a job on the *Buffalo Courier*, reporting on the local court proceedings and covering the financial news.[25]

In 1962, when *The Light of Other Days* was published and Tugwell was 71 years old, he reflected on his high school years and concluded that, in 1910, he wanted "to change things, not destroy them." What to change, how to do it, and when it would be done—these were questions that time would answer for him.[26]

Looking closely at the sentiments that statements such as these express demonstrates clearly that Tugwell's environment was affecting him. Between his birth in 1891 and his first couple of years in college, numerous changes and momentous movements had already taken place in America. Tugwell lived in the time of Populism, Progressivism, the presidencies of Theodore Roosevelt, William Howard Taft, and Woodrow Wilson, the technological revolution, and the overriding wave of American industrialization. To Tugwell, these years were the transition between the older, fast-fading agricultural order in which he grew up and the new, highly mechanized industrial society of the future. The years 1907-1909 were particularly important in his thinking because it was during these years that technology increased, the United States underwent a severe depression, Taft defeated William Jennings Bryan (thus ending Populism), and Progressivism was under way.

Although he would write on each of these movements as he grew older, his having witnessed them affected his thought. Years later, for example, Tugwell would write about Populism as reactionary, wanting to go back and wanting progress only for small farmers. Yet he would also remember hearing Bryan speak in 1908 and watching his father support Bryan; ultimately Tugwell concluded that Bryan represented America's chance to change, to adjust to the new world that was developing. Taft's victory destroyed that chance. Similarly, he would argue later that Progressivism wasn't much better than Populism because the Progressives "attempted to distinguish between what was good and what was bad in a system" that was totally immoral. Still, Tugwell would also remember that Woodrow Wilson did adopt a moderate form of Bryanism and left it to Franklin D. Roosevelt to continue.[27] Similarly, Tugwell delineated Progressivism and defined it in terms of individuals he came to know and identify with, such as Robert LaFollette. The reflections, experiences, and eyewitness accounts of the 17-year-old boy would affect the judgments of the older man, not in a contradictory way but in a manner that made his thoughts real and alive, ideas that developed gradually over time. This process of learning from what he experienced and from what he lived, combined with the evolution of thinking things through, was fully ingrained in young Tugwell before he left for college.

By his eighteenth birthday, ideas that would characterize his professional life had already begun to germinate. It is not that Tugwell spent a lot of time thinking about them—he was still too interested in enjoying life—yet the early stages of those thought patterns were present. Even before he entered college, he was thinking of democracy and its emphasis on freedom and its toleration of unwise majorities. He had gone through educational systems that were not relevant to the world, wondering about their consequences. His early distaste for and frustration with American businessmen's profit maximization had already appeared. His realization that order and some form of planning could improve life, that economics could help in that process, and that America's free enterprise system needed some changes —all of this was on Tugwell's mind by 1911.[28] He needed and he sought to find direction for all of this. In 1911, he decided to go to the Wharton School for these reasons.

NOTES

1. Rexford G. Tugwell, *The Light of Other Days* (Garden City, N.Y.: Doubleday, 1962), 11-12, 110-11, 230; Tugwell, *A Chronicle of Jeopardy, 1945-1955* (Chicago: University of Chicago Press, 1955), 1, 4-5, 37. This theme of the atomic bomb and its impact on Tugwell will be discussed in more detail in Chapter 7.

2. Tugwell, *The Light of Other Days*, pp. 70-71.

3. Ibid., pp. 20-23, 44, 77-80.

4. Ibid., p. 26.

5. Ibid., pp. 21-22, 27-28, 62, 71-72, 80-82; Rexford G. Tugwell, *The Stricken Land: The Story of Puerto Rico* (Garden City, N.Y.: Doubleday, 1947), 660ff.; Tugwell, *To The Lesser Heights of Morningside: A Memoir* (Philadelphia: University of Pennsylvania Press, 1982), 87.

6. Tugwell, *The Light of Other Days*, p. 220.

7. Dad to Rex, August 9, 1934; Dad to Rex, June 7, 1937; Dad to Rex, August 24, 1937—all in Tugwell papers, folder "Tugwell, Charles H. 1933-1946," FDR Library, Hyde Park, N.Y., box 26; Tugwell, *The Stricken Land*, p. 660.

8. Tugwell, *The Light of Other Days*, p. 73.

9. Ibid., pp. 36-39.

10. Ibid., pp. 119, 123-24.

11. Ibid., p. 174.

12. Ibid., pp. 41-43.

13. Ibid., p. 157.

14. Tugwell, *The Stricken Land*, p. 663; Tugwell, *The Light of Other Days*, pp. 52, 64, 68, 84, 119, 125-34.

15. Tugwell, *The Light of Other Days*, pp. 58-59, 192.

16. Ibid., p. 268.

17. Ibid., pp. 198, 201-02, 206.

18. Ibid., pp. 219-20.

19. Ibid., pp. 186, 208-09.

20. Ibid., p. 270.

21. Ibid., pp. 293-95.

22. Ibid., pp. 297-302ff.; Bernard Sternsher, *Rexford Tugwell and the New Deal* (New Brunswick, N.J.: Rutgers University Press, 1964), 3; Blair Bolles, "The Sweetheart of the Regimenters: Dr. Tugwell Makes America Over," *American Mercury* 39 (September 1936): 79ff.

23. Tugwell, *The Light of Other Days*, pp. 296-97.

24. See, for example, Tugwell papers, folder "The Masten Park Chronicle," FDR Library, box 51; Tugwell, *Light of Other Days*, pp. 371, 375, 378, 380ff.

25. Tugwell, *Light of Other Days*, p. 397.

26. Ibid., p. 328.

27. Ibid., pp. 57, 60, 84, 228, 234, 238-55; Rexford G. Tugwell, "The Reminiscences of Rexford G. Tugwell," p. 15, Oral History Research Office, Columbia University.

28. Tugwell, *The Light of Other Days*, pp. 82-86, 111-14, 134, 142-44, 237-38.

2

Wharton, War, and Wilson: 1911–1920

The Past improves. Soldiers find that even the squalors and boredoms of war after a while seem to have been incidents in a romantic enterprise; adults forget the terrors and tensions of childhood and recall mostly interludes of security and gaiety. Mean seasons seem presently to have had a high interest, and even personal enmities soften and seem in time to have been more comic than tragic. No wonder the bright college years of song and study seem in retrospect so idyllic. The light of other days is kindly and mellowing.

Rexford Tugwell, *To the Lesser Heights of Morningside*, p. 3

Tugwell wrote this at the very end of his long life. The sentiments expressed in this statement clearly reflect his years in college and the years immediately after. Between 1911 and 1920, Tugwell finished his undergraduate and master's degrees in economics, married and became a father, went to the University of Washington to explore the inner depths of the casual worker, served in a noncombatant capacity in World War I, and returned to Wilson, New York, at first to join his father's business and shortly thereafter to return to academe. These were formative years—years of change and growth, years of frustration and disappointment, but, in the long run, also years in which the light of other days was kind, mellow, and instructive.

In September 1911, Rexford Tugwell entered the Wharton School at the University of Pennsylvania. Although he realized then and later the disparity between what Wharton was and what he was looking for, he never regretted his decision to go there. In many ways, he believed Wharton prepared him for the positions he later expounded on the American business system and the free enterprise economy.[1] Founded in 1881, the Wharton School was the creation of Joseph Wharton, the wealthy ironmaster who gave the University of Pennsylvania a substantial part of his stocks and bonds in the Delaware and Bound Brook Railroad Company and the Schuylkill Navigation Company, valued at $79,000 then, and additional assets eventually totaling nearly $810,000 by 1948. A good practitioner of what he preached, Joseph Wharton wanted a school to train young men "of the well-to-do" families for careers in business, teaching, and public service. He also insisted that all who went through its doors be ingrained with the fundamental truth of tariff protection. This point was so important that Simon Nelson Patten was appointed the first economics professor at Wharton because of his brilliant defense of the tariff in his *Economic Basis of Protection*.[2] Whether the tariff was a fundamental axiom of economics or not, Wharton, by 1911, was in the forefront of producing high-quality business executives and industrial technicians, and promoting true research in the social sciences.

Coming from a "middle-income family," being "used to prosperity," and ingrained in a tradition of "working hard and being generously rewarded for it," Tugwell entered Wharton to prepare himself for public service. Eager to be accepted and wanting to be a "conforming member" of his new world, he soon realized that Wharton "was different and better—than high school life." It was what he always wanted.[3]

True to his Sinclairville and Wilson form, however, Tugwell's first two years in college were directed at enjoying life and exploring the social scene. Involved in extracurricular activities, he devoted most of his time to serving on the prom committee, being an editor of *The Daily Pennsylvanian*, and membership in Delta Upsilon. At the same time, he pursued his interests in English and literature and continued to develop his writing, winning a prize for a piece of work submitted in his freshman year (he was taking a second-year English course). Years later, Tugwell felt that it was in his freshman year that he realized "writing would be a means to an end," not the end itself. Economics was to replace that, especially as he acquired his mentors at Wharton.[4]

Looking back, Tugwell believed he was "a normal, and none-too-studious freshman," but also one whose asthma became so serious that it restricted his participation in sports. While academic subjects were treated as they had always been, Tugwell continued his avid reading. A noticeable change appeared, however, in that he became quite interested in "a literature of revolt and reconstruction."[5] Always sensitive to what went on in his environment, he began to read more deeply in American history as well as current and past political movements such as Populism, socialism, Fabianism, Henry George's single-tax movement, syndicalism, communism, anarchism, and the then popular muckraking journalists such as Lincoln Steffens. While it is nearly impossible to ascertain exactly what impact all this had, there is no question that it showed Tugwell was reflecting on and absorbing what he experienced and read, always formulating opinions and ideas.

Along these lines, it is not surprising that Tugwell supported Robert LaFollette's bid for the Republican presidential nomination until it collapsed, and then voted for Woodrow Wilson in 1912, his first time to vote. Since he saw Theodore Roosevelt as a true political adventurer, Tugwell's actions in 1912 coincided with his past as well as his growing concern for social justice and his growing distaste for profit maximization. His courses in economics and sociology reinforced his growing social conscience and facilitated his actions.[6]

By his junior year, Tugwell had become a serious student, following the advice of his teachers, especially Scott Nearing, Clyde King, and Simon Nelson Patten.[7] Forgoing just about all his extracurricular activities, including the school newspaper but not the *Red and Blue* (a literary magazine), he started concentrating on his studies,[8] as is shown by his being elected to Phi Kappa Beta. Tugwell was beginning to develop intellectually.[9]

Everyone is influenced by someone or something. Tugwell was no exception. What distinguished him was not only the depth these influences would have, but also their type. During his years at Wharton, Tugwell was influenced both personally and intellectually. The personal influences were teachers such as Clyde King (constitutional law), Leo Rowe (political science), G. W. McClelland (English), Scott Nearing (economics), and Simon Nelson Patten (economics). Of these, Nearing and Patten had by far the most effect on him. Tugwell was also influenced by the intellectual currents he was introduced to at Wharton, specifically the Veblen critique of American capitalism, Taylorism, and institutional pragmatism. The latter was reinforced in the 1920s at Columbia University, when Tugwell would encounter John Dewey. Combined with his reading and his tendency to be aware of and affected by his life experiences, these personal and intellectual influences facilitated Tugwell's growth. Undoubtedly, of the two the personal were the more important, especially Scott Nearing and Simon Patten.

Scott Nearing taught freshman economics. The supplementary reading lists for his class provided Tugwell with a wealth of knowledge he was eager to acquire. Meeting with Tugwell in class and at his home, Nearing became not only his teacher but his friend as well. Himself a student of Patten and known for his emphasis on factual information to sustain one's arguments, Nearing was a liberal crusader at Wharton, commenting on a wide variety of subjects ranging from a critique of the American business system to condemnation of child labor. In 1912 he published a short monograph encompassing his ideas and calling for the development of a super race through the aggregation of supermen. These supermen would be characterized by physical normality, mental capacity, concentration, aggressiveness, sympathy, and vision.[10] Nearing argued that the United States could sustain this super race through its natural resources and other abundant gifts. Looking back, at the end of his life, Tugwell admitted that Nearing's book reflected his undergraduate reformist beliefs and that it inspired his poem "Making America Over."[11]

Nearing's impact on Tugwell was strengthened by a small group of Wharton faculty who met to "discuss matters of common interests." This included Tugwell since, in his senior year, he was an instructor.[12] Being a crusader in a conservative environment such as Wharton did not bode well for one's survival. Nearing learned this when, in the spring of 1915, the board of trustees dismissed him. His firing created such a stir over academic freedom that the American Association of University Professors investigated his case, and students protested the board's actions. Tugwell, years later, believed that Nearing was dismissed because he wanted businessmen to act in the general interest, because he agitated against child labor, because he was generally labeled a radical, because he spoke to church groups about reform (thereby threatening at least George Wharton Pepper, a prominent Episcopal layman who was on the board of trustees) and because Nearing criticized the "best families" for their extravagance and waste.[13] Nearing survived his dismissal, crusading in other places and for other causes. Yet, the effect on Tugwell was serious. He became disillusioned with Wharton, intent on making the economics profession accountable, and determined to leave such a stifling environment. He left for the University of Washington when the opportunity presented itself.

Nearing promoted reformism in the young student, but it was Patten who guided him intellectually then and later. Calling him not only a "great teacher" but a "great philosopher" as well, Tugwell believed that Simon Nelson Patten was the "greatest single influence" on his thinking.[14] Born on May 1, 1852, at Cossayuna, New York, Patten grew up on his father's farm in Sandwich, Illinois. His mother having died when he was four years old, Patten was reared by a strict father and stepmother. His father had early chosen a career in law for him and Patten, at age 17, enrolled in the Jennings Seminary at Aurora to study it. Once there, his interest in philosophy and social science was far stronger. After one more year on his father's farm, he went to Northwestern University and then to Halle, Germany, where he studied under Johannes Ernst Conrad and received his Ph.D. in 1878. Back in the United States, he temporarily lost his eyesight. After recovering it, he began to publish his works in political economy until, in 1888, he was offered the chair of political economy at Wharton.[15]

By the early 1900s, Simon Nelson Patten was one of the leaders of the growing institutional movement in economics. "A brilliant personality," he led the attack on the classical economics developed by David Ricardo, Thomas Malthus, and others. Rejecting their economics of scarcity, he emphasized the abundance of nature and man's ability to exploit it.[16] In his view, economics was not a dismal science "foretelling disaster and showing the fundamental limitations that are set on progress." It was, rather, a science of optimism that pointed the way to unending progress by showing man how to multiply nature through his intelligence.[17] As such, it had to concentrate on society and man, using other disciplines, such as psychology, to understand human motivation.

In the modern industrialized economy, man had been unable to adjust psychologically to the new environment because he still believed in outmoded laissez-fairist ideas, such as competition and profit. He had to learn to harness industrialism as well as to "co-adapt" to the societal changes caused by it. An experimental attitude was, therefore, necessary, and economics had to help develop that attitude by studying the operation of the market scientifically. Although Patten was not a "rigid inductivist," he did believe that the test of fact was the ultimate criterion for any economic analysis.[18] He also felt that economic theory should deal with institutional reform, not human nature. To him, economics had to be functional, experimental, and institutionally oriented as well as interdisciplinary if it was to comprehend the economic system and man's relation to it. For Patten, in short, man had reached the age of surplus and could now exploit it, especially in light of the growing sophistication of economics and its practitioners.

As a student of Patten, Tugwell absorbed these ideas almost completely. Throughout the rest of his life, Patten's influence would permeate his thinking. Tugwell's inclination to see patterns, his view of society as an organism, his emphasis on technology and its potential, his optimism for man's future (at least until 1945), and his call for an economy of abundance—these and many more facets of his thinking stemmed directly from Patten.[19] "Permanently biased," Tugwell was appalled when Patten was forced to retire from Wharton shortly after Nearing's dismissal. The "old man," however, took it in stride and would continue to watch over and aid his young protégé, helping young Tugwell to secure a job at Columbia in 1920.

As Nearing and Patten affected the young student in a personally intellectual way, Tugwell was also influenced by ideas. While at Wharton, he was introduced to the ideas of Thorstein Veblen, Frederick W. Taylor, and the instrumental pragmatists. To Tugwell, Veblen was a "strange creature" whose economic studies were animated by a racial bitterness and a need for intellectual revenge. Impressed by Veblen's scientific insight and reliance on social science, Tugwell felt he painted capitalism as it was and not as economists wanted it to be. The dominance of the machine process, the barbaric origins of business, and the fallacious government policies sustaining the capitalist system—all Veblen's themes—demonstrated the brilliance of the man and his analysis. Tugwell, however, later concluded that Veblen was too much of a theorist, relying on broad and vague generalizations without attempting to verify them.[20] An institutionalist, he refused to accept the implications of experimentalism and quantitative analysis, thereby diminishing the efficacy of his arguments. Veblen's one saving factor was that his idea of the dominance of business in industry and all its implications was true. And Tugwell, like Patten, later absorbed that idea into his own economic philosophy.

If Veblen's system lacked a methodology, Tugwell found one by studying Taylorism and instrumental pragmatism. Although pragmatism would not exert a significant influence on his thinking until the 1920s, he had at least some knowledge of it at this time. Both Patten and Nearing had emphasized it in their classes and in their economic theories, so much so that Tugwell could not help but learn about it.[21] By the time he met John Dewey at Columbia, he was favorably disposed to the pragmatic approach and willing to incorporate it into his own system, something he readily did in the 1920s. Taylorism, however, offered a unique approach. Tugwell had a good knowledge of Taylorism and its implications while in college, since it had been brought to the public's attention in 1911 during the Interstate Commerce Commission's investigation of the railroads. By 1912, the Taylor Society had been formed and had become the focus of the movement.[22]

Concerned with progress through efficient industrial management, Taylorism sought to increase industrial productivity by using technology and scientific labor policies. Tugwell was particularly impressed by its experimental attitude and its reliance on experts, although he believed Taylor had erred in "trying to confine his procedure to a set of principles." If Taylorism were thoroughly applied in the industrial system, Tugwell believed, industry in general would progress rapidly. But in the early twentieth century, this was not happening because organized labor opposed it; the Taylorites had not yet perfected their techniques; and business still refused to accept the machine completely.[23] The economy was, therefore, not reaching its potential and exploiting the abundance of the United States. In the 1920s and 1930s, Tugwell developed this idea further, calling it planning in an economy of abundance.

Having been exposed to such personal and intellectual influences definitely had an immediate effect on Tugwell. By the end of his junior year at Wharton, he had completed the requirements for his degree. Much to his surprise, he was offered an instructorship at $600 per year. He accepted, especially since in June 1914 he married Florence Arnold, of Buffalo, New York. With his father supplementing his income and his bride remaining in Buffalo, Tugwell spent his senior year at Wharton teaching, studying, and receiving his B.A. degree in 1915.

In 1915-1916, Tugwell remained at the University of Pennsylvania, serving as an instructor while completing his master's degree in economics. During this time he worked as a special investigator for the Governor's Tri-State Milk Commission and a fact finder for Gifford Pinchot, then president of the Pennsylvania Rural Progress Association. His work in this regard was significant in that it not only coincided with his observations of the political world around him but also gave him an opportunity to put some of his thoughts in writing.

Although teaching occupied most of his time, Tugwell was still watching events around him, particularly the Progressive movement and the presidency of Woodrow Wilson. In later years, Tugwell argued that Progressivism had developed out of the reactionary Populist revolt of the 1890s. Obsolete in its economic reasoning, it sustained a business system that was wasteful, corrupt, and exploitative. It sought to protect atomism in the economy instead of promoting cooperation and integration. It was not a reform movement, but a self-centered attempt on the part of business to increase its profits. What was so disillusioning was that the presidents of the time seemed to aid business in doing this. Although Theodore Roosevelt and Woodrow Wilson increased the powers of the executive, they failed to lead the country properly. The United States needed to change its values during their administrations and adjust to the modern industrialized system.[24] The United States could have become more "socialized" (a term meaning cooperation), but it did not, primarily because of these two men. The unfortunate result was that the American people suffered, especially the farmer, as Tugwell learned while working for the Milk Commission and Pinchot.[25]

With Charles Reitel, a fellow instructor at Pennsylvania, Tugwell wrote articles on the milk farmers. In them, he argued that instead of enjoying the prosperity of the times, the farmer was continually in debt and facing poverty. Not understanding the operation of the market, he sought government help in vain. Frustrated and depressed, his only recourse was violence, as in the milk strikes of 1917. These farmers had not yet recognized the benefits of cooperation and organization, depending instead on their individual initiative and strength to face their economic crises. When this failed, they became desperate and went on strike.

In Tugwell's opinion, this was unwise. Strikes were ineffective in dealing with the primary problem the farmer had consistently been facing—the disparity between his costs and his income. While prices for feed and livestock, farm equipment, and farm labor rose, the price for milk remained the same. The milk farmer was not receiving enough for his product to meet his cost. To resolve this, Tugwell believed these farmers had to learn to consider their costs in setting prices and to cooperate in sales organizations so that they could bargain with milk dealers as equals. Their future depended on cooperation, not individual enterprise.[26] Although written in 1917 by a young economics instructor, these articles clearly showed early intimations of Tugwell's later economic thinking on cooperation and planning.

Tugwell's participation in the milk strike issue and his subsequent writings followed the distress caused by Nearing's dismissal. By early 1917, other things began to occupy his attention. He had a daughter, was completing his M.A. in economics, and was working toward his Ph.D. Yet his feelings toward Wharton were bitter. Angry and frustrated, he was looking for an out. He got it with Carl Parker.

Carlton H. Parker was an enthusiastic, effervescent economics scholar who had been at the University of California and then became dean of the new School of Commerce at the University of Washington in Seattle. In the winter of 1916-1917, he was visiting the Wharton School, making a grand tour of intellectual leaders who might help him in his understanding of human behavior in economic life. Having studied migrant labor in California since 1913, he was going beyond the traditional limits of economics and exploring the psychological implications of issues such as labor-industry relations, wages, and working conditions. As an instructor, Tugwell participated in Parker's meetings with the Political and Social Science Conference at Wharton. The result was, as Tugwell later put it, that he became Parker's slave.[27]

Since Parker was combining anthropology and psychotherapy to study labor-employer phenomena, Tugwell began to read extensively in abnormal psychology and related areas. With his own questioning of classical economics and its assumptions of rationality already appearing, Tugwell was attracted even more by Parker and what he was trying to do. When Parker asked the young instructor to go with him to Washington, Tugwell agreed, a decision he later regretted. Young and inexperienced, frustrated and bitter over Nearing's dismissal and Patten's retirement at Wharton, he thought Parker might create a new and better Wharton School at the University of Washington.[28] Seattle, unfortunately, proved to be far less than he had hoped for.

Arriving there, Tugwell was appointed an assistant professor of economics and placed in charge of the Department of Marketing. Instead of reading and studying psychology, as he had planned, Tugwell spent his first year preparing course outlines and teaching, tasks he resented more and more each day.[29] One of the consolations he had was his friendship with William F. Ogburn (Department of Sociology), who would later be with Tugwell at Columbia and Chicago, and Ferdinand Silcox, whom Tugwell would later appoint head of the Forest Service in the 1930s. While in Seattle, Tugwell worked with Parker for the War Labor Board, which investigated labor conditions in the lumber camps. During this investigation, he met Silcox and Felix Frankfurter. While visiting the camps and observing conditions there, he got firsthand knowledge of conserving natural resources, the causes of the casual workers, and the dynamics of employer-employee relations. Looking back, at the end of his life, Tugwell was certain that this experience made him a "convinced collectivist," realizing that men must have "a higher goal than profit, than loafing on socially necessary jobs, than exploiting each other."[30]

By 1918, Tugwell's Seattle experience was teaching him more than this. Realizing the mistake he had made in going there, he was determined to leave, especially after Carl Parker's death. He had also become convinced that psychology, while helpful, was not the complete answer to labor problems. Workers still needed better wages and working conditions. Economists had to find ways to achieve them, a task Tugwell had to put off because of World War I.

On Felix Frankfurter's recommendation, Tugwell was offered a civilian job in Paris with the American University Union. Since his asthma was so severe, he could not serve in a combat capacity and no armed service would accept him. This job was the next best thing, so he accepted it. Essentially, he helped run a "kind of combined club and service station for university men who would be temporarily in Paris."[31]

Since the job was not very demanding, Tugwell used his time in Paris to study French culture and society, visit with friends who were passing through, and reflect on the war and its consequences. Again influenced by Patten, he blamed British imperialism for World War I. Germany had grasped the technological imperatives of the twentieth century and was, as Patten believed, progressing toward unification. Yet German militarism eventually overshadowed this, and Tugwell accepted Wilson's explanation for American entry into World War I. England and the United States had to cooperate, suppress militarism, and make the world safe for democracy.[32] When the war ended, Tugwell thought collectivism (world cooperation) had advanced and that, under Wilson's leadership, a renewed civilization was about to dawn. It was short-lived, though. Imperialism, in a new guise, reappeared, and the lesson of war had been lost.

On a more personal note, the war raised questions for Tugwell himself. With the failure of the Treaty of Versailles, he asked himself a very telling question and answered it in a very logical way:

Was I, also, a conservative? I found communism basically even less attractive than capitalism as a philosophy. Capitalism had the seeds in it of self-destruction, but communism had a kind of iron logic I instinctively distrusted. . . . I was . . . an incorrigible experimentalist.[33]

Although he wrote this at the very end of his life, it still follows the logical progression of his thinking in 1917-1918. Tugwell may have used words that sounded "radical," such as "socialism" and "communism," but he also had his own definitions and ideas about their meanings. He was not then, nor was he ever, either of those extremes; rather, as he said, he was an experimentalist, and one who wanted cooperation and all that implied.

The war stimulated other thoughts for Tugwell. Despite the enormous waste and bloodshed, he believed that World War I served a useful purpose in modifying the erroneous laissez-fairism of the people. America's wartime "socialism" had been predicated on the assumption that coordination within business and between business and government would lead to increased productivity.[34] Not only did productivity increase, but the economy in general functioned quite smoothly. The War Industries Board had run the industrial system like a "well-oiled machine," more on a voluntary basis than on a forced one. Control of production, prices, and consumption had been achieved to a large degree, although Tugwell did feel more enforcement in the consumption sector was necessary. All in all, the war had accelerated American economic growth greatly while allowing business to experiment with a "kind of voluntary socialism," which it liked.[35] We became more "socially-minded" as a nation, while our "organization became functional and experimental."[36] We had, in short, recognized the benefits of planning, at least for a short time.

Tugwell soon learned, however, that the lessons of the war would be easily forgotten. Ironically, he too would forget some things. Tired and sick with influenza, he returned home in January 1919.

In November 1918, Tugwell had written to his father that he was ready to come home and work in the family farm and canning business. Excited to say the least, Charles Tugwell gave his son what he had requested—one-third of the business. Yet, while he fought off sinus and respiratory problems and while he truly tried to farm, Rexford realized that living comfortably in Wilson, New York, was not what he wanted.[37] He needed more, and it seemed that the university would provide it.

Tugwell soon learned that what one wants is not necessarily what others are willing to give. Although he decided that he needed to return to the University of Pennsylvania for his Ph.D., Tugwell was not welcomed with open arms by Ernest Patterson, then chairman of the Economics Department. Patterson pointed out to Tugwell that his undergraduate and graduate work had been mediocre at best, and that Tugwell seemed to have a penchant more for causes than for scholarship. Years later, Tugwell felt that Patterson really feared he was another Nearing in the making.[38] Tugwell's other teachers, especially Patten, encouraged the young man to return and complete his degree. He did so, and by the spring of 1920, he had passed his exams in economics, sociology, and English. Perhaps even more encouraging was Columbia's offer of an instructorship for the 1920 academic year. Tugwell believed that Patten had secured the position for him.[39] With his life in order, his goals established, and his determination set, Tugwell left for Columbia, where, in the 1920s, he would establish himself not only as a scholar but also as an adviser to a future president.

NOTES

1. Rexford G. Tugwell, *To the Lesser Heights of Morningside* (Philadelphia: University of Pennsylvania Press, 1982), p. 4.

2. Ibid., pp. 5-8.

3. Ibid., pp. 12-13.

4. Rexford G. Tugwell papers, folder *"The Red and Blue,* March 1913," FDR Library, box 51, and "Scrapbook, University of Pennsylvania, 1911," FDR Library, box 123; Tugwell, *Lesser Heights,* pp. 19-20; Bernard Sternsher, *Rexford Tugwell and the New Deal* (New Brunswick, N.J.: Rutgers University Press, 1964), 3ff.; Blair Bolles, "The Sweetheart of the Regimenters," *American Mercury* 39 (September 1936): 79ff.; Russell Lord, *The Wallaces of Iowa* (Boston: Houghton Mifflin, 1947), 348-50.

5. Tugwell, *Lesser Heights,* pp. 22, 24-25.

6. Ibid., pp. 35ff., 46.

7. Ibid., p. 51; Sternsher, p. 5.

8. Rexford G. Tugwell papers, "Scrapbook, University of Pennsylvania, 1911," FDR Library, box 123. See especially the folder containing copies of *The Red and Blue.*

9. Tugwell, *Lesser Heights,* pp. 51-53. Tugwell made lifelong friends at Wharton, such as John Lansel, who would serve with him in the Resettlement Administration.

10. Scott Nearing, *The Super Race: An American Problem* (New York, B. W. Huebsch, 1912), 20-24, 75ff.

11. Rexford G. Tugwell to Scott, April 25, 1972, Rexford G. Tugwell papers, folder "Nearing, Scott, 1942-1973," FDR Library, box 17; Tugwell, *Lesser Heights,* p. 27.

12. Scott Nearing, *The Making of a Radical: A Political Autobiography* (New York: Harper and Row, 1972), 56-57, 84ff.

13. Tugwell, *Lesser Heights,* pp. 66-69.

14. Simon Nelson Patten, *Essays in Economic Theory,* edited by Rexford G. Tugwell (New York: Alfred A. Knopf, 1924), v; quote is from a letter written by Tugwell to Allan G. Gruchy, published in Gruchy's *Modern Economic Thought: The American Contribution* (New York: Augustus Kelley, 1947), 408.

15. Henry Seagar, "Introduction" to Patten, *Essays in Economic Theory,* pp. xi-xvii.

16. Simon Nelson Patten, *The New Basis of Civilization* (New York: Macmillan, 1907), chs. 9 and 10; Rexford Tugwell, "Some Formative Influences on the Life of Simon Nelson Patten," *American Economic Review,* Suppl. (March 1923): 282-85; Gruchy, *Modern Economic Thought,* pp. 408-415.

17. Rexford Tugwell, "Notes on the Life and Work of Simon Nelson Patten," *Journal of Political Economy* 31 (April 1923): 175-76. See also Tugwell, "A Bibliography of the Works of Simon Nelson Patten," *Annals of the American Academy of Political and Social Science* 107 (May 1923): 358-67.

18. Tugwell, "Notes on the Life and Work of Simon Nelson Patten," p. 185.

19. Tugwell, *Lesser Heights*, p. 43.

20. Thorstein Veblen, *The Theory of the Leisure Class* (New York: Macmillan, 1899) and *The Theory of Business Enterprise* (New York: Scribner, 1904) are the works that particularly influenced Tugwell. Quoted materials are from Rexford Tugwell, "The Theory of Occupational Obsolescence," *Political Science Quarterly* 46 (1931): 170-227, and "Veblen and Business Enterprise," *New Republic* (March 19, 1939): 215-19. See also Rexford Tugwell to Paul Homan, January 21, 1931, Rexford Tugwell papers, folder "Homan, Paul T. 1930-1952" FDR Library, box 11; Mrs. G. W. Kenrick (private secretary to the governor) to Professor Allan G. Gruchy, July 16, 1946 with attachment, Tugwell papers, folder "Gr-Gu" FDR Library, box 9. On p. 3, no. 1, of this attachment, Tugwell indicated that he had never been influenced by Veblen. The explanation for such a statement is the time at which it was written. By 1946, Tugwell was very much disillusioned with economics as a profession, even going so far as to consider himself a political scientist. Thus, his dissociation from Veblen is not surprising. Also, Tugwell was overemphasizing his association with Patten to such an extent that he was underplaying everyone else's influence. The personal influence was far outweighing the intellectual. In spite of this one statement, the intellectual influence of Veblen is there, especially in Tugwell's attitude toward business and the free enterprise system.

21. Sternsher, *Tugwell and the New Deal*, p. 13.

22. Rexford Tugwell, *Industry's Coming of Age* (New York: Harcourt, Brace, 1927), 120-21.

23. Ibid., pp. 123-24.

24. Tugwell, *Light of Other Days*, pp. 230-55; Rexford Tugwell, "The New Deal: The Progressive Tradition," *Western Political Quarterly* 3 (September 1950): 390-427.

25. Tugwell, *Light of Other Days*, pp. 235, 288. For his views on Roosevelt and Wilson extending executive power, see Tugwell, *The Enlargement of the Presidency* (Garden City, N.Y.: Doubleday, 1960), chs. 33-38.

26. Rexford Tugwell and Charles Reitel, "Meaning and Making of Milk Strikes," *Pennsylvania Farmer* 42 (September 22, 1917): 1, 4ff.; Tugwell, "Marketing Farm Products," *Pennsylvania Farmer* 42 (December 22, 1917): 12.

27. Tugwell, *Lesser Heights*, pp. 69-75.

28. Ibid., pp. 79-81.

29. Ibid., p. 90.

30. Ibid., pp. 89-90. The casual worker will be dealt with in Ch. 3.

31. Ibid., p. 99.

32. Ibid., pp. 61-66.

33. Ibid., pp. 119-20.

34. Rexford Tugwell, "America's War-Time Socialism," *The Nation* 124 (April 6, 1927): 365.

35. Ibid., pp. 365-66.

36. Rexford Tugwell, "The Paradox of Peace," *New Republic* 54 (April 18, 1928): 264.

37. Tugwell, *Lesser Heights*, pp. 122-26.

38. Ibid., p. 128.

39. Ibid., pp. 128-29.

3

Columbia University: 1920–1932

What I wrote was not always publishable, but much of it was; and since it was fairly successful, it became a regular and cultivated occupation.

What I had done [in the 1920s] was to follow my normal tendency to think as I wrote and to work out my ideas from one tentative statement to another. What I was intent on was distant and difficult; I only glimpsed it myself at times of sustained effort.

Rexford G. Tugwell, *To the Lesser Heights of Morningside*, pp. 173, 187

It is difficult to pinpoint precisely the date when Rexford Tugwell wrote these two statements. Both were in his last autobiography, published posthumously in 1982 and written when Tugwell was nearly 82 years old. Nevertheless, despite this difficulty and his apparent age, these statements best describe his years at Columbia and his natural tendency to write out his thoughts as they were developing, evolving, and taking on new and deeper meanings. From 1920, when he was appointed an instructor on Columbia's teaching faculty, until 1932, when he joined Governor Franklin D. Roosevelt's Brains Trust, Tugwell had written four books as sole author, was a joint author of a major textbook on economics, directed a symposium on economics and edited the publication from it, was a joint editor and contributor to a book on Soviet Russia, and wrote over 45 articles that were published in professional journals, magazines, and academic society bulletins. During this same period, he finished his Ph.D. in economics at the University of Pennsylvania and ascended the academic ladder at Columbia to full professor. The Columbia years were good years, productive years, successful years for a young scholar. They were also a time for reflection, maturing, and thinking ideas through.

It was during this Columbia era that distinctly Tugwellian themes appeared and unfolded: his attacks on classical economics; his assault on laissez-faire and the American business system; his analysis of

Taylorism, technology, and cultural lag; his call for order and planning; his defining of the economist's role in society; his demand for revitalizing America's educational system; and his in-depth appraisal of the Great Depression and Herbert Hoover's handling of it. Tentative, evolving solutions for American agricultural problems and industrial development were offered, suggested, and worked on in his thinking and writings.

In all of this, Tugwell's maturation as an economic thinker and a political economist occurred. It was all done in an academic environment, and the lessons Tugwell learned about academics were hard and painful. Jealousy, pettiness, and small-mindedness affected him adversely at first, but positively in the long run, toughening his skin and firming up his self-confidence. By the time he joined Roosevelt's Brains Trust, Tugwell was not only well known but also a mature, hardened, and self-assured individual. The Columbia years were good, and they were preparatory for his future in government service.

While an instructor at Columbia in 1920, Tugwell was still working on his Ph.D. in economics at the University of Pennsylvania. With Leo S. Rowe and Clyde King encouraging him, he faced the less encouraging Patterson and the constitutional lawyers at the university. Looking back at the end of his life, Tugwell felt that he had made a "tactical" error in the choice of his subject. Interested "in the direction and control of economic enterprise" and how much "could be done, short of public ownership, to contain and coordinate the rapidly expanding industrial system," he chose to study the economic basis of the public interest in light of the Supreme Court's handling of antitrust laws.[1]

At the same time, he recalled, he felt the antitrust laws were ineffective in protecting the public interest, although reformers had done "fairly well in regulating traction, water, power, and warehouse interests." How to have the federal government do this for "oil, steel, sugar, etc. monopolies" was the problem. To resolve it, Tugwell examined common-law regulations of business to ascertain the claim government had to regulate economic affairs. After analyzing court decisions and surveying economic theory, he concluded that government, representative of the people, could watch over services and prices. In his opinion, services had to be adequate for what the public needed while prices had to be reasonable. Although business theoretically could govern itself vis-à-vis services and prices, Tugwell concluded it was better for the government to regulate, since business consistently refused to adopt policies promoting low prices, high wages, and no speculative profits. Thus, only government, thinking of the public interest, would keep production high and prices low.

The antitrust laws, moreover, tended to be ineffective because size of corporations, in Tugwell's thinking, was irrelevant. The Supreme Court was regulating business, not with common law but with the police-power clause of the Constitution. Inconsistent in doing so, it was using economic, not legal, bases for regulation. Regulation was absolutely necessary so as to assure the general welfare, but not in the manner the Court had done it.[2] This attitude regarding antitrust laws and their implementation goes a long way toward explaining Tugwell's later opposition to the antitrustism of the New Deal. At the time he wrote his Ph.D., and later as a New Dealer, he consistently believed that it did not work.

Although Patterson had grave doubts, Tugwell's dissertation was accepted and a synopsis of it was published. With Ph.D. in hand, the young instructor was promoted to assistant professor at Columbia in 1922. Between 1922 and 1932, Tugwell ascended the professorial ladder at a regular pace. He became an associate professor in 1926 and full professor in 1931. Rewards for his teaching and publication, his promotions were an indication of just how good the Columbia years were.

Throughout his tenure at Columbia, Tugwell, despite his pronouncements to the contrary, had a relatively light teaching schedule, thereby allowing him to concentrate on research and writing. As a teacher, he was at his best when he taught in moderation. Preferring to work with bright students, he was never one to volunteer for heavy teaching loads. His one saving grace at Columbia was his role in the Contemporary Civilization classes. Under the direction of Herbert Hawkes and John Coss, Tugwell was brought in early in his instructorship days. Feeling it replaced "department store education," he believed, then and later, that it was a course that prepared students for "life in a democracy."[3] He enjoyed it, taught it, helped prepare the syllabus for it, and prided himself on it. Contemporary Civilization was supposed to be "a detached approach to industrialism and the contemporary problems it had brought with it." It was a course in which Tugwell and his fellow instructors tried to integrate the social sciences and philosophy in dealing with industrialism's problems. It taught students American values, the American free enterprise system, American business, and their consequences. Students were also taught to think of alternatives and the future.[4]

Although he taught graduate-level economic theory and later worked in the senior honors program, Tugwell was so enthralled with

Contemporary Civilization that he wrote a textbook for it. Coauthored with Thomas Munro (Department of Philosophy) and Roy E. Stryker, *American Economic Life and the Means of Its Improvement* was a novel approach to economics, detailing poverty, riches, and comfort in America while suggesting ways those who lived in poverty might move or be moved upward by "increased productivity, by more equitable sharing, and by more reflective uses of goods and services."[5] In assessing Contemporary Civilization and *American Economic Life*, Tugwell's enthusiasm for them is not surprising, since they both typified his desire to "find wider and wider generalizations containing and giving meaning to the contemporary world . . . as well as tying together and finding direction" for progress.[6] Years later, Tugwell felt this was what was happening to him in the 1920s, and Columbia provided him with the time and environment to think, reflect, and sort all of this out. This freedom, paid for by Charles Beard in 1917 when he resigned over the Board of Trustees' actions interfering with academic freedom, was crucial for Tugwell, or at least he thought so.[7]

In searching for answers, Tugwell looked to others for help, something he was used to doing. At Columbia, he found help from colleagues who were cordial and friendly, such as Hawkes and Coss. Yet, of all those he knew at Columbia, the men who would truly help him and influence his future development were John Dewey and Wesley Mitchell.

To Tugwell, John Dewey was "the only philosopher" of his generation, and one "who was as difficult to read as he was to hear." He considered himself a disciple, and his interaction and reading of Dewey especially affected his experimental approach to economics. Tugwell felt that Dewey "encouraged" his turning away from classical economics and politics, and "his admission of the future as the chief influence on the present." Pragmatism "meant the future could be brought into focus, judged in advance as a working hypothesis, and altered before it was reached."[8] This was planning as Tugwell was beginning to understand it and as Dewey helped him to see it.

Wesley Mitchell, on the other hand, influenced Tugwell by his "search for uniformities in group behavior" and his tool of measurement. This latter was particularly ironic, since Tugwell seldom, if ever, utilized a quantitative approach in his research and writing. To Tugwell, Mitchell was an experimental economist who was "interested in policy, in fact, and in the future." A free spirit, he was "the best we have" in economics.[9]

It is one thing to say someone influenced you; it is something else to recognize just how that person affected you. While there is no doubt that Tugwell was affected in his economic thinking by Mitchell, he was probably more affected by Mitchell's being an older colleague watching out for him. By the mid-1920s, especially after the publication of *Industry's Coming of Age* in 1927, Tugwell felt his colleagues did not think he was much of an economist and that he did not have much of a future. In fact, Tugwell went so far as to say that his colleagues "wrote him off."[10] He was even encouraged by Hawkes and Coss to seek an administrative post, something he did unsuccessfully.

It was Mitchell who told him of his colleagues' disapproval and Mitchell who shielded him. There were several reasons why Tugwell was supposedly "written off," including his attacks on classical economics, his condemnation of economists who consulted for business while working for the university, and his experimental approach to economics. Also, his prolific writing probably had something to do with the coldness. All of it hurt Tugwell's feelings. In dealing with it, however, Tugwell delved into his work even more. He also saw Mitchell in a friendly light. How else was he to deal with these problems, especially since Simon Patten had died? Tugwell worked and published even more.

After 1925, Tugwell did a number of things to branch out. To earn extra money, he taught at the American Institute of Banking and wrote book reviews for the *Saturday Review of Literature*. He also began to do research, to study, and to write on a variety of topics, especially agriculture. His writings facilitated his being asked to meet with and talk to Governor Frank O. Lowden of Illinois, who was considering a presidential campaign. Although Lowden's hopes were dashed, Al Smith's weren't. In 1928, Smith's "alter ego," Belle Maskowitz, brought Tugwell in to advise Smith on agriculture. Tugwell recommended that a balance be achieved between industry and agriculture, and he even proposed his Advance Ratio Price Plan. Smith, unfortunately, chose to listen to George Peek, and Tugwell was out.[11] Nevertheless, others wanted to hear Tugwell. In 1928, Herbert Croly, editor of the *New Republic*, asked Tugwell to write two articles per month on economic issues of the campaign. Tugwell not only wrote the articles but also relished the social gatherings he attended as one of the contributing editors of the magazine.

If these 1928 activities were indicative of Tugwell's growing reputation, there was another that contributed to it in a different manner. In 1927, Tugwell was a member of a trade union delegation that spent ten weeks in the Soviet Union. The delegation was headed by Albert F. Coyle and included such notables as Robert Dunn of the American Civil Liberties Union, J. W. Fitzpatrick of the Actors and Artists of

America, and Stuart Chase, co-founder of Consumer's Research. Tugwell was to study agriculture. While there, he spent a fair amount of
time sightseeing and giving speeches. On his return, the delegation put
together a group of essays on Soviet Russia, with Tugwell writing a
chapter on agriculture. Neither then nor later was he a partisan of
Russian communism, nor did he accept Marxism. Nevertheless, what
was an innocent scholarly adventure later turned into a nightmare for
Tugwell. Critics in the 1930s would accuse him of being a Communist,
a regimenter, and a proponent of dictatorship, all of which was non-
sense. Years later, Tugwell indicated that he was "considered suspi-
cious by many" because of the trip. It was something he never lived
down.[12]

By 1929, Tugwell's Russian trip didn't matter. In that year, he received a fellowship to study agriculture abroad and, with his family,
he went to France. While he was in France, his sister died. On his return, he published his findings in a series of articles. The last excursion
Tugwell made before entering the Roosevelt coterie involved education. In 1931, E. E. Day, who was in charge of the Social Science
Division of the Laura Spellman Rockefeller Foundation, asked him
to undertake a reassessment of social science teaching in American
universities and to write a report. Traveling for nearly six months to
various universities, he talked to teachers in the social sciences and
found that they all agreed something needed to be done. The report
was prepared by Tugwell and Leon Keyserling, T. C. Blaisdell, C. W.
Cole, and Joseph McGoldrick. Tugwell wrote a chapter that revealed
his feelings on American education and its future. In light of his own
education and the economic crisis of the depression, Tugwell argued
strongly that there needed to be a definite turn toward the future.
Students needed to define and sort out alternatives and, using an experimental approach, they needed to plan. In his report, Tugwell suggested that an institute be established to collect materials for storage
and distribution on this new approach. Years later, Tugwell felt this
report and publication "was one of the most considerable efforts I
had ever made."[13]

It was also during this time that Tugwell thought about, researched,
and wrote on a variety of topics, including the economist's role in
society, farming, labor, planning, industry, laissez-faire and the business system, the depression, Hoover's handling of the crisis, and a
critique of Soviet Russia. All were part and parcel of his evolving economic thinking and his political economy.

Among the many problems Tugwell analyzed in his writings through-out the 1920s, the role of the economist in modern society was para-mount. Rejecting the classical theorists who made economics a dismal science, he preferred the institutionalism of Patten and his contem-poraries. Whereas the classicists like Adam Smith, Thomas Malthus, and James and John Stuart Mill were primarily moral philosophers who infused natural law into economics in order to develop a logical body of general laws, the institutionalists like Patten recognized the importance of human behavior in its effects on economic theory.[14] To Tugwell, this was particularly important. He consistently argued that economists, as social scientists, were "imperatively required . . . to say what it is the industrial system does to men and to define what it is men have a right to expect from industry." Economics is the only social science that predicts the future by determining what the eco-nomic system can and should do, since it alone provides "the plans for its doing."[15]

By developing a "psychological theory of man" and by accepting an experimental attitude in its approach to societal problems, Tugwell believed economics could meet this obligation as well as dispel its traditional image.[16] Also, modern experimental economics, by analyz-ing industrial forces with quantitative tools, discovering new bases for policy, and developing a body of relevant principles, would help man subject nature to his will, confront the inevitable problem of change in modern society, and sustain the basic human impulses of exploration, experimentation, and cooperation. In the age of surplus that the twentieth century represented, all this would make man's life more pleasant and fruitful.[17]

Throughout the 1920s, in his writings Tugwell applied this approach to the economic problems of the United States. Regarding the worker, for example, Tugwell felt that the basic human impulse to wander and seek adventure was being repressed by the "modern mode of life." Working in the gloomy interior of a factory, men were continually co-erced to lead monotonous lives, surrender their freedom, suffer "disas-trous psychic maladjustments," and observe the disruption of their home life.[18] Wages, although high in comparison with European wage levels, could not sustain a life-style equivalent to the worker's produc-tive contribution. Even the security of his job was uncertain because technology, while enhancing his efficiency potential, simultaneously threatened him with occupational obsolescence.[19] Frustrated and in-secure, he was developing into a potentially disruptive force in Amer-ican society.

In Tugwell's thinking, the masses of the American labor movement could be divided into three groups, each more or less inclined to utilize revolutionary violence to ameliorate its living conditions. First and foremost were the "bread and butter men" who were typically good unionists or possessed the characteristics of good unionists. Physically sound and psychologically normal, they were uneducated but skilled in their occupations. "Of good basic stuff," they could be "easily moulded into an effective and courageous, if slow-moving, army" that would eventually and peacefully move toward the acquisition of industrial control. All they needed was effective leadership. The second group, the migratories or industrial nomads, were neither as pliable nor as peaceful as the unionists.[20] Mentally inept and consistent wanderers, they were the casuals. Although Tugwell distinguished between the upper casual who periodically gave way under industrial pressure and the lower casual who continuously lacked any social roots, he believed both represented dangerous threats to the American economic system, the latter in particular. Victimized by industry and ignored by society, they comprised about 38 percent of the American work force. Alone and isolated, the casual was primarily a social illness. Under the authority of labor leaders, the third group in Tugwell's scheme, they might become revolutionaries.[21]

Tugwell generally believed American labor leaders possessed the "qualities of leadership men value." Combining the characteristics of demagogue, prophet, politician, and idealist, most labor leaders fought effectively for the rights and privileges of the average workingman. There were, however, some, like those in the IWW, who were not so trustworthy. Self-appointed martyrs, they were agitators and outlaws who offered "the dream of a worker's empire" as an escape for the casual. Preaching violence and revolution, they were responsible for "I.W.W.-ism" and its philosophy of despair and the tragic occurrences that the Centralia (Washington) clash between lumber workers and townspeople symbolized.[22] Unless their influence was neutralized, Tugwell feared, they might infect the entire American work force.

To accomplish this neutralization, he suggested that industry approach the problem rationally. In the short run, he believed, industry had to provide the casual with better working conditions, shorter hours, and higher wages so as to diminish the appeal of revolutionary leaders and the discontent they fed upon. In the long run, industry and American society had to develop a broad social program involving "the job, the home, the city environment, the possible uses of leisure, and the relation of men in industry to political authority," so as to eliminate the fundamental causes of casual labor. Although Tugwell admitted he did not have any specific suggestions to implement such a program, he felt this was the only way the dangers of the casual could be eliminated. The United States had to make an honest attempt to fit him into a "producing niche where he can function with reasonable efficiency, happiness, and permanency."[23]

As for the rest of the labor force, Tugwell argued that the conservative union, while weak, could promote labor's interests by fighting for bread-and-butter goals.[24] In this way, the union could at least improve the worker's immediate standard of living. Tugwell, however, did not believe these policies would resolve the weak position of labor vis-à-vis industry. Symptomatic of the inequities in the normalcy system, its position could be enhanced only by fundamental changes in America's economic philosophy and societal institutions.[25] Long-range in scope, these changes would establish the necessary equilibrium in the decision-making process between industry and labor and between industry and farming, so that the United States could achieve its economic potential.

While the normalcy system exploited labor, Tugwell argued that it also sustained industrial domination at the expense of the farmer. Unlike the worker, who confronted psychological frustration and job insecurity, the farmer encountered more serious threats to his lifestyle. To him, industrialization and urbanization spelled disaster. His family life, once closely knit and cooperative, became distant and isolated as his family and his neighbors migrated to the cities. His self-sufficiency, once dependent on the "diurnal rhythms" of nature, was transformed into a dependence on economic forces beyond his understanding. Even his traditions, once respected and valued by all, deteriorated into obsolete goals no one cared about. Alone and confused, the farmer had become a tragic figure in a society committed to industrial progress.[26]

For Tugwell, the practical implications of these developments were clearly illustrated throughout the 1920s. During this period, he consistently argued that the farmer confronted three critical problems. First, the agricultural-industrial relationship was imbalanced. Although World War I had witnessed an abnormal increase in farm prices, the general price decline beginning in 1919 affected the farmer almost immediately. Between 1919 and 1924, farm prices continued in a downward spiral and remained in it for the rest of the decade, despite the general rise in industrial prices and the overall standard of living. In view of his relatively stable costs, this constant price decline signified that the farmer's purchasing power was not keeping pace with "the increased purchasing power of the townsman's dollar." He was forced to accept low prices for his own goods while paying more for the industrial products he needed.[27]

To complicate matters, the basic inelasticity of agriculture, the farmer's second problem, intensified his already depressed condition in a distinctive way. Unlike industry, which could manipulate the supply and price of its products according to market demands, agriculture was inherently incapable of making such adjustments. In times of prosperity and rising prices, farm prices rose high above the general price level, while in times of depression, they fell significantly because farmers had to deal with nature, not people. Immune to market fluctuations, farmers were unable to control their supply of products easily or quickly in order to exploit or resist price changes. Tugwell did believe, however, that this phenomenon might be alleviated if the farmer confronted his last problem, organization.[28]

Adamant in economic thinking, the farmer had consistently refused to recognize that the more organized an economic group is, the more it adjusts to market changes. A staunch individualist, he let his physical isolation, dependence on weather, and occupational diversity distort his thinking about the economy until the technological revolution of the twentieth century. With the growing use of automobiles and telephones, farmers began to communicate more frequently, learning that not only was there little or no difference between the problems of a wheat farmer and a corn farmer, but also that cooperation was necessary. In the 1920s, this realization was laying the foundations for an agrarian revolt that, Tugwell hoped, would go beyond the activities of legislative farm blocs and farmer-labor movements in its demands for agricultural relief.[29]

To provide that relief, Tugwell suggested that the basic causes of farm distress be removed. In the short run, farmers' incomes had to be increased by diminishing the farm surplus, even at the expense of the consumer, while in the long run, a "delicately balanced system" had to be established in which "not only farmers' production and consumption schemes but also those of other groups of the community [would] be brought into some kind of harmonious operation that would yield a balanced, orderly, and sane system of economic life." A concert of interests, this equilibrium would not only assure an equitable price relationship between industry and agriculture but also guarantee continuous progress for the American economy as a whole.[30]

As an economist, Tugwell believed that the implementation of this concert implied introducing fundamental changes in agriculture. A long-range process, agriculture had to undergo a basic reorganization in which its technical efficiency would be increased, the costs and prices of its products lowered, and the extent of its markets widened. Involving immense research and extensive capital outlays, such a program was the farmer's only hope to increase his purchasing power and to provide agriculture with the ability to stand on its own feet.[31] In Tugwell's opinion, this program demonstrated the importance of planning in the modern economic process, since planning was the means on which the concert of interests and agricultural reorganization depended.

In all of his writings on the farm question in the 1920s, Tugwell consistently emphasized that planning was the only way to effectively help the farmer. All-inclusive, it implied production and price controls, revision of the tariff structures, the possible consolidation of farm units, the use of scientific experts in policy making, and the adoption of an experimental attitude. Agricultural planning, however, did not necessarily imply ruthless collectivization and revolutionary violence, as had happened in Russia. Based on the cooperativeness of farmers and the extension of governmental authority, it would succeed in a democratic country like the United States.[32]

Tugwell suggested that planning be implemented in a number of ways. In the 1928 presidential election, for example, he proposed the Advance Ratio Price Plan to Al Smith. The purpose of the plan was to determine scientifically the number of acres, the amount of production per acre, and the consumption of farm goods so that a ratio price for farm products could be established a year in advance. By adjusting farm production to actual consumption, farmers were guaranteed a base price proportionate to industrial prices. To administer the program, Tugwell suggested that a corporation be established to distribute the contracts and funds to farmers cooperating in the plan. Although difficult to administer, the scheme made the farm surplus problem more manageable.[33] In the long run, it also demonstrated the feasibility of restricting production.

If this scheme proved unacceptable, Tugwell suggested that the government conduct a survey of the amount of land necessary to meet normal consumption needs at profitable prices. Notices of limitations on planting, on a basis of ten-year averages, would then be given by local or county agents of the Farm Board to individual farmers. If any farmer produced more than his allotment, he might be penalized by being denied the use of railways and warehouses.[34] In either scheme, Tugwell emphasized that the government had to play a stronger role than it had in the past. It had to conduct the statistical surveys, restrict production accordingly, control prices, and experiment in its programs. If the evidence indicated, the government had to facilitate the consolidation of farm units.[35] Although Tugwell was convinced by this time that the family farm should be abandoned in the future, he believed the farmers' individualism and the general laissez-faire philosophy of the United States opposed such a step. These forces hindered the implementation of planning and relied instead on tariff revision and McNary-Haugenism as prime solutions to the farm problem.

Despite their popularity in the 1920s, Tugwell did not consider tariffs and McNary-Haugenism as primary amelioratives for farm distress. He argued that, if used selectively, the most the tariff could accomplish was to "artificially" raise domestic prices, restrict markets, and make the problem of overproduction worse. With the Hawley-Smoot Tariff, nothing was accomplished, since it neither helped American industry nor promoted the "cause of international harmony."[36] McNary-Haugenism, on the other hand, seemed to be much more promising, although it, too, left much to be desired.

In an effort to help the farmer, four bills sponsored by Sen. Charles McNary and Rep. Gilbert Haugen were passed by the Congress between 1924 and 1928. Although each differed in detail, they all contained the basic feature of a Federal Farm Board. Established to buy up the surplus of designated farm commodities at a price based on pre-World War I averages, this board had the option of selling the surplus abroad or storing it in warehouses until prices rose. An equalization fee was levied on producers of the various commodities so that the government would not incur any financial losses. Essentially providing for a combination of price fixing and dumping, the bills were consistently vetoed by President Coolidge, who applied what Tugwell called his "Vermont shop-keeping economics" to agriculture.[37]

Seeing McNary-Haugenism as a step in the right direction, Tugwell believed that it offered only mild palliatives for a serious problem. By concentrating on the surplus, it failed to recognize the basic weaknesses in agriculture itself, failed to provide for the extension of government authority in assuring general price regulations, and failed to develop a cooperative structure for those farmers affected by it.[38] Planning, mechanization, and consolidation, and all they implied— these were the answers to the farm question. Eventually, they could be applied in agriculture and industry, once the American people discarded their philosophy of laissez-faire and recognized the inequities produced by an industry-dominated system.

More than anything else, Tugwell consistently emphasized that industrial reform was the key to the American economy's functioning properly. As the twentieth century progressed, Tugwell reasoned, technology and Taylorism in industry had begun to characterize American economic growth. Life was becoming more and more dependent on machines. In and of itself, this was good because not only were machines "accurate, tireless, and self-operative," but they also were enhancing America's productive potential to the point that it was within a "stone's throw" of abolishing human work and labor.[39] Taylorism, moreover, by expertly studying better means to increase productivity, was enabling industry to mature in such a way that, by the 1920s, the United States had arrived at an era of economic surplus and maintenance.[40] Theoretically at least, an economy of abundance had been achieved. In reality, this was not the case.

In spite of this phenomenal potential, Tugwell argued that "the most puzzling phenomenon associated with this efficiency is that it has not made us wealthier than we are." The United States still confronted the problems of poverty, overwork, and illness. Industries, overequipped with plant, machinery, and men, still produced more than the market could absorb, and the economy in general still failed to distribute its wealth equitably. Instead of letting the machines work for him, man in effect was working for the machine.[41] Tugwell believed there was only one explanation for this intolerable situation: A cultural lag had developed in the United States.

As an institutional economist, Tugwell believed that man, although incapable of altering his nature, could change his environment. In doing so, he also had to adjust his thinking so as to reap the full benefits of those changes. When he refused to do so, a cultural lag or imbalance developed, as had happened in the United States. What happened is that as technology increased America's productive potential, American values remained constant. Social and political institutions failed to adapt to the complexity of modern life, so that America fell behind the technology that was inevitably being developed. Intellectually, spiritually, and morally, the United States continued to adhere to a nineteenth-century value system in a twentieth-century world. Nowhere was this more clearly illustrated than in technological unemployment.[42]

Traditionally, the classicists had argued that technological improvement, by reducing costs, and consequently prices, increased incomes, which, when spent, created a demand for more products. This increased demand, moreover, would eventually cause business to invest its income in more plant capacity, which, in turn, would create more jobs. A cyclical phenomenon, the economy continued to grow because the technological improvement was helping everyone.[43] In Tugwell's thinking, nothing was further from the truth. Despite the simplicity of its cause-and-effect analysis and its general acceptance by the American people, he emphasized that there were fundamental flaws in the theory.

Tugwell reasoned that technological improvement did not automatically reduce costs, because capital was needed to implement the change, and business, uncertain whether the new machinery would be profitable, would ordinarily be reluctant to introduce it. Although businessmen in the 1920s were optimistic about the advantages of machines, this did not necessarily imply that prices might be lowered. In Tugwell's view, business would lower prices only when there was a promise of full continuity in the productive process. In light of the individualistic character of American industry, this meant that businessmen reduced prices only if and when they were certain that consumers would buy more of *their* products and not their competitors'. Similarly, businessmen, instead of reinvesting their profits in industry, continually sought to increase their surplus reserves. In the 1920s, Tugwell was certain that those reserves were being invested in corporate securities, buying on the open market, advertising, foreign loans, speculation on the stock market, and, only minimally, for plant expansion. Businessmen were not doing what the classical theory said they would naturally do. As a result, technological unemployment worsened.

To resolve the problem, Tugwell suggested that the United States adjust to the inevitable changes taking place and recognize that unemployment is only incidental to, not caused by, technology. In the short run, this implied alleviating occupational obsolescence by reeducating the worker for a new job and by establishing a social security system in which both the government and business paid to support the displaced worker until he found a new position. In the long run, this meant that the United States, and business in particular, had to learn to adjust demand to supply and cost to price through planning.[44] Although convinced that planning was the only solution, Tugwell was not certain that it would be adopted, because its implementation depended upon America's discarding its philosophy of laissez-faire.

As the traditional business theory, Tugwell felt laissez-faire was responsible for all the problems confronting the United States, ranging from the cultural lag to the basic disequilibrium within the economic decision-making process. A simplistic theory, it emphasized that the national welfare was best served by the individual businessmen who competed among themselves for profit without restrictive government interference. The government's function, in fact, was to sustain business interests within the economy by preventing monopolization and by keeping "economic affairs in a continual state of conflict."[45] To go beyond that was unacceptable, even if the government considered regulation to be necessary. Competition, profits, and individualism— these were the means by which the economy was supposed to grow, at least theoretically.

Although useful in the revolt against mercantilism and divine right monarchy, Tugwell argued that this theory was not applicable to the economic conditions of the modern world. Even its assumptions "that men, businesses, and regions are free to volunteer for any activity, that they possess a perfect mobility in seeking out the most effective occupation . . . [and] that men's economic activities are dominated solely by this single self-interest motive . . ." were highly questionable. In Tugwell's thinking, history had shown that the "free competitive order" had never existed in pure form, that employers had always had the upper hand over their employees, and that perfect mobility never existed because men had to work wherever they could. Monopolies, moreover, had destroyed whatever competition there was even before the twentieth century.[46] In spite of all this, the theory of laissez-faire had adherents, especially in the United States, where it not only sustained the inequitable normalcy system but also was responsible for the disastrous depression of 1929.

Specifically, Tugwell argued that the American economy in the 1920s presented a deceiving facade. Seemingly prosperous, it had experienced a period of expansion between 1922 and 1929 due to increased mechanization and scientific management. "Factories ran, railways were busy . . . and credit remained liquid." But, as industrial efficiency increased, business neither lowered the prices for products nor increased the wages of workers in proportion to increased profits and reduced costs.[47] Keeping profits in reserve, expending some of them uselessly in speculation, and investing in unplanned expansion, business failed to realize that "what consumers had to buy with had become disproportionate to the goods being produced."[48] To make matters worse, technological unemployment and the depressed condition of farmers further reduced mass purchasing power. Although business sought to stifle this decline by overextending credit to sell its products, the process of overproduction and underconsumption had already gone too far. A spiral of decline had set in, and depression inevitably followed.[49]

Since the depression had been caused by a disruption of the price-wage-profit relationship, Tugwell suggested in 1932 that "values had to retreat until goods could issue from the industrial process priced so that their purchase was possible with the available funds of consumers." In the immediate post-1929 period, this meant that a policy of deflation, "of capital values, of securities, of retail prices, of industrial excrescences such as advertising and huge reserves . . . ," had to be implemented along with public works programs for the unemployed workers and relief for the farmer.[50] In the long run, this meant that the United States had to learn to maintain an equilibrium among industry, labor, and agriculture through planning. Tugwell was suggesting not only that the tenets of laissez-faire be rejected, but also that Hoover's approach to the economic crisis be reevaluated.

Although his ideas mellowed with time, Tugwell consistently criticized Hoover between 1928 and 1932. Seeing him as a lifelong exponent of laissez-fairism, Tugwell believed that Hoover fundamentally remained in the tradition of Harding and Coolidge. Like them, he was orthodox in his economics, inflexible in his approach to problems, and committed to the American capitalistic system.[51] Unlike them, however, he presented the image of "the engineer pragmatist, the examiner of reality, [and] the man of action guided by fact." Superficially, Hoover was the businessman par excellence in government. In reality, he was quite different. A dogmatic personality, Hoover always assumed that the facts supported his ideas and that his economic programs were theological in origin and form, especially the ones he developed during the depression.[52]

In analyzing those programs, Tugwell emphasized that Hoover sought to resolve the crisis in an unrealistic, traditional way. Assuming that business units had to remain small and independent, that the government had to protect business in every way possible, and that competition had to be maintained, Hoover formulated policies designed to restore prosperity through business confidence.[53] For that reason, he supported such programs as the Hawley-Smoot Tariff, despite the experts' opposition to it; the Reconstruction Finance Corporation, the National Credit Corporation, and the War Finance Corporation for business and banking, not worker or farmer relief; all attempts to balance the budget; and the moratorium on debts. This also explained why he refused to support direct federal relief, whether in the form of non-self-liquidating public works or outright doles.[54]

To do any more or go any further, whether in extending government authority or coercing businessmen to cooperate, was dangerous, in Hoover's thinking, because such policies smacked of communism and socialism. Hoover believed such policies were useless anyway, because prosperity was "just around the corner." It had to be, since Hoover, as president, said so. Even when the facts on unemployment and productivity demonstrated that the promised recovery was not in sight, that his programs were not working, and that the crisis was deepening, Hoover continued to believe this. In Tugwell's opinion, the only reason he did so was that he had no alternative. Having gone far within his own ideological limits, he concluded that there was little or nothing he could do. By 1932, Hoover, once the Horatio Alger of the twentieth century, was transformed into Hoover the tragic Canute. His dignity "lost in a spate of ridicule," he did not understand why the American people constantly criticized him. Tugwell, of course, could.[55]

In assessing Hoover's performance, Tugwell emphasized that Hoover failed to resolve the depression because he had too much faith in the laissez-faire American system and too much trust in the business community. Instead of attempting to sustain the normalcy system that had caused the depression, Tugwell felt that Hoover should have sought to change it by initiating policies that would have diminished business domination while increasing the influence of the other groups in American society. This might have been easily accomplished by approaching the crisis in a more realistic manner: by restoring mass purchasing power and creating an equilibrium among industry, labor, and farming as soon as possible; not by reducing wages through work-sharing schemes or by adopting inflation and/or taxation as the only approach to alleviating distress within the economy, but by forcing down retail prices to equal wholesale prices; by organizing federal relief programs in the form of public works; by instituting income and inheritance, not sales, taxes; by avoiding budgetary deficits; and by government "take-over of any necessary enterprises which refuse to function when their profits are absorbed by taxation."[56] A deflationary process, these programs, when combined, would at least stabilize the economy and allow recovery to begin. Tugwell, however, did not believe that these policies eliminated the fundamental weaknesses in the economic system that had caused the depression. To do that would involve a long-range program involving the abandonment of laissez-faire and the implementation of planning.

In offering planning as the primary solution to the crisis, Tugwell was reiterating what he had been saying throughout the decade. To him, planning was so important that he believed it alone offered the United States the opportunity to adjust to the realities of the twentieth century and, thereby, achieve its economic potential. Implying cooperation, not conflict; consolidation, not competition; the public interest, not selfish profit making; experimentalism, not blueprints; and institutional change, not revolution, it was the logical alternative to America's philosophy of laissez-faire.[57] As such, it required changes in the traditional attitudes of business and government before it could succeed.

In practical terms, Tugwell argued, this meant that the United States had to recognize that business had been immoral, irresponsible, ruthlessly selfish, and unsportsmanlike throughout the 1920s and even after the onset of the depression. If planning were to be instituted, all this had to change.[58] Instead of competing against one another for selfish profit, businessmen had to learn to cooperate for the general, public interest. Instead of planning within their individual concerns, where they had little or no conception of the entire economy, they had to learn to plan for all industry, emphasizing the whole over the parts. And, instead of relying on small, obsolete units of organization, they had to consolidate in the interest of efficiency.[59] Once this was done, the problems of overexpansion, overproduction, and unwise investment—characteristics of the normalcy system—would be resolved and a coordinated, balanced economy established.

To make certain that all this happened, Tugwell stressed, the government had to assume a different role in the decision-making process. Instead of being the traditional policeman of the Wilson-Brandeis school, it had to exert more authority over capital uses, profits, and prices so as to assure an equitable adjustment of production to consumption, cost to prices, and profits to wages.[60] This could be accomplished by the government's cooperating with business in coordinating planning, by its sanctioning of consolidation through incorporation laws, and by its taxing undistributed excess profits. In Tugwell's view, none of this activity on the part of the government implied either a government takeover of industry or a revolutionary break with the tenets of American democracy. Industry was primarily responsible for planning, with the government supervising the process and exercising its constitutional right "of surveillance of services and prices" to protect the general welfare.[61] As long as business governed itself in such a way that prices were low, wages high, and profits reasonable, Tugwell emphasized, there was no need for more extensive government interference, as was the case in Russia.

Although he admired the Russian form of planning for its reliance on experimentalism and scientific techniques, Tugwell *never* believed that it was a viable and/or acceptable form for the United States. Ruthless in implementation, political in purpose, and suppressive in action, it was totally alien to American democratic traditions.[62] It was not to be transplanted to the United States, where democratic liberties were highly valued and where problems were resolved without resort to violent tactics. Evolution, not revolution, was the American way, and Tugwell hoped that, in terms of planning, that method of change and adjustment would prevail. If, however, it did not—if the United States failed to adopt planning—then, he feared, the United States might be in serious trouble. Not only would the economy of abundance fail to materialize, but the nation would have to face recurring depressions and the possibility of revolution.[63] By 1932, Tugwell thought that even businessmen, the staunchest opponents of planning, recognized this and sought to avert it by suggesting their own proposals for instituting planning.

Despite the popularity of these proposals, Tugwell felt the programs offered, such as the Swope Plan, were ineffective because they were like a "Gosplan without power." Doing little or nothing to effect the institutional adjustments necessary to the success of the planning principle, they tended to sustain business dominance without government supervision or regulation. Instead of doing that, he suggested a procedure he thought was more in line with the implications of planning.[64]

In this planning program, Tugwell recommended that associations within each industry be set up by the businessmen of that industry. These associations would establish a planning board for the entire industry, composed of employers, workers, and consumers. This board would be responsible for centralizing management, "maintaining standards of competition," and controlling maximum prices and minimum wages.[65] Voluntary in essence, the boards would deal with all intra-industrial matters. For interindustrial affairs, they would create a central planning board that would serve as "a mediating and integrating body for the coordination of the several industries' plans and policies respecting production, prices, division of markets, working conditions, and the like."[66] The U.S. Industrial Integration Board would be primarily an investigative and coordinating body with authority to control the allocation of capital and the pricing policies of the industries. It would also have the power to "lay fines on corporations or members" who were not in line with the industry and to expel those who refused to cooperate.

With the boards so constituted, the government could exercise its authority by taxing undistributed profits so as to channel capital into the right places. It could also incorporate industry so as to provide some control over new capital issues.[67] The revenues received from this, moreover, could be placed in an Industrial Reserve Fund. Administered by a board composed of representatives from the government and the Industrial Integration Board, the Fund would be divided annually into three parts: one-third would be returned to industries that adhered to the plan, one-third would be retained until the fund equaled twice the paid-in capital of the member industries, and one-third would be used for unemployment insurance benefits. In allocating the fund in this way, Tugwell felt the complying industries would be rewarded, surplus funds of corporations would be eliminated, and money for workers without jobs would be available.[68] The entire planning mechanism was to be administered so that everyone, from industrial managers to workers to consumers, would benefit.

Essentially planning "from the bottom up," with the Industrial Integration Board overseeing interindustrial affairs from "the top down," success depended on business cooperation, government's exercise of its authority in price and capital investment, and the protection and recognition of the interests of weaker businesses, technicians, workers, consumers, and farmers.[69] Nevertheless, in line with his constantly evolving thinking and his writing things out, Tugwell emphasized that the plan was only suggestive. Experience was needed to fill in the details to assure effective implementation. Once that was accomplished, the benefits from it would be astounding.[70]

This was the Tugwell whom Raymond Moley brought to Governor Franklin D. Roosevelt in 1932. A well-known academic from Columbia, he had written on a variety of issues in the 1920s and had ideas on a variety of problems facing the United States. Yet his ideas, like his writings, were always in an evolutionary process. Time, experience, a willingness to try—all of these things, when combined with his suggestions, represented the Rexford Tugwell who was about to enter the Brains Trust.

NOTES

1. Rexford G. Tugwell, *To the Lesser Heights of Morningside* (Philadelphia: University of Pennsylvania Press, 1982), 146.

2. Rexford G. Tugwell, "The Economic Basis for Business Regulation," *American Economic Review* 11 (December 1921): 643-58; Rexford G. Tugwell, *The Economic Basis of Public Interest* (repr. New York: Augustus M. Kelley, 1968), iii-ix, 100ff.

3. Rexford G. Tugwell to Harry Carman, May 23, 1947, Tugwell papers, folder "Ca-Ce," FDR Library, box 4; Tugwell, *Lesser Heights*, pp. 141ff.

4. Tugwell, *Lesser Heights*, pp. 145, 163, 167-68; see also Tugwell papers, "Course Notes and Outlines," folder "Columbia College, 1922-1928," FDR Library, box 54.

5. Rexford G. Tugwell, Thomas Munro, and Roy E. Stryker, *American Economic Life and the Means of Its Improvement*, 3rd ed. (New York: Harcourt, Brace, 1925 and 1930), books II and III; Tugwell, *Lesser Heights*, pp. 149-50, 160; James Reid to Prof. Roy E. Stryker, May 29, 1933, Tugwell papers, folder "Stryker, Roy E.," FDR Library, box 25.

6. Tugwell, *Lesser Heights*, p. 165.

7. Ibid., pp. 152-55.

8. Ibid., pp. 143, 155-57. Tugwell was particularly impressed with John Dewey, *How We Think: A Restatement of the Relation of Reflective Thinking to the Educative Process* (New York: D. C. Heath, 1933).

9. Rexford G. Tugwell, "Wesley Mitchell: An Evaluation," *New Republic* 92 (October 6, 1937): 238-40.

10. Tugwell, *Lesser Heights*, pp. 184-85.

11. Rexford Tugwell to Gov. Frank O. Lowden, October 5, 1931, Tugwell papers, folder "Lo-Ly," FDR Library, box 14; Tugwell, *Lesser Heights*, pp. 192, 203, 210-14.

12. Rexford G. Tugwell, Stuart Chase, and Robert Denn, eds., *Soviet Russia in the Second Decade* (New York: John Day, 1928), 55-102.

13. Rexford G. Tugwell and Leon Keyserling, eds., *Redirecting Education*, 2 vols. (New York: Columbia University Press, 1934-1935), I, 3-112; Rexford G. Tugwell to E. E. Day, January 20, 1932, January 27, 1932, and March 15, 1932, all in Tugwell papers, folder "Rockefeller Foundation, 1932 and 1949," FDR Library, box 23.

14. Rexford Tugwell, ed., *The Trend of Economics* (New York: F. S. Crofts, 1924), 390ff; Tugwell, "Economics and Ethics," *Journal of Philosophy* 21 (December 4, 1924): 686; Tugwell, "Human Nature in Economic Theory," *Journal of Political Economy* 30 (June 1922): 318-25; Rexford Tugwell to Henry G. Leach, September 11, 1930, Tugwell papers, folder "Columbia University, 1929-1939," FDR Library, box 5; Rexford Tugwell to Willard Atkins, January 21, 1931, Tugwell papers, folder "An-Ax," FDR Library, box 1.

15. Tugwell, "Human Nature in Economic Theory," p. 343; Tugwell, "Economics as the Science of Experience," *Journal of Philosophy* 25 (January 19, 1928): 40; Rexford Tugwell, "The American Economic System," lecture notes, Tugwell papers, folder "Columbia College," FDR Library, box 54; Tugwell, *Trend of Economics*, p. 384.

16. Tugwell, "Human Nature in Economic Theory," p. 320; Tugwell, *Trend of Economics*, pp. 413ff.

17. Tugwell, *Trend of Economics*, pp. 384, 415; Tugwell, "Economics as the Science of Experience," p. 37; Rexford Tugwell to Horace Taylor, March 29, 1929, Tugwell papers, folder "Taylor, Horace, 1927-1933," FDR Library, box

25; Allan Gruchy, *Modern Economic Thought: The American Contribution* (New York: Augustus M. Kelley, 1967), 418-30; Tugwell, "Economics and Ethics," p. 690; Tugwell, "The Distortion of Economic Incentive," *International Journal of Ethics* 34 (April 1924): 280ff.

18. Rexford Tugwell, "The Gipsey Strain," *Pacific Review* 2 (September 1921): 177-83; Tugwell, "The Hired Man," *Nation* 121 (August 5, 1925): 164; Tugwell, "The Distortion of Economic Incentive," p. 280.

19. Rexford Tugwell, "Wage Pressure and Efficiency," *New Republic* 55 (July 11, 1928): 196; Tugwell, "The Theory of Occupational Obsolescence," *Political Science Quarterly* 46 (June 1931): 171ff.; Tugwell, "Occupational Obsolescence," *Journal of Adult Education* 3 (January 1931): 19.

20. Tugwell, "The Gipsey Strain," pp. 183-84.

21. Ibid.

22. Ibid., pp. 185-86; Rexford Tugwell, "The Outlaw," *Survey* 44 (August 16, 1920): 641-42; Tugwell, "The Casual of the Woods," *Survey* (July 3, 1920): 472-73.

23. Tugwell, "The Gipsey Strain," p. 196; Tugwell, "The Outlaw," p. 641.

24. Tugwell, "Wage Pressure and Efficiency," p. 198.

25. Tugwell, "The Theory of Occupational Obsolescence," pp. 223-26. The details of his program will be presented later.

26. Rexford Tugwell, "The Problem of Agriculture," *Political Science Quarterly* 39 (December 1924): 549-51; Tugwell, "The Woman in the Sunbonnet," *Nation* 120 (January 21, 1925): 73-74; Tugwell, "Country Life for America," *Pacific Review* (March 1922): 566-77; Tugwell, "The Man with the Hoe," *Nation* 121 (October 21, 1925): 467; Tugwell, "Distortion of Economic Incentive," p. 280.

27. Tugwell, "The Problem of Agriculture," pp. 554-58. Quotes are from pp. 558 and 554, respectively.

28. Ibid., pp. 566-68.

29. Ibid., pp. 570-75; Rexford Tugwell, "What Will Become of the Farmer?" *Nation* 124 (June 15, 1927): 666.

30. Tugwell, "The Problem of Agriculture," pp. 576-81; Rexford Tugwell, "Reflections on Farm Relief," *Political Science Quarterly* 43 (December 1928): 486.

31. Tugwell, "What Will Become of the Farmer?" p. 666; Tugwell, "Reflections on Farm Relief," p. 481, 489.

32. Tugwell, Chase, and Denn, *Soviet Russia in the Second Decade*, p. 100.

33. Rexford Tugwell, "The Reminiscences of Rexford G. Tugwell," p. 1, Oral History Research Office, Columbia University; Tugwell, "A Memorandum Concerning the Problem of Agriculture: A Summary Outline," Tugwell papers, FDR Library, box 70.

34. Tugwell, "Reflections on Farm Relief," p. 490.

35. Tugwell, "The Problem of Agriculture," p. 576; Tugwell, "Reflections on Farm Relief," p. 491; Tugwell, "Farm Relief and a Permanent Agriculture,"

Annals of the American Academy of Political and Social Science 142 (March 1929): 275-77; Rexford Tugwell to John D. Black, December 19, 1930, Tugwell papers, folder "Bi-Bl," FDR Library, box 3.

36. Rexford Tugwell, "The Tariff and International Relations" (January 1930), p. 6, Tugwell papers, FDR Library, box 53; Rexford Tugwell to Milledge Bonham, December 29, 1930, Tugwell papers, folder "Bo," FDR Library, box 3.

37. Tugwell, "Reflections on Farm Relief," p. 488; Tugwell, "What Will Become of the Farmer?" p. 665.

38. Tugwell, "Reflections on Farm Relief," p. 482; Tugwell, "Farm Relief and a Permanent Agriculture," p. 280; Rexford Tugwell, "A Memorandum Concerning the Problems of Agriculture," Tugwell papers, FDR Library, box 70.

39. Rexford Tugwell, *The Industrial Discipline and the Governmental Arts* (New York: Columbia University Press, 1933), 7, 25, 44.

40. Rexford Tugwell, *Industry's Coming of Age* (New York: Harcourt, Brace, 1927), 245-46.

41. Tugwell, *The Industrial Discipline*, pp. 19-28, 203; Rexford Tugwell, "An Economist Reads Dark Laughter," *New Republic* 45 (December 9, 1925): 87-88.

42. Tugwell, *Industry's Coming of Age*, pp. 244ff.; Tugwell, *The Industrial Discipline*, pp. 3ff.; Bernard Sternsher, *Rexford Tugwell and the New Deal* (New Brunswick, N.J.: Rutgers University Press, 1964), 11; Gruchy, *Modern Economic Thought*, p. 455.

43. Tugwell, "Occupational Obsolescence," pp. 20ff.; Tugwell, "The Theory of Occupational Obsolescence," pp. 183ff.

44. Tugwell, "Occupational Obsolescence," p. 21; Tugwell, "The Theory of Occupational Obsolescence," pp. 181-82, 216, 218-23ff.

45. Tugwell, *The Industrial Discipline*, pp. 19, 32-33, 41-46.

46. Ibid., pp. 46ff.

47. Rexford Tugwell, A. T. Cutler, and G. S. Mitchell, "Flaws in the Hoover Economic Plan," *Current History* 35 (January 1932): 525ff.; Tugwell, "Hunger, Cold, and Candidates," *New Republic* 54 (May 2, 1928): 324.

48. Rexford Tugwell, diary, folder "Introduction," pp. 6-7, Tugwell papers, FDR Library, box 30.

49. Tugwell et al., "Flaws in the Hoover Economic Plan," pp. 525ff.

50. Rexford Tugwell, *Mr. Hoover's Economic Policy* (New York: John Day, 1932), 24.

51. Rexford Tugwell, "Platforms and Candidates," *New Republic* 55 (May 30, 1928): 44; Tugwell, "What Is a Scientific Tariff?" *New Republic* 55 (June 13, 1928): 93. In later years, Tugwell modified his thinking to show that Hoover, in many respects, foreshadowed the Roosevelt presidency. See, for example, Tugwell, "The Protagonists: Roosevelt and Hoover," *Antioch Review* 13 (December 1953): 419-22.

52. Tugwell, *Mr. Hoover*, p. 5.

53. Ibid., pp. 6-7, 17.

54. Ibid., pp. 8-9, 14-18, 25; Tugwell et al., "Flaws in the Hoover Economic Plan," pp. 528ff. Ironically, Tugwell tended to be critical of Hoover's failure to balance the budget.

55. Tugwell, *Mr. Hoover*, pp. 22-28; Tugwell, diary, folder "Introduction," pp. 5-6, Tugwell papers, FDR Library, box 30.

56. Rexford Tugwell, "Discourse in Depression," *Teachers College Record* 34 (1932): 6, draft in Tugwell papers, FDR Library, box 69; Tugwell, "The Principle of Planning and the Institutions of Laissez-Faire," *American Economic Review, Supplement* (March 1932): 12-13; Tugwell and R. F. Ford to W. P. Wilson, May 11, 1931, Tugwell papers, folder "Wi," FDR Library, box 29; Tugwell to Frank O. Lowden, October 5, 1931, Tugwell papers, folder "Lo-Ly," FDR Library, box 14; Tugwell to Basil O'Connor, July 9, 1932, Tugwell papers, folder "O'Connor, Basil 1932-1963," FDR Library, box 17.

57. Tugwell, "Discourse in Depression," pp. 8, 14-16; Tugwell, *Industry's Coming of Age*, pp. 255-56, 266-67; Tugwell, "High Wages and Prosperity: Discussion," *Bulletin of the Taylor Society* (February 1928): 19-21; Tugwell, diary, folder "Introduction," p. 11, Tugwell papers, FDR Library, box 30; Tugwell to J. R. Brachett, April 11, 1931, Tugwell papers, folder "Br," FDR Library, box 4; Felix Morley to Tugwell, attached "Responsibility and Economic Distress," January 18, 1932, Tugwell papers, folder "Brookings Institution," FDR Library, box 4.

58. Tugwell, "Principle of Planning," p. 2; Tugwell, "Discourse in Depression," p. 10.

59. Tugwell, "Principle of Planning," pp. 17-20.

60. Tugwell, "High Wages and Prosperity," p. 19; Tugwell, "Governor or President?" *New Republic* (May 16, 1928): 381; Tugwell, *The Industrial Discipline*, pp. 199-202; Morley to Tugwell, "Responsibility and Economic Distress," pp. 4-5.

61. Tugwell, *The Economic Basis of Public Interest*, pp. v-ix, 101ff.; Tugwell, "The Economic Basis for Business Regulation," pp. 643-58.

62. Rexford Tugwell, "Experimental Control in Russian Industry," *Political Science Quarterly* 43 (June 1928): 161-87.

63. Tugwell, *Industry's Coming of Age*, pp. 244, 247, 261-62.

64. Tugwell, "Principle of Planning," 2ff., 6-8, 9-11.

65. Tugwell, *The Industrial Discipline*, p. 212.

66. Ibid., pp. 212-15.

67. Ibid., pp. 212-13.

68. Ibid.

69. Ibid., pp. 218ff.

70. Ibid., pp. 227ff.

4

Brains Trust/New Deal: 1932–1935

I could not be so much in love with this land, so fiercely concerned
for the honor and welfare of the people I belong to, if it were not
part of me and I part of it.
>   Rexford G. Tugwell to Jacques Barzun, April 19, 1954,
>   Tugwell papers, FDR Library, box 1.

Any contributions to scholarship and literature [or public service] I
am likely to make will consist in the development of alternative suggestions—something strange and new—which I shall probably leave as
mere suggestions rather than as finished tasks.
>   Rexford G. Tugwell, diary, December 31, 1932,
>   Tugwell papers, FDR Library, box 30.

As complicated a man as he was, Tugwell succinctly said in these two
statements much of what he was and much of what he would do in
his life, particularly in the New Deal years. Underneath all the rhetoric,
writings, speeches, news conferences, and other forms of communica-
tion he used, Tugwell was a man deeply in love with his country, a
nation he believed capable of doing so much, yet oftentimes being
thwarted in achieving its potential. His role in helping it to achieve its
potential and his role in helping others was, as he said, to offer new
and strange suggestions, not finished tasks but ideas he developed,
offered, and, when possible, sought to implement himself. Both themes
or characteristics, if you will, represented the Tugwell of the New
Deal. If the New Deal did anything for him, it gave him an opportunity to do more than talk.

As an academic he had devoted himself to studying the American
economy, analyzing its intricate operations, and suggesting alternatives to make the system more equitable, efficient, and humane. He
had had little or no opportunity, however, aside from the 1928 presidential campaign, to discuss his ideas with political leaders who could

do something about them—at least not until he met Franklin D. Roosevelt. After that, everything changed. As an original member of the
Brains Trust, assistant secretary and under secretary of agriculture,
and director of the Resettlement Administration, Tugwell not only
offered his ideas to Roosevelt but also had a chance to implement
some of them himself. The political novice of 1932 soon learned,
though, that what he thought was necessary for the American political
and economic system might not be politically feasible. Whether it was
his ideas on planning, his programs for Pure Food and Drug, or his
agricultural suggestions, Tugwell soon learned the realities of American political life. In this sense, the New Deal, and especially Franklin
D. Roosevelt, educated him as much as he had sought to educate the
presidential candidate of 1932 and the American people. It was a difficult and disillusioning experience at times, but Tugwell did not easily
forget the practical lessons he had been taught by his political mentor.

In retrospect, Tugwell's entry into the Roosevelt inner circle was
quite natural. A reputable economist, he had spoken out against
Hoover's depression programs, publicly offered his own explanations
for the economic crisis confronting the nation, and confidently suggested his own solutions for restoring prosperity. As a member of the
Columbia University faculty, moreover, he was in a position to attract
the attention of his colleague Raymond Moley, who in 1932 was a
close adviser of the governor of New York and, with Samuel Rosenman and Doc O'Connor, was responsible for organizing the group of
advisers later known as the Brains Trust.[1]

The idea of recruiting university professors for advice on campaign
issues originated with Rosenman and O'Connor, and it was Moley's
task to locate these experts, assist in screening them for possible use
in the upcoming campaign, and, if they were acceptable, introduce
them to Roosevelt for final approval. Since everyone agreed that agricultural policy was going to play a prominent role in the campaign,
Moley suggested that Rexford Tugwell be considered as a possible
adviser in this field. Although he knew Tugwell only casually as a colleague at Columbia, Moley had been impressed enough by his writings
on agriculture and the depression that, after a few preliminary meetings, he asked Tugwell to meet with Rosenman and O'Connor for
further discussions.[2] Tugwell jumped at the opportunity.

At a meeting in Rosenman's apartment, Tugwell spoke convincingly
on the plight of the farmer, the causes of the depression, and what he
believed was necessary to restore prosperity. Reiterating much of
what he had said in his writings and speeches, he related in detail how

the discrepancies in costs-prices-wages-profits had caused the economic breakdown. Businessmen had to bear the primary responsibility for what had happened, and in the future, Tugwell argued, they had to be more disciplined. Specifically, he indicated that business had taken advantage of the wartime productivity by refusing to lower prices and/or significantly raise wages in relation to their savings in cost.

Eventually, as the 1920s progressed, "what consumers had to buy with had become disproportionate to the goods being produced." Some industrial production had increased so much without a corresponding increase in purchasing power that these goods could not be sold. Instead of accepting lower profits or prices, businessmen reacted to this situation by laying workers off. As unemployment increased and purchasing power diminished, Tugwell argued, it was inevitable that a "spiral of decline" set in. To make matters worse, banks, consistent in their overinvestment and speculative activity throughout the postwar period, began to demand repayment on their loans, thereby squeezing the life out of commercial credit. "With loaning stopped, production restricted, [and] unemployment growing," Tugwell concluded, "there was only one possible means of relief—to reestablish consumers' buying power."[3]

In Tugwell's thinking, the only way to accomplish this objective was for the federal government to assume more authority in the economic system. Relying on its power to issue currency and its responsibility to represent the national interest, it could discipline business to act in the public interest and supervise the economic process so that a balance between production and consumption would be created. Farmers had to be helped in such a way that the relationship between industry and agriculture could be restored. Since the depression had fundamentally originated from this disruption, Tugwell suggested that the government needed to forgo the traditional farm remedies and adopt more modern ones, such as crop reduction and restriction. In essence, what Tugwell was saying to Moley, Rosenman, and O'Connor was that a concert of interest had to be established, one in which "everybody could employ everybody else and everybody work for everybody else." With business refusing to do this in 1931 and 1932, Tugwell emphasized, the government now had to do it.[4]

In many respects, this was a stark and revealing exposition for the governor's advisers. Impressed by his "profound" understanding of the economy and by his "progressive," not radical, suggestions for reactivating it, they decided to bring Tugwell to Roosevelt for final approval.[5] A meeting was arranged and Tugwell, escorted by the others, went to Albany. Looking back at this meeting with Roosevelt, Tugwell recalled that he was nervous and somewhat unnerved by Roosevelt. As the conference progressed, his confidence was restored and he restated practically everything he had told the governor's advisers regarding the depression, his suggestions for a concert of interest, and his belief that the government had to act decisively to confront the economic crisis.[6] He even suggested to Roosevelt that the latter's ideas on retiring submarginal lands and resettling farmers were not enough to restore the farmer to his rightful position in the economic process. Instead, Tugwell argued, much more was needed in terms of agricultural-industrial balance if the farmer, and the economy generally, were to revive.[7] Without explicitly agreeing or disagreeing with this, Roosevelt listened to the rest of the young professor's disquisition and, by the end of the evening, concluded that he would be a valuable asset in the upcoming campaign. With the governor's final blessing, Tugwell was admitted into the Brains Trust.[8]

Since 1932, Tugwell was consistent in emphasizing that the purpose of the Brains Trust was to help Roosevelt understand the causes of the depression and what needed to be done to restore prosperity. Under Roosevelt's direction, it was "to furnish materials when asked, ideas when allowed, and conclusions and programs when they seemed called for." As a source of information during both the convention and the national campaign, it was designed to serve the candidate by preparing background information on the issues, statements for the candidate to make (including speeches), and memoranda on campaign topics, all of which would "arm [Roosevelt] for emergence into a public forum he had not yet to contend in." Through innumerable informal meetings, discussions, and conferences, Tugwell believed, the Brains Trust succeeded in its primary objective.

Tugwell also felt that he and Adolph Berle were serving another purpose: to educate Roosevelt so that he might reject many of his obsolete ideas, such as balanced budgets, tariffs, and atomism. In their place, they hoped to have him adopt ideas that were more conducive to the realities of the twentieth century, such as the recognition of the inevitability of consolidation, the need for extensive government activity within the economy, and the necessity for planning and its implementation. By the end of the 1932 campaign, and even of the New Deal, Tugwell believed that he and Berle had failed, that Roosevelt had not gone far enough in reforming the system as it should have been. But neither did he believe that their failure was complete, because Roosevelt not only had started the process of change that they dreamed of, but he also had accepted many of those changes, although political considerations prevented him from espousing them publicly or implementing some of them legislatively.[9] It was a bittersweet failure, and Tugwell, then and later, accepted it because he believed it was the American system, not Roosevelt, that was responsible.

In the prenomination campaign, Tugwell was assigned to work on the farm problem, providing background memoranda on the causes of the farm depression and any possible ways to restore the farmer to a more prosperous position. He also worked on a scheme to implement industrial cooperation for overall recovery.[10] Tugwell consistently advised Roosevelt that farm production had to be adjusted to consumer demand, and that the only way this could be accomplished was through a system of crop reduction and control. In Tugwell's view, the problem was not whether controlled production and the reduction of surpluses were necessary, but whether "a plan for control that was politically feasible" could be devised. If one was developed, he believed, it not only would help the farmer immediately with emergency relief, but it also would establish the foundation for a permanent land-use program that, in the long run, would prevent the farmer and the country from experiencing another catastrophic depression.[11]

Although Tugwell did not offer any such program himself, he suggested that the domestic allotment ideas of Beardsley Ruml, M. L. Wilson, Henry Wallace, and others might be just what was needed. To find out more about them, he, at Roosevelt's request, attended an agricultural conference in Chicago and talked with the sponsors of domestic allotment. It did not take Wilson and Wallace long to convince Tugwell that their program was what he was looking for. Tugwell returned to Roosevelt and became an outspoken exponent of the domestic allotment plan, serving as a medium through which the sponsors of the idea could meet with Roosevelt himself. In doing so, however, Tugwell encountered the opposition of Henry Morgenthau, Jr., who was also assigned to work on the farm problem and advise the governor of his suggestions.[12]

Representing the Cornell group, Morgenthau believed that agricultural recovery depended on "tax relief, credit reform, reduction of distribution costs, and monetary measures."[13] By inflating the prices of his products, Morgenthau felt, the farmer's purchasing power would be so increased that recovery would have to follow (at least theoretically). Tugwell argued that realistically no such thing could happen. Although he agreed with Morgenthau that changes in the tax and credit policies were necessary and desirable, he was appalled by Morgenthau's suggestion that inflation be used as the primary means to restore farm prosperity. In Tugwell's analysis, permanent inflation would neither restore the necessary agricultural-industrial balance within the economy nor do anything "toward mitigating the disparities which existed" in the system. A sound money man, Tugwell wanted to establish a concert of interest.[14]

Although the Tugwell-Morgenthau dispute was resolved with the passage of the Agricultural Adjustment Act in 1933, Tugwell was quite worried in 1932 that Roosevelt was not saying or doing what he should. In agriculture, for example, Tugwell wanted Roosevelt to publicly commit himself to domestic allotment, something the governor chose not to do. Nor was Roosevelt willing to give up his ideas on subsistence homesteads, despite Tugwell's arguments. Tugwell was particularly upset by Roosevelt's refusal to outline specifically a program for industrial recovery based on a concert of interest. Although Tugwell suggested the program he had outlined in *The Industrial Discipline* as a starting point for a scheme of industrial cooperation, the farthest Roosevelt went was to announce his acceptance of a concert of interest in a speech he gave at St. Paul on April 18.[15]

Tugwell was pleased that Roosevelt had used part of a draft speech he had written on the economy, calling for the implementation of planning and the action necessary to carry it out. But, just as there was hope in the speech, Tugwell found disappointment as well. Without offering any specific program, Roosevelt indicated that some form of planning was necessary if the United States was to survive.[16] Tugwell believed the governor should have gone beyond that. Specifically, he wanted Roosevelt to say that "modern concentrations could be taken advantage of . . . [and that] government could become a senior partner in industry-wide councils [where it could] maneuver their member elements into such arrangements that fair exchanges could go on continuously." The government, moreover, would make certain that a new price structure was established, new incentives for producers were developed, and protection of the consumer was assured. Above all, Tugwell wanted the governor to say that all this was to be accomplished, not by adhering to either blueprint planning or the traditional atomistic approach to industrial relations, with its concomitant reliance on balanced budgets and tariffs, but by experimentation in approach and policy. It was a long-range process that could resolve the depression and create an American economy of abundance, if given the chance.

Although Tugwell was certain that Roosevelt was privately committed to this approach in April 1932, he did not believe that the governor was willing to admit it publicly for political reasons.[17] At first, this situation proved to be a problem for Tugwell because, as a political amateur, he did not understand or accept Roosevelt's strategy of not alienating anyone. As time went on and as Roosevelt quietly instructed him on the facts of political life, he acquiesced in the approach of expediency and quietly resigned himself to the personal disappointment it entailed. For the remainder of the prenomination campaign, he continued to advise the governor on what he wanted him to say, but never to the point of endangering his personal relationship with Roosevelt or the campaign strategy being pursued.

Between the St. Paul speech in April and the Democratic convention in July, Tugwell's dislike of Roosevelt's strategy of expediency intensified. With the exception of a speech at Oglethorpe University, Georgia, where the governor had called for "bold, persistent experimentation," Tugwell felt that Roosevelt's speeches were becoming more vague, meaningless, and even openly contradictory. He began to worry that the governor might use the presidency for "Wilsonian purposes," attempting to complete the program of orthodox progressivism, especially in terms of the antitrust tradition, instead of seeking to reform the American economic system. For Tugwell, not only was this Wilsonian philosophy dangerous and obsolete as a policy for handling the depression, it might even cost Roosevelt votes among the progressives in the country. Hoping to prevent that, he advised the governor to be more explicit in offering a recovery program and more firm in rejecting orthodox progressivism. Although he failed to affect Roosevelt in this matter, his fear of the governor's losing votes was mistaken. In July, Roosevelt won the Democratic nomination at Chicago and his national campaign for the presidency began.[18]

At the Chicago convention, Tugwell was a spectator. He watched the delegates play politics without fully understanding what was going on. When Roosevelt gave his acceptance speech, Tugwell was pleased that he had used some draft paragraphs he had written on agriculture and the theme of the concert of interest, but he was disappointed in Roosevelt's failure to commit himself explicitly to domestic allotment or to outline a recovery program. What disturbed him even more was the platform adopted by the party. Instead of stating the need to bolster purchasing power, to bring the price structures into balance, and to foster the growth of large-scale industry, it simply gave an "old-fashioned free-enterprise, balanced-budget pronouncement" without recognizing the obvious contradictions in such a program. There was little doubt in Tugwell's mind that such a platform was a serious liability in the forthcoming campaign.[19]

Angered and worried by what had happened at the convention, Tugwell renewed his campaign to have Roosevelt confront the issues head-on. In a memorandum presented to the nominee, Tugwell suggested that Roosevelt publicly endorse the creation of a National Economic Council to deal with the problems caused by the depression. In clear language, Tugwell told Roosevelt that integrated "industrial planning is necessary if we are not periodically to suffer from inflation, wrongly directed productive efforts, waste of capital resources, and consequent periods of stagnation for the redressing of past mistakes." Although industry generally had recognized this need to plan its production schedules, industrialists were implementing their programs in such a way, Tugwell felt, that economic disaster was inevitable. Instead of coordinating their planning programs, each industry planned only for itself, with the result that "surpluses are built up during failing demand and . . . excessive advertising budgets are maintained in the futile hope of persuading consumers to buy."

This distressing situation, Tugwell believed, could be alleviated if a more national course of action were followed. In practical terms, this meant that the "average of demand must be gauged in advance by experts, co-ordinated production programs must be based on them, and it must be made certain that the amount of goods flowing into the markets is proportional to the purchasing power of consumers." With present-day industry so constituted that private self-interest was paramount and with nationwide monopolies outside the accepted realm of American democracy, Tugwell concluded that a Federal Economic Council had to be created to carry out this integrated program.[20]

Attached to the executive and "operating under his direction to secure the needed coordination, the Council would be composed of economists and representatives from industry." Including 21 members, it would have 9 subordinate divisions:

1. Statistical, with the duty of gathering and interpreting information relative to current production, distribution, capital issues, monetary supplies, domestic and foreign trade, and consumption;

2. Production, with the duty of planning the national output of staple goods, agricultural and manufactured;

3. Consumption, with the duty of estimating future needs of the population;

4. Domestic trade, with the duty of estimating the ability of distributive resources to care for the streams of commerce;

5. International trade, with the duty of formulating policies with respect to our international economic relations;

6. Prices, with the duty of watching and advising concerning the general and specific relationships among various prices for the preservation of balance;

7. Capital issues, with the duty of encouraging or discouraging the flow of capital into various industries;

8. Natural resources, with the duty of estimating the rate of use and the efficiency with which resources are used;

9. Finance, with the duty of co-ordinating the work of the Council with that of the national banking system.[21]

Once the council was established, Tugwell suggested, the federal government should "press for a reorganization of industry somewhat on the model of the Federal Reserve System in banking." The antitrust laws were to be repealed and "each industry [would] be encouraged to divide itself into suitable regional groups on which will sit representatives of the Economic Council."[22]

Since the creation of the council would take some time, Tugwell emphasized that "in its experimental stages," its powers should be advisory only. Later, it might be necessary to enhance those powers "by constitutional change and enabling legislation." Whether that happened depended on business. In Tugwell's thinking, if reasoned planning and expert persuasion were executed with sufficient care, and if American businessmen at the executive levels would "sink [their] differences in a national program of expansion and stabilization," the enhancement of the council's powers would be neither necessary nor desirable. But, if they did not, "if business continued to display the divisive policies of self-interest in spite of governmental cooperation and administrative leadership," then "resort to compulsion in the public interest" had to follow. Until that happened—and Tugwell hoped it would not—he believed that his conservative program was the answer. All it needed was a chance to prove itself.

To make certain that Roosevelt understood what he was saying, Tugwell concluded his memorandum by flatly stating:

It is not proposed to have the government run industry; it is proposed to have the government furnish the requisite leadership; protect our resources; arrange for national balance; secure its citizens' access to goods, employment and security; and rise to the challenge of planning.[23]

Together, government and business could overcome the administrative, financial, and constitutional difficulties the proposal entailed. More significantly, both, through cooperation and sacrifice, could assure that the United States would achieve its destiny of well-being and abundance. For Tugwell, America's course of action was clear. All he asked was that Roosevelt take the first step by calling a group of economists and industrialists together to determine how this course was to begin and how his proposal was to be implemented.[24]

Roosevelt thought enough of this proposal to have Adolph Berle review it. Berle's memorandum indicated that "the liberal wing of the party, particularly the intellectuals, are very firm in favor of an economic council." Berle felt that although in theory they were "right," the practical problems involved in Tugwell's suggestion were "Herculean." He concluded by saying that a slow development of such a group might take place.[25]

The Tugwell memorandum was a significant document not only because of Berle's comments but also because it indicated what Tugwell was thinking and suggesting in 1932. It explicitly demonstrated that he was still defining planning in terms of cooperation, experimentation, balance, expertise, and the service ideal; that he was not radical, but relatively conservative, in his ideas on planning, calling for business to assume its responsibility or face government compulsion and authority; and that he was not yet certain how the planned economy should be implemented. Like the Industrial Integration Board of *The Industrial Discipline*, Tugwell's Federal Economic Council was only a suggestion, a brief outline of a possible program, and not a detailed procedure of implementation.

In retrospect, it is ironic that while he consistently demanded that Roosevelt be specific in offering industrial and agricultural recovery programs, Tugwell himself was not specific in regard to planning. To call for experimentation in the midst of the Great Depression was not a feasible alternative and/or method for implementing a new, all-inclusive approach to economic affairs. Much more was necessary, at least in terms of institutional structure. Detail, in short, was just as important as the principle, and although Tugwell realized that, he was not willing or able to do anything about it. He needed more time and experience to develop and understand planning in its theoretical and practical aspects, and time was the one commodity Roosevelt did not have.

Throughout the national campaign, Tugwell continued to voice his opposition to Roosevelt's policy of ambivalence and uncertainty on the issues. Frustrated and disappointed, he pleaded with Roosevelt to talk of specific remedies, to emphasize the need for planning and balance within the economy, and to offer an alternative to Hoover's policies. Although Roosevelt refused to do so in every case, he did assign Tugwell the task of writing a speech "outlining the causes of the depression, attacking the Republican position, and presenting an alternative plan for recovery." Eagerly grasping this opportunity, Tugwell wrote the speech, only to discover that when Roosevelt gave it on August 20 in Columbus, Ohio, it was modified considerably.[26]

If the Columbus address was disappointing in its failure to be specific, Tugwell felt that Roosevelt's speeches at Pittsburgh and Baltimore toward the end of the campaign were disastrous. In both instances, Roosevelt committed himself to the wrong policies, calling for reductions in the government's budget, the restoration of business confidence, and the strengthening of the tariff.[27] Tugwell felt that these speeches indicated the growing influence of people like Bernard Baruch in the Roosevelt circle. By catering to these more conservative influences and by advocating many of their obsolete programs, Tugwell was afraid that Roosevelt might be limiting his freedom of action after the election, that he might find it harder to listen to those advocating planning—Henry I. Harriman, Gerard Swope, and Fred Kent, all of whom Tugwell agreed with—and that he might alienate the progressives, who daily were expressing their disillusionment with Roosevelt's pronouncements.[28]

Even though he believed Roosevelt was privately committed to planning and the principles enunciated in the Oglethorpe speech, Tugwell was not certain that anyone else could share that belief, based on what the candidate had been saying. His only hope was that once the election was over, Roosevelt's actions would dispel any doubt about his belief in and commitment to these ideas. In November, the American electorate gave him the opportunity he was looking for, and Tugwell looked longingly to the inauguration for his satisfaction.[29]

Having fulfilled its responsibilities, the work of the Brains Trust ended on Election Day. As an advisory group, it helped Roosevelt understand the depression's impact on the country as a whole, but as a policy-making group (as Tugwell defined it), it failed to convince him that offering specific remedies or rejecting many of his old-line progressive ideas was either necessary or desirable. Tugwell believed that he failed personally in this respect, and as a result, he decided to continue his efforts to help Roosevelt overcome his conservative inclinations and views of public opinion. In Tugwell's opinion, Roosevelt would eventually implement planning, even if, in 1932 and early 1933, "it was not at all clear how it could be done or how far we would have to go."[30] With Roosevelt's victory in November, Tugwell therefore turned his attention to helping the president-elect fill in the details of this program.

Between the November election and the March 1933 inauguration, Tugwell's responsibilities changed somewhat. In addition to advising the new president on agricultural and industrial policies, he was assigned to work on the preparations for the forthcoming London Economic Conference, to help develop a program for dealing with the deteriorating banking situation, and to assist in developing what later became the Civilian Conservation Corps. In regard to the London Conference, Tugwell initially took a nationalistic economic position. Since the London Conference was designed to deal with the depression from an international perspective, he believed that it would have to deal with three separate areas: the war debts, disarmament, and "the general regularization of commodity production throughout the world to reduce surpluses, the problem of stability of exchanges . . . the matter of negotiated tariffs, and other matters which could be said to be much more strictly economic and less involved in controversies of a political nature."

Considering Europe's abandoning of the gold standard as well as its general desire to use the United States for its own purposes, especially in monetary policy, Tugwell recommended to Roosevelt that he support the payment of the debts, that he isolate the question of disarmament from the debt problem, and that he foster the acceptance of bilateral agreements on commodity production and tariffs instead of an international free-trade policy. Although this program was in opposition to what businessmen and Cordell Hull were advocating, Tugwell, along with Moley and Berle, felt that no other alternative existed. In the midst of the Great Depression, the United States had to resolve its own problems first, without much regard to the rest of the world.[31]

In a similar vein, Tugwell suggested that Roosevelt approach the banking situation resolutely and in terms of the national interest. Since the Federal Reserve System had not operated so as to prevent the banking problem confronting the nation, he felt that the government now had to. Arguing that the government was probably a better banker than the private owners of banks, he recommended that the president-elect utilize the post offices, establish a corporation to issue scrip, and establish a national bank. Such a program not only would relieve the currency problem but also would provide more stability for the banking system. Uncertain whether the president had the authority to do these things, Tugwell, at Roosevelt's request, checked the terms of the 1917 Trading with the Enemy Act. His opinion was that the president could do these things, and take the United States off the gold standard as well. In the end, though, it didn't matter, because Tugwell realized that others were advising Roosevelt on these questions and that the crisis might very well force the president-elect to act quickly.[32]

Although Tugwell had made these suggestions privately and he knew of other proposals being offered to Roosevelt at this time, he made a serious tactical error when he indirectly revealed these tentative policies publicly. On February 25, 1933, he had lunch with James H. Rand, Jr., chairman of the board of Remington Rand. Without knowing that Rand intended to report their conversation to President Hoover, Tugwell told Rand not only what the president-elect had in mind vis-à-vis the banking situation, but he also stated that Roosevelt realized the banking structure would collapse shortly and that this would place the responsibility on Hoover. In Tugwell's own words, Roosevelt would worry about rehabilitating the country after March 4.[33] It was a foolishly arrogant remark, a characteristic of Tugwell's appearing at times throughout his life and sometimes causing him more problems than he could handle.

Rand and Hoover exploited this mistake for all it was worth politically. Depicting Roosevelt as callously political in his motivation, the press, with Hoover's acquiescence, tried to place the responsibility for the banking system's inevitable collapse on his shoulders. For a short time they embarrassed the president-elect and diverted attention from the basic weaknesses in the banking system. For Tugwell, the Rand incident had longer-lasting effects. Newspaper reporters Mark Sullivan and Frank Kent used it, in conjunction with their pure food and drug campaign, to sustain their unjustified allegations that Tugwell was a radical Bolshevik seeking to overthrow the American system of government. Employing every talent at their disposal, they tried to convince the American people that "Tugwell, Rex," "Rex the Red," and "Rex, the Sweetheart of the Regimenters" was dangerous, sinister, and highly influential in governmental circles. By 1936, their anti-Tugwell campaign was so incessant that they contributed to Tugwell's resignation.[34]

Although Tugwell regretted incidents like the Rand episode for the effects they had on Roosevelt, in early 1933 he did not have much to worry about. In light of his past service as a Brains Truster and his activity during the interregnum, his relationship with the president-elect was still strong and friendly. In fact, Roosevelt considered Tugwell so valuable that he was considering him for a position within the administration. As early as December 1932, Moley was the first to suggest that Tugwell be appointed to the Commerce Department as an under secretary. Apparently Roosevelt agreed, because within two months, Moley informed Tugwell that his appointment as an assistant secretary of commerce was certain. What was not so certain, however, was whether Tugwell would accept any position.[35]

Initially, Tugwell's reaction to the news of his pending appointment was mixed. Although happy at the prospect of serving Roosevelt, he was worried that his official position might force him to compromise too much, that his political naiveté might continue to embarrass the president, and that his commitment to Columbia University might be endangered. This last concern was especially significant. When his appointment to the Department of Agriculture was assured, he went to see President Nicholas Murray Butler to request a leave. Tugwell was so moved by Butler's concern for him and Columbia that he withdrew his name, only to change his mind that night after talking with Roosevelt. Roosevelt's argument was short and sweet—the time for talking was over; the time for action was now. Also, Roosevelt told Tugwell that he needed him for jobs he couldn't trust to anyone else. Tugwell understood and related to that well, but in the long run his decision to leave Columbia for Washington was one he always regretted. When the time came for him to return, Columbia didn't want him. It was a deeply felt hurt that Tugwell carried with him for the rest of his life.

While Tugwell eventually moved into the Department of Agriculture, after the offer of a position in the Department of Commerce fell through, the initial offer and his reaction to it were significant. In considering the offer, he indicated that changes in the Commerce Department had to be implemented before he could accept an appointment. Specifically, he felt that business had to be brought under closer "general government direction" and that the government had to "change over from the old anti-trust law repressions to recognition and control of present trends and scale." One way to do this was for the government to revive the Bureau of Corporations, place the investigative staff of the Federal Trade Commission under its authority, and begin carrying out the planning program he had outlined in *The Industrial Discipline*. If that was done, and if an acceptable secretary of commerce was placed in charge, then he could accept the appointment in good conscience and work to accomplish the goals Roosevelt stood for.[36] If not, he might better serve the president by being a critical, outside observer.

In retrospect, what Tugwell was saying in this regard was highly revealing. By laying down conditions for his acceptance of a position in the Department of Commerce, he was clearly demonstrating that he felt the primary responsibility for planning remained with business. The government's role was to be supervisory and regulatory rather than compulsory and directive. Cooperation between business and government was the key to success. His suggestion for a revived Bureau of Corporations also indicated his basic inclinations. While serving the old Rooseveltian purpose of being a "watchdog" over business, Tugwell now demanded that it act in the public interest and not for the benefit of private industry. Along with the intra- and interindustrial councils of *The Industrial Discipline*, he was confident that planning would be implemented within the American democratic system without any resort to more extreme measures.

While his appointment to Commerce never materialized, this did not stop Tugwell from continuing to advise Roosevelt on the importance of planning and on the need to adopt a specific program for confronting the immediate problems caused by the depression. With a profound sense of uneasiness gripping the country as the crisis deepened, Tugwell feared a revolutionary sentiment might be developing in the midst of widespread unemployment and hunger. If it was left unchecked, not only would the American government be endangered, but there was the possibility of American society being undermined. To prevent this, he recommended that a program to increase purchasing power be enacted immediately once Roosevelt took office and that he pursue it diligently once the New Deal was under way.[37]

Specifically, Tugwell recommended that such a program encompass relief, fiscal, and monetary policy. Designed primarily to achieve a short-term objective, he felt a $5 billion public works program and direct federal relief through the Reconstruction Finance Corporation or some other agency was necessary. In Tugwell's view, the Robert Wagner-Robert LaFollette-Edward Costigan proposals could serve as a beginning in this direction.[38] In fiscal matters, he suggested that redistribution of income through graduated income and undistributed profits taxes might be beneficial, forcing industry to invest its money where it was most needed. As an emergency measure, moreover, he reluctantly encouraged the government to institute deficit spending.

Tugwell thought that, in the short run, unbalancing the budget would stimulate the recovery process, but in the long run it would be "a crude device for correcting" the permanent disparities within the economy. He also feared that permanent deficit spending would create too much social unrest, particularly among industrial and higher-income groups.[39] To Tugwell, what Roosevelt had to do was "make a grand effort toward the resumption of industrial activity in normal ways," and permanent deficit spending was not one of those ways.

Along the same lines, he suggested that Roosevelt "ought to take over immediately large blocks of paralyzed industries" that were operating at "15 to 25 percent of capacity." Either by outright nationalization or, at the very least, by lease, he argued, this expanded fiscal policy would support and further the initial stages of the recovery process. He did not recommend this as a permanent policy, especially in light of the constitutional, financial, and practical problems involved. Just like his suggestions for public works and deficit spending, Tugwell considered that here short-term objectives were more important than long-term considerations.[40] The same was true for monetary policy.

Throughout 1931 and 1932, Tugwell had opposed outright inflation as a policy for relieving the economic crisis. Instead of helping the farmer or worker, it hurt those on fixed incomes, depreciated the value of fixed investments, and endangered the recovery process by perpetuating a rising price level, something no society could afford. Inflation did not increase purchasing power, which, in Tugwell's opinion, was the key to the economy's revival.[41] With Hoover's refusal to adopt policies that would have lowered prices and increased purchasing power, however, a new situation developed. By late 1932 and early 1933, Tugwell argued that the economy had become so deflationary that the only way to resolve the crisis was for the government to design a policy of reflation and a managed currency. In practical terms, this meant that selective price adjustments had to take place, with some prices going up while others went down. The United States also had to go off the gold standard internationally so as to manage its currency at home.[42] Later, when Roosevelt did institute reflationary policies and abandoned the gold standard, Tugwell supported these only as emergency measures and not as permanent, long-term programs.[43] In and of themselves, Tugwell did not believe they could restore recovery, although they might contribute to it.

Essentially, Tugwell was saying that the depression was a complex phenomenon that did not lend itself to simple, utopian formulas. Public works programs, direct federal relief, deficit spending, progressive taxation, government operation of depressed industries, reflation, and currency management—all of these suggestions, if carried out simultaneously, could alleviate the symptoms of the crisis. In doing so, they aided in preventing a revolutionary ferment from developing any further while also helping to create a more viable economic framework in which the causes of the depression could be dealt with. For Tugwell, only planning could eliminate those causes by correcting the basic disparities within the American economic system and by restoring the fundamental balance between industry and agriculture. A long-range program, he was convinced, had to be adopted because it represented America's only alternative for surviving in the twentieth century. With a sense of urgency, he persisted in his efforts to convince Roosevelt of the need for planning, especially after the president-elect took office on March 4, 1933.

After Roosevelt's inauguration, Tugwell's role as an adviser changed again. Instead of merely offering proposals for dealing with the agricultural and industrial crisis, he became actively involved in formulating and administering policies adopted by the president for overcoming the depression. This was particularly true in the case of the Agricultural Adjustment Administration (AAA) and the National Recovery Administration (NRA). In both instances, Tugwell aided in drafting the legislation, worked to make the programs effective, and advised the president on alternatives after the Supreme Court declared them unconstitutional. In both instances, he publicly defended the principles on which they were based while privately criticizing their administrators. For Tugwell, the AAA and NRA represented America's first steps toward the planned economy and, being so, he felt a personal responsibility for their survival in the American system.

Without a doubt, Tugwell was one of the men most responsible for the creation of the AAA in 1933. As a professional economist in the 1920s, he had written prolifically on the farmer's problems stemming from World War I and the basic inelasticity of agriculture. As an adviser in the 1928 presidential campaign, he had unsuccessfully suggested his Advance Ratio Plan to Al Smith. And, as a Brains Truster, he had persistently advised Roosevelt on the importance of reestablishing an equilibrium between industry and agriculture in addressing the crisis of the depression. In all these activities, Tugwell had not been able to offer a politically acceptable and economically feasible farm program because he believed the resolution of the farm problem depended on long-term land-use policies involving planning and not short-term, "fly-by-night" panaceas, such as McNary-Haugenism and other dumping schemes. He believed the latter proposals, based on political considerations and "negative" policies, dealt with symptoms of farm distress, not its causes.[44] This was not true of a farm proposal Tugwell considered more noteworthy: voluntary domestic allotment.

Although he had heard of the plan in late 1931, Tugwell did not seriously acquaint himself with its principles until the spring of 1932. He met with three of its sponsors—Beardsley Ruml, M. L. Wilson, and Henry Wallace—in April and May, and then, at Roosevelt's request, in June he attended an agricultural conference where the domestic allotment idea was explained to him in detail.[45] From then on, Tugwell became the chief exponent of the plan among Roosevelt's advisers as well as the primary medium through which the sponsors of the idea could interact with Roosevelt. Tugwell's actions in this regard are not surprising, since the domestic allotment plan coincided with many of the suggestions he had been making throughout the 1920s and early 1930s.

Like Tugwell's Advance Ratio Plan (ARP), the purpose of domestic allotment was to equalize farm supply with consumer demand through a system of voluntary agreements among farmers. The domestic allotment proposal, however, was more detailed and specific. According to it, agricultural experts, "using historical amounts of production as base figures," would calculate "the total prospective sale of export crops in the domestic market" and then allocate specific amounts of production for each cooperating farmer. In return for agreeing not to plant more than his specified amount, the farmer was to receive "payments which, when added to the selling price," would give him a parity return "on the domestically consumed portion of his product." If, however, a farmer produced more than he agreed to, his excess production would receive only the prevailing world prices and nothing else.[46]

Completely dependent on his cooperation, the domestic allotment idea was designed to convince the farmer that the less he produced, the more money he would make. It also attempted to demonstrate to the farmer that the problem of the surplus was to be resolved by himself.[47] In view of Europe's inability to buy American goods in the midst of the world depression and the saturation of the American market itself, the advocates of domestic allotment hoped to convince the farmer that his only hope lay in cooperation and restricted production, at least in the immediate future. Cooperation, planning, and expertise—these were the keys to farm prosperity as far as they, and Tugwell, were concerned.

In Tugwell's opinion, domestic allotment was impressive because it was specific in its implementation procedures and politically feasible in its voluntarism. By making the farmer socially conscious, he felt, it relieved the immediate burden of farm distress, aided in laying the foundation for a long-range land-use program, and facilitated the establishment of a "regulated and balanced" economy. At the same time, he believed it would encounter quite a bit of opposition. A new approach to the farm question, it ignored the traditional remedies of tariffs and dumping, thereby incurring the wrath of the more conservative farm leaders.[48] To counter this, Tugwell began a vigorous campaign to sell the domestic allotment idea to the American people.

Between November 1932 and March 1933, he collaborated closely with M. L. Wilson, Mordecai Ezekiel, and Frederick Lee, a Washington attorney, in writing propaganda supporting domestic allotment, in drafting legislation incorporating its principles, and in encouraging the lame-duck Congress to act quickly. In view of the deteriorating farm situation, Tugwell was particularly adamant in demanding that the Congress act on domestic allotment.[49] With farm prices declining, foreclosures increasing, and farm discontent intensifying, he feared violence might erupt and spread quickly throughout the country. Unfortunately, political considerations were more important to the Congress than actual conditions, and as a result, nothing was done.

After Roosevelt's inauguration on March 4, the status of domestic allotment changed drastically. Under the supervision of Henry Wallace, the new secretary of agriculture, the supporters of the proposal held conferences and produced a compromise draft bill for congressional consideration. Introduced on March 16 in the House of Representatives, the bill immediately ran into the opposition of inflationists and conservative farm leaders. Objecting to the restrictive production features of the bill and its taxing provisions, they sought to kill it in committee. By early April, this strategy seemed to be working so well that President Roosevelt intervened. Having committed himself to domestic allotment, he sought to salvage as much of it as he could. To placate the inflationists, he accepted the Thomas amendment to the AAA, which allowed him, as president, to expand the currency. To placate the opponents of controlled production, he ordered Wallace, Tugwell, Jerome Frank, and Frederick Lee to meet with George Peek, a prominent McNary-Haugenite, to work out their differences. Although several conferences were held in April and May, Peek refused to compromise on production control, arguing instead for marketing agreements. On May 3, however, he accepted provisions of the bill for restrictive production as a last resort, while simultaneously agreeing to be the chief administrator of the program. Within ten days of his decision, opposition to the bill subsided and the AAA became law.[50]

In its final form, the AAA was a hodgepodge of ideas and methods designed to satisfy everyone. Purporting to bring about a balance between the production and consumption of farm goods so that farm income would have the same relative purchasing power as existed from 1909 to 1914, it empowered the secretary of agriculture to do any of several things. For basic farm products, such as wheat, cotton, corn, hogs, tobacco, milk, and rice, the AAA could enter into agreements with individual farmers by which the AAA would pay the farmer to limit his production. The AAA could also buy up agricultural surplus and/or lend money to farmers, accepting their crops as collateral until prices rose. In this instance, the Commodity Credit Corporation, created in the fall of 1933, was to act as the lending agency. Finally, the AAA, through the secretary of agriculture, could subsidize agricultural exports if it so desired. The entire program was to be financed from revenues acquired through a special tax on food and fiber processors, who could pass the tax on to the consumers.[51]

Although the AAA was legally supposed to be administered by Secretary of Agriculture Henry Wallace and AAA Administrator George Peek, this did not happen once it was in operation. As Assistant Secretary of Agriculture, and later as Under Secretary of Agriculture, Tugwell played a prominent role in the overall and daily operation of the program. The reason for this was quite simple. Tugwell was appointed to Agriculture because he had helped Roosevelt in the campaign; he had consistently championed domestic allotment before its passage; and he got along rather well with Wallace. Wallace himself had requested that Roosevelt appoint Tugwell as assistant secretary because he needed help in dealing with the administrative details of running his department. Recognizing his own limitations in this area, Wallace believed Tugwell would prove a valuable asset. Roosevelt agreed, and he offered Tugwell the position. In accepting the appointment, Tugwell naturally defined his responsibilities very broadly, believing he would assist the secretary in all activities within the department, including the AAA. Although this interpretation of his authority eventually led to serious problems within Agriculture, Tugwell, in May 1933, was justified in thinking the way he did. For all practical purposes, the AAA was within his jurisdiction and, as such, subject to his influence and direction.[52]

In all his speeches and writings as assistant and under secretary of agriculture, Tugwell consistently defended the AAA. Emphasizing its voluntary, experimental nature, he continuously characterized it as a temporary program seeking to achieve a dual purpose. In the short run, it was attempting to assist the farmer by reducing the "spread between costs and retail prices" and the "spread between the prices which farmers receive and those which consumers pay." In the long run, it was laying the foundation for the permanent land-use planning necessary to sustain agriculture's survival in the modern world.[53] Although the short-run objective conflicted in some instances with the longer-range goal, Tugwell did not believe that the clash seriously endangered the effectiveness of the overall program. Many of the shorter-term devices being employed, such as crop reduction, would be abandoned once the more permanent land policies were adopted and put into practice.

In many respects, Tugwell argued, the explanation for this clash lay in past government land policies. Between the founding of the republic and the onset of the depression, Tugwell believed, the government, especially on the federal level, had pursued reckless, wasteful, and irrational programs in distributing the public domain. Without any concern for the future, the government gave the land to anyone who would settle it, whether individual farmers or, in the late nineteenth century, industrial concerns. By 1900, land exploitation by private interests had reached such alarming proportions that a conservation movement was started to salvage what was left. Demanding that the government assume its responsibility in protecting the nation's most abundant resource, the conservationists successfully pressured the government on all levels to adopt a more scientific and efficient approach to land utilization.

Tugwell felt, however, that their success was temporary because, with World War I and the return to normalcy in the 1920s, private interests again took control of the public domain and exploited it for their own benefit. Encouraged by the federal government in particular, these private interests speculated in wild-eyed enterprises, ruthlessly stripped the land of its wealth, and ignored the basic principles of land use to such an extent that they contributed to the outbreak of the depression. Tugwell emphasized that this private exploitation forced the American people generally to reexamine their attitudes toward the land and to demand that the federal government devise new programs for developing it in the general interest. With the Hoover administration refusing to do this, Tugwell concluded, the New Deal had to, and it was in this context that it devised the AAA.[54]

In Tugwell's argument, the basic principles underlying the AAA and the New Deal farm program were the simple assumptions that land is a commodity affecting the entire economic system, that the federal and state governments can "go a long way in planning the use of the public domain," and that an agriculture-industry balance had to be established before the depression could be resolved. In attempting to reduce acreage so that "probable production" would be brought more closely in line with "probable consumption," the AAA was trying

to persuade the American farmers to work together so as to cultivate the soil of the United States as though it were one single farm, to keep out of certain kinds of production fifty million acres of land, to assure the production of food and fibres we need, with ample reserves both for export and carryover, to protect drainage and water supplies through a great program of reforestation, and through special credit and financial institutions to keep the farmer on his farm and the farm family in the farm home during a period of terrible economic insecurity throughout the world.[55]

In this sense, the New Deal and the AAA were trying to save American capitalism, not destroy it.

Tugwell argued that the methods employed by the government to achieve this objective were in the American democratic tradition. Without coercing the farmer to do anything, the government was asking him to cooperate in its grand planning effort to restore the economic system.[56] If it succeeded, everyone would share in the results; if it failed, the farmer would have to assume some of the responsibility for that failure.

Tugwell also felt that the processing tax used in the AAA was constitutional and within the American framework. Although representing "a shift in purchasing power from one group [the consumer] to the other [the farmer]," it did not imply class legislation. For Tugwell, there were two reasons why this was so:

First, no recovery can occur until farmers are able to buy industrial products on an ample scale, so that the temporary disadvantage to the consumer will be overcome just as fast as an increased farm buying power gets to work. Second, an increase in farm income means a direct expansion of purchasing power—much of it, as in the case of farm machinery, of special importance to the capital-goods industries.[57]

In practical terms, Tugwell suggested, this meant that there was a direct correlation between mass production and mass consumption. Each depended on the other and, considering the effect the depression had on the farmer, it was of the utmost importance to make certain that farm income increased proportionately. The AAA, through the processing tax, was doing that, and therefore it was justified in attempting to shift purchasing power from one group to another.

In defending the AAA in this way, Tugwell was saying that the devices employed by the program were temporary expedients that, in the short run, facilitated the restoration of the farmer to a more equitable position within the economic system while, in the long run, they had little or nothing to do with eliminating the basic causes of farm distress. To accomplish that, more permanent policies had to be implemented, and those policies had to deal with the basic problem of the land itself, especially in terms of retiring submarginal land, reorienting the family farm, and revising the American value system.

Despite arguments to the contrary, Tugwell emphasized that the American individualistic philosophy contributed to the outbreak of the depression generally and the agricultural crisis specifically. By promoting the individual's rights, this philosophy encouraged the government to pursue lax land policies that, in turn, encouraged private interests to abuse the land. Individual farmers especially were responsible for this land misuse because they planted more land than they had to. They thereby not only created a surplus problem but also contributed to soil erosion. By 1933, Tugwell indicated, so much of the land had been damaged that a significant portion of the farm population migrated to the cities in order to escape the poverty-ridden existence they were leading—all to no avail. Ill-prepared for industrial occupations, they could not adjust to urban life and their situation worsened. Those who stayed on the farm were suffering as well, because the land could no longer produce a livelihood. Desolate and barren, it had lost much of its productive power. In Tugwell's opinion, until that power was restored, the farm depression would continue indefinitely, regardless of any artificial means employed to sustain the farmer.[58]

In light of this, he recommended that the federal government act quickly to initiate a permanent land-use program. Specifically, he wanted the government to withdraw approximately one-seventh of the public domain from use, including the submarginal lands of the Appalachian highland, the Piedmont plateau, the Great Lakes, and the Great Plains. Here, the government would restore the soil through massive reforestation projects. In addition, the government had to move people from the submarginal lands to better, more productive lands. By relocating these farmers, the government was providing a "real alternative to poverty living" while simultaneously making them more productive in the economic system. The government had to consider seriously whether consolidated farms should replace the more inefficient individual ones. In Tugwell's words:

If individual agricultural workers are to operate at a high level of productivity, if at the same time agricultural production is to be limited to the effective demand for agricultural products, there must be a very appreciable reduction in the proportion of American workers engaged in commercial agriculture—preferably by the gradual transference of some farm laborers and tenants who are now operating at a low level of productivity, with low incomes, and some farm operators who are working on submarginal lands, into at least part-time production of goods and services for which there is a more elastic demand. Part of these goods and services may be directed toward retaining the population remaining in agriculture, resulting in better housing for rural families, better schools for rural children, more nurses, doctors, telephones, books, and clothes, and more adequate diets both for farm families and for city families.[59]

More important, having fewer commercial farmers might be the only way to sustain an equitable, lasting balance between industry and agriculture. With technological efficiency daily enhancing industrial productivity, Tugwell emphasized, it was essential for agriculture to follow suit, and considering the sophistication of the American economic system, farm consolidation might be the only way to do it.

Although land withdrawal, resettlement, and farm consolidation were the initial steps in a land-use program, Tugwell did not believe they were the only ones. Much more was necessary, although he was not certain what, specifically, had to be done. In this respect, Tugwell argued, experience would fill in the details and farmer-government cooperation would determine how successfully the program was progressing. Like any long-term planning program, land use needed time and experience to make it work.

In spite of Tugwell's public optimism that the New Deal, through the AAA, was striving to help the farmer in the short and long runs, he privately expressed serious reservations about the way the program was being administered by the Washington bureaucrats, especially George Peek. Ironically, Tugwell had initially supported the appointment of Peek as administrator of AAA, only to find that, within a very short time, he became his chief opponent.

Before the passage of the AAA, Tugwell believed Peek was the logical choice for administrator. Although disagreeing with him on several critical issues, he considered Peek to be a forceful, intelligent person who had the "best grasp of anyone" of the AAA's potential, even though he did tend to be too conservative in philosophy and too international-minded in temperament. Both Tugwell and Wallace felt that Peek, a veteran of McNary-Haugenism and a close friend of Bernard Baruch, was the only one who could quash congressional opposition to the AAA and assure its passage.[60] In May 1933, this was a valid assumption.

Considering the novel features of the proposed AAA and the strong adherence to traditional farm remedies within the Congress, the probable appointment of Peek as administrator would, and eventually did, facilitate the acceptance of the program. What neither Wallace nor Tugwell realized was that Peek was determined to implement only the provisions of the AAA that coincided with his own ideas on farm recovery.[61]

A strong-minded individual, Peek believed the primary way to agricultural recovery was to treat agriculture as a separate, integral unit within the economic system and to give it every possible advantage. In terms of the AAA, he felt this meant utilizing the marketing agreements as soon as possible. These agreements were designed to allow the processors and middlemen an opportunity to develop codes of fair competition and, in return, to receive antitrust exemption. Like their counterparts in the NRA, they implicitly served as the basic vehicles for price fixing. In Peek's thinking, this latter characteristic of the codes was particularly important because it assured high prices for American farm goods, facilitated the maintenance of high levels of production, and prevented lower-priced foreign competition from infiltrating the American market.[62] If the codes, moreover, proved successful operationally, they would eliminate any need for restrictive crop control. As far as Peek was concerned, the domestic allotment provisions of the AAA were unnecessary and dangerous, and he was determined to avoid them at all costs. In doing so, he would cause his own downfall.

Of all those in the Department of Agriculture who opposed Peek's refusal to institute domestic allotment, no one was more critical than Tugwell. Using every talent at his disposal, he publicly and privately criticized Peek for not seeing the economy in holistic terms and for accepting marketing agreements, tariffs, and dumping as the primary means for resolving the agricultural crisis. Tugwell was even more disturbed by Peek's resistance to the attempts of the AAA's Consumers' Council to establish standards of "quality, identity, [and] labelling" for farm products and to have them written into the marketing agreements.[63] Tugwell believed that there was no justification for any such action. Peek seemed to be sacrificing the farmer and the consumer for the processor's benefit and perverting the basic principles underlying the AAA. Sooner or later, he had to be stopped, and in September 1933, Tugwell felt the time had come to do that.

By September-October 1933, the AAA had split into two opposing groups. The liberal faction, headed by Tugwell and Wallace, "wanted to exploit the sense of crisis to push through long-needed reforms to relieve the poverty of sharecroppers, tenant farmers, and farm laborers, and to crack down on packers, millers, and big milk distributors to make sure that increased farm prices came out of middlemen and not the consumer." Supported by Jerome Frank, Frederick Howe, Paul Appleby, C. B. Baldwin, Mordecai Ezekiel, and Louis Bean, it stood solidly behind the principles of domestic allotment. The conservative faction, headed by Peek, included Chester Davis and Charles Brand. Unlike the liberals, they were favorably inclined toward the big farmer and processor, and more limited in the scope of their approach. Up to the fall of 1933, neither faction openly feuded with the other, although privately each sought to gain an advantage. This situation changed drastically, however, when the sugar and tobacco marketing agreements were being formulated and when Peek proposed his butter-export scheme.[64]

In the former incident, the Legal Division of the AAA, headed by Jerome Frank, advised Wallace to reject the sugar marketing agreement because it did not provide enough protection for the growers, while in the tobacco agreement, it suggested that the AAA be given permission to check all company books. As secretary of agriculture, Wallace had the authority to approve or disapprove a code, and in these instances, he agreed with the Legal Division and acted accordingly. Upset and angry, the processors appealed to Peek for help. Sensing that the agreements were really a test of strength, Peek reprimanded the Legal Division, especially Frank, and appealed to the president for approval. Recognizing the appeal for what it was, Roosevelt decided to support Peek in order to prevent an open break involving Wallace-Tugwell-Peek. The tobacco code was accepted without the provisions for access to company books, and the sugar code was sent back to the processors for further consideration. All in all, the controversy appeared to have resulted in a significant victory for Peek.

Encouraged by what had happened, Peek decided to move against Jerome Frank. In a memorandum to Wallace, he demanded that Frank be removed immediately as general counsel. When Wallace refused, Peek prepared himself for a final showdown. In late November and early December, instead of reopening the Frank question, he decided to make his butter-export scheme the final test case. According to this proposal, the United States would export a large quantity of butter to Europe in order to resolve the surplus problem at home. Since this would probably involve a loss to the American farmer, Peek requested that the secretary of agriculture subsidize the export and advance $500,000 out of processing tax revenues to make up the difference between the foreign and domestic prices. Essentially a dumping scheme, Peek thought it would prove to be a highly beneficial endeavor.

Although Peek had proposed the idea in a memorandum to Wallace, it was Tugwell who considered it. Since Wallace was with Roosevelt at Warm Springs, Georgia, Tugwell was the acting secretary and, as such, responsible for handling all departmental business. In this instance, however, he felt it was wiser for him to discuss the memorandum with Wallace before making any decision. Contacting him by phone, he told the secretary of Peek's request, and together they decided that he should turn it down. On December 2, Tugwell informed Peek of his decision not to advance $500,000 because the scheme was too costly and involved dumping.[65] Without considering the reasons behind the decision, Peek threatened to go directly to Roosevelt for final approval. He also indicated that, as far as he was concerned, the president's decision would resolve once and for all the power struggle between the AAA administrator and the secretary of agriculture.

Although Roosevelt had consciously avoided interfering in the Wallace-Tugwell-Peek disputes in the past, there was no way he could get around this one. The controversy was widely publicized by the press, and the authority of his secretary of agriculture was being challenged. In light of this, he decided that Peek had outlived his usefulness, and on December 7, he asked for his resignation. He also publicly announced his support of the Wallace-Tugwell opposition to the butter scheme and their decision to redirect the AAA away from the marketing agreements.[66] By supporting Wallace and Tugwell in this way, the president hoped that the controversy within the AAA and between the USDA and the AAA would subside, and that the implementation of the New Deal farm program would be smoother and more coordinated, at least in the immediate future.

If Tugwell and Wallace construed the Peek resignation as a victory, they soon learned that it was only a shallow, temporary one. Events were about to unfold that not only would disrupt the Tugwell-Wallace rapport but also would result in the decline of Tugwell's influence in the USDA and AAA. Weakened and ineffective, Tugwell would then turn his attention to the Resettlement Administration.

After Peek resigned on December 11, 1933, Roosevelt appointed Chester Davis as his successor. A mild-mannered, shy person, Davis had been a close adviser of Peek's, a member of the conservative faction in the AAA, and an experienced agriculturalist. Unlike his predecessor, he was a good administrator and a convert to the principles of domestic allotment. Although still committed to marketing agreements, tariffs, and dumping, Davis believed that anything that helped the farmer was acceptable if it could be implemented properly. On taking office, he told AAA personnel that he was seeking to resolve the differences among them and, thereby, to make the AAA an effective, efficient agency within the New Deal.[67]

Throughout most of his first year as administrator, Davis did not encounter any problems with the young liberals in the Legal Division or with Tugwell, who originally supported his appointment as Peek's successor. Aside from a few skirmishes over marketing agreements, the AAA carried on its business in an orderly, routine way.[68] All of this changed, however, at the beginning of 1935. In January and February, the young liberals in the Legal Division took it upon themselves to reinterpret an agreement the AAA had worked out with southern landlords employing tenant farmers. Originally, the agreement was that landlords who signed acreage-adjustment contracts would not reduce the number of their tenants during the first year's operation. While Davis and Tugwell were away on trips, however, the Legal Division reinterpreted the provisions and ordered state AAA administrators to force southern landlords to keep the same tenants on the same land for the second year of operation. In doing so, they caused a tremendous uproar throughout the South.

On hearing the news, Davis returned to Washington immediately. Furious over their insubordination, he was convinced that the Legal Division had gone too far in reinterpreting the AAA and that his own authority as administrator had been seriously challenged. He requested permission from Secretary Wallace to handle the liberals in any way he saw fit. Wallace agreed with Davis and therefore granted the request. On February 4, Davis made his move. He fired Jerome Frank, Lee Pressman, Victor Rotnem, Francis Shea, and Alger Hiss of the Legal Division, and removed Frederick Howe as head of the Consumer Council. At a press conference the next day, he and Wallace justified the purge by saying that it was the only way to preserve harmony within the AAA, and denied that the economic and social views of Frank and his colleagues had anything to do with it.[69] When asked what effect the purge would have on Under Secretary Tugwell, neither commented. For all practical purposes, Wallace and Davis did not have to offer any opinions; Tugwell did that himself.

Bitterly upset over the firings, Tugwell returned to Washington in a hostile mood. Accusing Davis of planning to "rid the Department of all liberals and to give the reactionary farm leaders full control of policy," he demanded that Wallace overrule Davis or, at the very least, transfer Frank and his colleagues to other positions within the government. When Wallace refused to do so because of his relationship with farm leaders and his own political ambitions, Tugwell went to Roosevelt and submitted his resignation.[70] Dramatically, he told the president that he had no other alternative: The purge had been directed against him; Wallace had publicly assumed that he (Tugwell) would no longer have anything to do with the AAA; and the Wallace-Davis rapport would create more problems for him in the future. Tugwell stated that he would prefer to be transferred to the Department of Interior, where he could work with Secretary Ickes in implementing a long-range conservation program. Although Roosevelt agreed that Tugwell's usefulness in the USDA was in question and that a transfer to Interior might help everyone involved, he was not certain that it could be done, since no funds had been appropriated for the position. Without ruling out the possibility, however, he told Tugwell to talk with Wallace and sit tight until he could get back to him.[71]

While waiting for the president, Tugwell consulted with Wallace about his future within the USDA and the AAA. In clear and direct language, Wallace told Tugwell that he wanted him to remain as under secretary of agriculture only if he (Tugwell) would relinquish all his authority over the AAA. In light of his relationship with Davis, Wallace argued, this was the only way to preserve any harmony within the New Deal farm program. In Tugwell's opinion, however, nothing was further from the truth. As Davis' technical superior, he felt that he had the right and the obligation to participate in the operation of the AAA whether or not overall coordination was achieved. Considering Davis' inclination to cater to the interests of the conservative farm leaders, Tugwell was adamant on this score. As far as he was concerned, Wallace would either have to accept him as he was or find a new under secretary. Disagreeing over fundamentals, neither Tugwell nor Wallace was willing to compromise. As a result, a stalemate set in. To make matters worse, Tugwell's hopes for a position within the Interior Department were soon dashed; Ickes informed him that he was unable to secure the necessary congressional approval. Without any authority in the USDA and without any possibility of being transferred, Tugwell resigned himself to the defeat the purge had inflicted on him.[72]

In assessing the purge and its effects, there is little doubt that Tugwell has to assume some of the responsibility for what happened. Almost from the beginning, he had created ill feeling among the bureaucrats in the USDA by his activity in the Peek resignation and by his shielding of the young liberals in the Legal Division. His refusal either to dissociate himself from the petty quarreling within the AAA or, at the very least, to exert some influence over the Frank group also hurt him because it created a situation in which he became the target for those in the USDA seeking a scapegoat. And his unwillingness to compromise on the objectives of the AAA with either Peek or Davis made it seem as if he were interfering in something that was not his business. To many in the USDA and the AAA, Tugwell was a radical social reformer who was trying to use the AAA for his own purposes without any regard for the objectives they were striving to achieve. A distorted, unreal image, it was nevertheless the one that Tugwell had helped to create, and the one that contributed to his downfall.

Although the purge seriously undermined Tugwell's influence within the USDA and the AAA, it did not completely destroy him as a New Dealer. He still had a good enough rapport with Roosevelt that his usefulness in the New Deal was apparent in a number of other areas and in a variety of ways.

NOTES

1. Raymond Moley, *After Seven Years*, (New York: Harper and Brothers, 1939), 1-24; *The First New Deal*, (New York: Harcourt, Brace, and World, 1966), 11-16; Samuel Rosenman, *Working with Roosevelt*, (New York: Harper and Brothers, 1952), 59ff.; Tugwell, diary, folder "Introduction," p. 3, Tugwell papers, FDR Library, box 30; Rexford Tugwell, *The Brains Trust* (New York: Viking Press, 1968), xi-xiii, 6, 9; Tugwell, *To the Lesser Heights of Morningside* (Philadelphia: University of Pennsylvania Press, 1982), 232-33.

2. Moley, *After Seven Years*, p. 15; Tugwell, *The Brains Trust*, pp. 12-18; Tugwell, "The Reminiscences of Rexford G. Tugwell," pp. 4-5, Oral History Research Office, Columbia University; Bernard Sternsher, *Rexford Tugwell and the New Deal* (New Brunswick, N.J.: Rutgers University Press, 1964), 39-40.

3. Tugwell, diary, folder "Introduction," pp. 6-7, Tugwell papers, FDR Library, box 30; Tugwell, *The Brains Trust*, pp. 12-18.

4. Tugwell, "The Reminiscences of Rexford Tugwell," pp. 4-5.

5. Moley, *After Seven Years*, p. 15; Tugwell, *The Brains Trust*, p. 19.

6. Tugwell, *The Democratic Roosevelt* (Garden City, N.Y.: Doubleday, 1957), 212ff.; Sternsher, *Tugwell and the New Deal*, pp. 40-41.

7. Tugwell, *The Brains Trust*, pp. 21ff. Tugwell recalled here that he had touched a nerve, and that it was his objective to show Roosevelt that agriculture and industry together needed help.

8. Rexford G. Tugwell to A. A. Berle, March 6, 1964, Tugwell papers, folder "Berle, Adolph," FDR Library, box 3; Tugwell, diary, folder "Notes from a New Deal Diary," December 20, 1932, pp. 2ff., Tugwell papers, FDR Library, box 30; Tugwell, "Reminiscences," p. 19. See also Tugwell, *The Brains Trust*, pp. xi-xiii, and Tugwell papers, "New Deal Materials, 1932-1933," FDR Library, box 38.

9. Rexford Tugwell to Adolph Berle, November 14, 1939, and Berle to Tugwell, November 15, 1939, both in Tugwell papers, folder "Berle, Adolph," FDR Library, box 3; Tugwell, *The Brains Trust*, pp. 32-33, 76-77, 153, 216, 268ff., 373, 520-22.

10. Tugwell, *The Brains Trust*, pp. 128-29; Sternsher, *Tugwell and the New Deal*, p. 41.

11. Tugwell, "Reminiscences," p. 12; Tugwell, *The Brains Trust*, p. 206.

12. Tugwell, "Reminiscences," pp. 10, 13, 14-15, 20, 24-25; Tugwell, *The Brains Trust*, pp. 206-10; see also Tugwell papers, folder "Correspondence: November 1931-February 1933," FDR Library, box 41. Tugwell freely admitted that he did not know specifically how to control production.

13. Sternsher, *Tugwell and the New Deal*, p. 186.

14. Tugwell, "Reminiscences," p. 9; Tugwell, *The Brains Trust*, pp. 44ff.

15. Tugwell, *The Brains Trust*, pp. 69, 71, 176ff., 192. Although *The Industrial Discipline* was not published until 1933, Tugwell said he told Roosevelt of it in 1932.

16. Ibid., pp. 47-50; Sternsher, *Tugwell and the New Deal*, p. 42. For the complete text of the speech see Samuel Rosenman, ed., *The Public Papers and Addresses of Franklin D. Roosevelt*, I, *The Genesis of the New Deal, 1928-1932* (New York: Random House, 1938), 623-39.

17. Tugwell, *The Brains Trust*, pp. 59, 63, 93-97, 123, 158; Tugwell, diary, folder "Introduction," p. 11, Tugwell papers, FDR Library, box 30.

18. Tugwell, *The Brains Trust*, pp. 104, 112, 126-27, 144ff. Although Tugwell liked the Oglethorpe address, he later felt that it failed to recognize that planning in the methods, not the objectives, was needed. For a complete text of the speech, see Rosenman, *The Public Papers . . . Roosevelt*, pp. 639-47.

19. Tugwell, "Reminiscences," pp. 27-31; Tugwell, *The Brains Trust*, pp. 233, 255ff., 378-79; Sternsher, *Tugwell and the New Deal*, p. 42.

20. Tugwell, *The Brains Trust*, pp. 525-26.

21. Ibid., p. 526.

22. Ibid.

23. Ibid., p. 527.

24. Ibid., p. 528.

25. Ibid., pp. 277-78; Adolph Berle, memorandum to Franklin D. Roosevelt, August 17, 1932, "The Economic Council," in Beatrice A. Berle and Travis Jacobs, eds., *Navigating the Rapids, 1918-1971: From the Papers of Adolph A.*

Berle (New York: Harcourt Brace Jovanovich, 1973), 59. See Elliot Rosen, *Hoover, Roosevelt, and the Brains Trust: From Depression to New Deal* (New York: Columbia University Press, 1977), for a different view.

26. Tugwell, *The Brains Trust*, pp. 294-95, 299, 304, 309, 345, 392-93. For a complete text of the Columbus speech, see Rosenman, *Public Papers . . . Roosevelt*, pp. 669-84.

27. Tugwell, *The Brains Trust*, pp. 473, 481-84; Rosenman, *The Public Papers . . . Roosevelt*, pp. 795-812, 831-42.

28. Tugwell, *The Brains Trust*, pp. 416, 417, 446-47, 404-05, 496-97, 512.

29. Tugwell, diary, folder "Introduction," p. 10, Tugwell papers, FDR Library, box 30; Tugwell papers, folder "The Contributions of Herbert Hoover," pp. 10ff., FDR Library, box 70; Tugwell, *The Brains Trust*, pp. 422-34.

30. Tugwell, diary, folder "Introduction," pp. 10ff., Tugwell papers, FDR Library, box 30; Tugwell papers, folder: "The Contributions of Herbert Hoover," pp. 30-31, FDR Library, box 70; Tugwell, *The Brains Trust*, pp. 405, 430, 444, 464, 466. Quote is from p. 430.

31. Tugwell, diary, folder "Notes from a New Deal Diary," December 20, 1932, pp. 8-10, and diary, folder "Notes," January 24, 1933, p. 78, Tugwell papers, FDR Library, box 30; Tugwell, diary, folder "Hundred Days/Addendum to the Hundred Days," pp. 9-10, Tugwell papers, FDR Library, box 30; Tugwell, *The Brains Trust*, pp. 475-76; Sternsher, *Tugwell and the New Deal*, pp. 54-56; Tugwell, "Reminiscences," pp. 57-58. Later, after the London Conference failed and once the New Deal was under way, Tugwell did support an international approach to the depression. See Tugwell, "The New Course of International Trade," address to the International Institute of Agriculture at Rome, October 24, 1934, pp. 4, 9, 17, Tugwell papers, FDR Library, box 56. Tugwell was responsible for changing the date of the conference from April to June. See also Rexford Tugwell, *Roosevelt's Revolution: The First Year, A Personal Perspective* (New York: Macmillan, 1977), 7ff.; Tugwell, *Lesser Heights*, pp. 234-35.

32. Tugwell, diary, folder "Notes from a New Deal Diary," February 18, 1933, p. 99, Tugwell papers, FDR Library, box 30; Tugwell, "Reminiscences," p. 38; Sternsher, *Tugwell and the New Deal*, p. 124. See also Tugwell, diary, April 21, 1933, p. 14, Tugwell papers, FDR Library, box 30; Tugwell, *The Battle for Democracy* (New York: Columbia University Press, 1935), 29-33; Tugwell, *Roosevelt's Revolution*, pp. 22-23.

33. Tugwell, *The Democratic Roosevelt*, pp. 261ff.; Sternsher, *Tugwell and the New Deal*, pp. 73-76.

34. For an excellent discussion of Tugwell's treatment by the press, see Sternsher, *Tugwell and the New Deal*, pp. 223-51.

35. Tugwell, diary, folder "Notes from a New Deal Diary," December 30, 1933, pp. 91-92, Tugwell papers, FDR Library, box 30.

36. Ibid., February 12, 1933, p. 94, and February 1, 1933, p. 95, Tugwell papers, FDR Library, box 30; Tugwell, *Lesser Heights*, pp. 241-42.

37. Tugwell, diary, folder "Notes from a New Deal Diary," December 24, 1932, p. 18, Tugwell papers, FDR Library, box 30; Tugwell, *The Industrial*

Discipline (New York: Columbia University Press, 1933), 228-29; Sternsher, *Tugwell and the New Deal*, pp. 143-46.

38. Tugwell, diary, folder "Monetary Preliminaries," article "Roosevelt Advisor Outlines Seven Point Program for Recovery," *New York World Telegram*, January 29, 1933, pp. 94-95, Tugwell papers, FDR Library, box 30; Arthur M. Schlesinger, Jr., *The Crisis of the Old Order* (Boston: Houghton Mifflin, 1956), 449ff., and *The Coming of the New Deal* (Boston: Houghton Mifflin, 1958), 95; Sternsher, *Tugwell and the New Deal*, p. 149.

39. It is important to remember that what Tugwell was saying during the interregnum coincided with what he was saying once the New Deal was under way. See Tugwell, diary, folder "Notes from a New Deal Diary," April 3, 1933, pp. 6-7, and April 14, 1933, p. 11, Tugwell papers, FDR Library, box 30; Tugwell, "Economy or Efficiency," n.d., Tugwell papers, FDR Library, box 55; Sternsher, *Tugwell and the New Deal*, pp. 107-08, 133-39, 316-19; Arthur M. Schlesinger, Jr., *Politics of Upheaval* (Boston: Houghton Mifflin, 1960), 506. Tugwell did not completely understand Keynesian deficit spending in February-March, 1933. One man who saw that was Marriner Eccles, *Beckoning Frontiers* (New York: Alfred A. Knopf, 1951), 114-15, 134.

40. Tugwell, diary, folder "Notes from a New Deal Diary," April 12, 1933, p. 14, Tugwell papers, FDR Library, box 30. Tugwell did feel, then and later, that certain industries, such as public utilities, would be more efficiently operated by the government.

41. Rexford Tugwell to Frank O. Lowden, October 5, 1931, folder "Lo-Ly," Tugwell papers, FDR Library, box 14.

42. Tugwell, diary, folder "Notes from a New Deal Diary," December 20, 1932, p. 4, December 28, 1932, pp. 27-30, and January 14, 1933, p. 60, Tugwell papers, FDR Library, box 30; Rexford Tugwell to Clyde King, January 23, 1933, folder "Ki-Kl," and Fiorello LaGuardia to Rexford Tugwell, March 13, 1933, folder "La," FDR Library, boxes 12 and 13, respectively.

43. Rexford Tugwell, "The Process of Recovery," August 14, 1933, pp. 6-10, Tugwell papers, FDR Library, box 55; Tugwell, address to Adult Education Association (October 29, 1933), USDA press release, Tugwell papers, FDR Library, box 55; Tugwell, "The President's Monetary Policy," November 5, 1933, p. 3, Tugwell papers, FDR Library, box 55; Tugwell, "Managing Money," November 14, 1933, pp. 1-7, Tugwell papers, FDR Library, box 55; Tugwell, diary, folder "Diary 1934," April 26, 1934, p. 3, Tugwell papers, FDR Library, box 31; Tugwell, "Prices and Dollars," and "Our Weight in Gold," both in Tugwell, *The Battle for Democracy* (New York: Columbia University Press, 1935), 48-51, 25-28, respectively.

44. Tugwell, diary, folder "Notes from a New Deal Diary," December 31, 1932, p. 35, and January 6, 1933, p. 46, Tugwell papers, FDR Library, box 30. See also David L. Wickens to Rexford Tugwell, December 20, 1932; Mordecai Ezekiel to Rexford Tugwell, December 31, 1932; Wickens to Tugwell, January 3, 1933; and Ezekiel to Tugwell, January 10, 1933, all in Tugwell papers, folder "Correspondence: November 1931-February 1933," FDR Library, box 41.

45. Tugwell, *The Brains Trust*, pp. 453, 457, 459. The actual originators of the plan were John Black, William J. Spillman, M. L. Wilson, Beardsley Ruml, Mordecai Ezekiel, and Henry Wallace—all working cooperatively, for the most part. See Edward L. Schapsmeier and Frederick Schapsmeier, *Henry A. Wallace of Iowa: The Agrarian Years* (Ames: Iowa State University Press, 1968), 125ff. See also Mordecai Ezekiel to Rexford Tugwell, January 15, 1933, "Facts on the Domestic Allotment Act," folder "Ezekiel, Mordecai," Tugwell papers, FDR Library, box 7; Ezekiel to Tugwell, October 20, 1939, folder "Agriculture, Department of," Tugwell papers, FDR Library, box 1.

46. Sternsher, *Tugwell and the New Deal*, p. 173.

47. Ezekiel, "Facts on the Domestic Allotment Act," pp. 7-10, folder "Ezekiel, Mordecai," Tugwell papers, FDR Library, box 7; Ezekiel to Tugwell, October 20, 1939, pp. 1-9, folder "Agriculture, Department of," Tugwell papers, FDR Library, box 1.

48. Tugwell, diary, folder "Notes from a New Deal Diary," January 6, 1933, pp. 46-52, Tugwell papers, FDR Library, box 30.

49. Schapsmeier and Schapsmeier, *Wallace*, pp. 169ff.; Lord, *The Wallaces of Iowa* (Boston: Houghton Mifflin, 1947), 326ff.; Sternsher, *Tugwell and the New Deal*, pp. 185ff.

50. For a detailed discussion of the Peek-Wallace et al. conferences, see Schapsmeier and Schapsmeier, *Wallace*, pp. 170-73, and Sternsher, *Tugwell and the New Deal*, pp. 188-90. Tugwell never denied that he was one of the authors of AAA. See Tugwell, "Reminiscences," pp. 42-43.

51. Schapsmeier and Schapsmeier, *Wallace*, pp. 173-74; Sternsher, *Tugwell and the New Deal*, p. 190. Tugwell later stated that he and Jerome Frank conceived the Commodity Credit Corporation. Tugwell, "Reminiscences," pp. 50-51.

52. Tugwell, diary, folder "Notes from a New Deal Diary," January 7, 1933, p. 48; January 24, 1933, p. 77; February 17, 1933, p. 97; February 18, 1933, p. 99, Tugwell papers, FDR Library, box 30; Henry A. Wallace to Franklin D. Roosevelt, memorandum, May 14, 1934, FDR papers, FDR Library, OF-1; Henry A. Wallace to Rexford Tugwell, January 28, 1933, Tugwell papers, folder "Wallace, Henry," FDR Library, box 28. Tugwell, of course, supported Wallace's appointment as secretary of agriculture in February 1933.

53. Rexford Tugwell, "Our Lands in Order," USDA press release (August 4, 1933), pp. 1-3, and "Diversified Attack," column (October 15, 1933), p. 3, both in Tugwell papers, FDR Library, box 55. See also Tugwell, "Taking the Initiative," column (October 28, 1933), pp. 2-3, Tugwell papers, FDR Library, box 55.

54. Rexford Tugwell, "The Place of Government in a National Land Program," address to a joint meeting of the American Economic Association, the American Statistical Association, and the Farm Economic Association (Philadelphia, December 29, 1933), USDA press release, Department of Agriculture, National Archives, box 293. Also in Tugwell, *The Battle for Democracy*, pp. 143-64.

55. Rexford Tugwell, remarks as assistant secretary of agriculture on the NBC "Farm and Home Hour" (February 2, 1934), p. 4, Tugwell papers, FDR Library, box 56; Tugwell, "Address over CBS" (July 31, 1934), USDA press release, Department of Agriculture, National Archives, box 302.

56. Rexford Tugwell, "Renewed Frontiers," *New York Times*, January 14, 1934, pp. 1, 3, 7, Tugwell papers, FDR Library, box 56; Tugwell, "Address Before the Niagara County Pioneer Association" (New York, August 8, 1934), pp. 2-3, 11, and "Address at Clemson College" (August 15, 1934), pp. 3ff., both USDA press release, Department of Agriculture, National Archives, box 302.

57. Rexford Tugwell, "The Price also Rises," *Fortune* 9 (January 1934): 108.

58. Rexford Tugwell, "National Significance of Recent Trends in Farm Population," *Social Forces* 14 (October 1935): 1-7.

59. Tugwell, "The Place of Government in a National Land Program," in *The Battle for Democracy*, pp. 158ff.; Tugwell, "The Planned Use of the Land," *Today* 1 (January 20, 1934): 7, 23-24, Tugwell papers, FDR Library, box 56; Tugwell, "The Farmers' Control of Industry" (June 1934), p. 5, and "Nature and Agricultural Adjustment," address to Annual Farm and Home Picnic (Brookings, South Dakota, June 29, 1934), pp. 4ff., both in Tugwell papers, FDR Library, box 56; Tugwell, "National Significance of Recent Trends," p. 6. Quote is from the latter. Tugwell's ideas on resettlement will be developed further in Chapter 5. As early as March 1934, Tugwell had intimations of such an agency. See Tugwell to the president, March 3, 1934, FDR papers, FDR Library, OF-1, box 2. See also Tugwell, "The Outlines of a Permanent Agriculture," pp. 53-63, Tugwell papers, FDR Library, box 69.

60. Tugwell, diary, folder "Notes from a New Deal Diary," April 3, 1933, p. 8, Tugwell papers, FDR Library, box 30.

61. Ibid.

62. Schapsmeier and Schapsmeier, *Wallace*, pp. 175ff.; Sternsher, *Tugwell and the New Deal*, pp. 194-95.

63. Tugwell, "Reminiscences," p. 66; Tugwell, "Consumers and the New Deal," address to Consumers League of Ohio (Cleveland, May 11, 1934), in *Battle for Democracy*, pp. 280ff.; Sternsher, *Tugwell and the New Deal*, pp. 180, 181, 194, 196.

64. William Leuchtenburg, *Franklin D. Roosevelt and the New Deal* (New York: Harper and Row, 1963), 75-76; Sternsher, *Tugwell and the New Deal*, p. 198; Louis Bean, "The Reminiscences of Louis Bean," pp. 154ff., Oral History Research Office, Columbia University.

65. Tugwell, "Reminiscences," pp. 46, 65-66; Jerome Frank, "The Reminiscences of Jerome Frank," pp. 76ff., Oral History Research Office, Columbia University.

66. Sternsher, *Tugwell and the New Deal*, p. 201. Roosevelt, after accepting Peek's resignation, appointed him as a special adviser on foreign trade.

67. Ibid., p. 203.

68. Tugwell, "Reminiscences," pp. 65-66; Chester Davis, "The Reminiscences of Chester Davis," pp. 341ff., Oral History Research Office, Columbia University.

69. Chester Davis, "Reminiscences," pp. 372ff., 412; Jerome Frank, "Reminiscences," pp. 149ff.

70. Tugwell, diary, folder "Diary 1935," February 10, 1935, pp. 45ff., Tugwell papers, FDR Library, box 32; Tugwell, "Reminiscences," pp. 46, 67-69.

71. Tugwell, diary, folder "Diary 1935," February 10, 1935, p. 45, and February 16, 1935, p. 50, Tugwell papers, FDR Library, box 32.

72. Sternsher, *Tugwell and the New Deal*, pp. 205-06.

Photograph 1. Rexford G. Tugwell. Photograph courtesy of the Franklin D. Roosevelt Library.

Photograph 2.   Rexford G. Tugwell, Great Plains Drought Area Committee, 1936. Photograph courtesy of the Franklin D. Roosevelt Library.

Photograph 3.   Rexford G. Tugwell, Ponce Losey Field, 1943. Photograph courtesy of the Franklin D. Roosevelt Library.

Photograph 4.   Rexford G. Tugwell, Governor of Puerto Rico. Photograph courtesy of the Franklin D. Roosevelt Library.

Photograph 5. Mrs. Rexford G. Tugwell, 1943. Photograph courtesy of the
Franklin D. Roosevelt Library.

Photograph 6.   Rexford G. Tugwell, 1942, with Charles Taussig (standing, second from right). Photograph courtesy of the Franklin D. Roosevelt Library.

Photograph 7. Rexford G. Tugwell and Cabinet, LaFortaleza, Puerto Rico, June 1946. Photograph by the Office of Information for Puerto Rico, courtesy of Franklin D. Roosevelt Library.

Photograph 8. Rexford G. Tugwell, University of Puerto Rico, 1955. Photograph by Samuel A. Santiago, University of Puerto Rico, courtesy of the Franklin D. Roosevelt Library.

Photograph 9. Rexford G. Tugwell, Center for the Study of Democratic Institutions, 1970s. Photograph courtesy of the Center for the Study of Democratic Institutions.

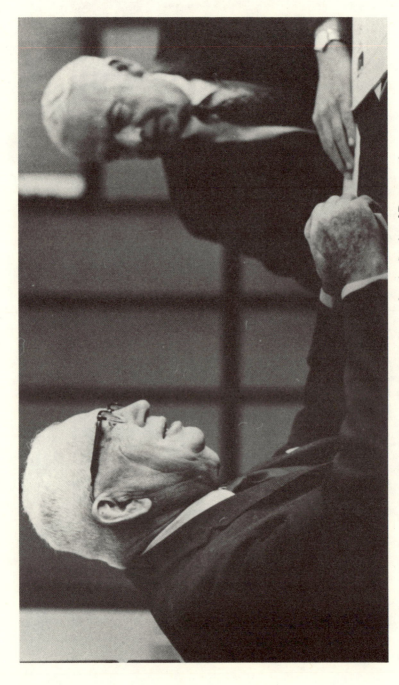

Photograph 10. Rexford G. Tugwell and Robert Hutchins, Center for the Study of Democratic Institutions, 1970s. Photograph by Donald Timm, courtesy of the Center for the Study of Democratic Institutions.

5

The New Deal: 1933–1936

I could see afterward how little chance I had had to accomplish what Roosevelt wanted; but, of course, I could not see it then. I was badly placed, for one thing. I was a subordinate appointed official rather than an elected one. But also I made the mistake of attempting too much at once—of undertaking battles on more fronts than were necessary or could be successfully fought; and once engaged, I could not or would not withdraw. So I would become not so much a symbol of progressivism as a kind of crackpot radical. Most of this transition happened in 1933 and 1934. By the end of my first year I was confirmed as a notorious character.

Rexford Tugwell, *Roosevelt's Revolution: The First Year, A Personal Perspective,* p. 276

Although Tugwell wrote this comment about his role in the New Deal and his personal actions at the very end of his life, he certainly hit the nail on the head. Although appointed to the USDA as assistant secretary of agriculture, his role in the New Deal was more varied and widespread. Acting on Roosevelt's direct orders or on what he perceived to be the president's desires, Tugwell wore many different hats and played several different roles. He acted as a spokesman and defender of the New Deal as well as a liaison with the congressional progressives. He also participated in the formation of the National Recovery Administration (NRA), its implementation, and eventually its demise. Within the USDA, moreover, he was involved in reorganization, budget cutting, bureau revitalization, the early stages of the Civilian Conservation Corps, the creation and transfer of the Soil and Conservation Service to USDA, the Surplus Relief Corporation, the appointment of Ferdinand Silcox to the Forest Service, and a tour of ten western states.

In 1934, Tugwell's long-term involvement with Puerto Rico started when he studied sugar quotas. Even more important than all of these activities, he attempted to implement his own ideas and programs with the Pure Food and Drug bill and the creation of the Resettlement Administration. By 1936, his activities were so well known, and for the most part controversial, that he resigned. While Roosevelt may have appreciated him—as evidenced by his promotion to under secretary of agriculture in 1934—the pressure on the president became intense. Press attacks on Tugwell were so vehement that Roosevelt had little choice. Tugwell, however, did not resign until his mark within and on the New Deal had been made.

Tugwell's activities were clearly visible in the pivotal role he played in formulating the NRA. Throughout April and May 1933, he collaborated closely with Assistant Secretary of Commerce John Dickinson and Senator Robert F. Wagner of New York in drafting their proposal for industrial recovery, while simultaneously maintaining a liaison with the study group headed by Hugh Johnson and Donald Richberg. After both drafts were presented to the president, Tugwell attended the conference ordered by Roosevelt to iron out the differences between the two. Here, Tugwell acted more as a mediator than as a sponsor of either version. It was at the conference in Lewis Douglas' office that he offered his suggestions for implementing industrial recovery through planning.[1]

Tugwell believed that those who attended the conference—Wagner, Dickinson, Johnson, Frances Perkins, Richberg, Douglas, and himself —all had one thing in common. They were realists who

thought the Anti-trust acts had failed and that a change was long overdue. They proposed to recognize that there were technical reasons for concentration; and they felt that public policy ought to be so arranged that large scale organization could go on to its natural apotheosis. Their idea was that control had been exercised at the wrong level. It had sought to prevent the development of large scale industries. If combinations, consolidations or associations were recognized, then it would be possible to secure the public interest in reduced costs and prices, and progress could be encouraged rather than suppressed.[2]

They also believed that the trade association movement of the 1920s had been the first step in this direction. By fostering consolidation, it enabled industry to reduce costs. But trade associationism did not result in lower prices or higher wages, because industry abused its rights and refused to accept its responsibilities. In the future that had to be stopped, although the Dickinson-Wagner and the Johnson-Richberg groups could not agree on how to do it. It was a fundamental disagreement that Tugwell believed was the crux of their problem.

Although he liked the cooperative features of the Dickinson proposal, Tugwell felt that it was unworkable. Calling for interindustry cooperation through trade associations, the plan contained no compulsory provisions to assure that industry would act in the public interest. The Johnson plan, on the other hand, provided for federal licensing of all codes and guaranteed the government an active role in the recovery process generally and in the code-making process specifically. "With more teeth in the penalties," Tugwell believed the plan would work, and for that reason he supported the Johnson plan over the Dickinson. This did not imply, however, that Tugwell was completely satisfied with the Johnson plan. Even here, he demanded that more be done. He offered two suggestions that he believed would make it stronger.[3]

Specifically, Tugwell recommended that the conferees incorporate into the Johnson draft a "tax and reserve fund scheme" and a Bank for Corporate Surpluses (BCS). In the former instance, he suggested that a processing tax be placed on industrial goods so that a reserve fund could be built up that would "be distributed periodically to those who had complied with the code provisions." A disciplinary device, it rewarded the compliant businessmen while punishing those who refused to cooperate. The BCS, on the other hand, would coerce businessmen into investing their profits. According to this proposal, all undistributed industrial surpluses would be deposited in a special bank, the BCS. An industry could borrow from the bank for expansion purposes at reasonable interest rates, but if it sought to withdraw its money, it would have to give a 60-day notice and pay a tax of up to 25 percent. The revenue from the tax would be returned to the BCS for use by more productive industries.

In offering these suggestions and in supporting the Johnson proposal, Tugwell was again revealing his belief that planning would resolve the depression, that business would have to assume the primary responsibility for implementing it, and that the government would have to make certain that industry acted in the public interest. His tax and reserve fund and BCS schemes indicated that he identified planning with cooperation, the service ideal, and economic balance. Together, industry and the government would institute planning, but if industry refused to do its part, then the government would have to coerce it. Business, in short, had a choice, and if it made the wrong one, it would face the consequences.[4]

Although the conferees rejected Tugwell's specific proposals to bolster the Johnson plan, and although Tugwell was forced by his administrative duties to withdraw from the conference, the final compromise bill was very much in line with his basic ideas on planning. The establishment of the codes, the suspension of the antitrust laws, and the provisions for federal approval and supervision of industry were all acceptable as far as he was concerned. The fundamental principles of the NRA, in fact, were so agreeable that Tugwell consistently defended them in his speeches and writings between 1933 and 1935. This role as public apologist for the New Deal, something he had already been doing in AAA, was one Tugwell readily accepted, feeling that Roosevelt wanted him to do it.[5]

Generally, Tugwell persistently characterized the NRA as a cooperative, experimental program designed to restore recovery and maintain an economic equilibrium within the American economic system. Depending upon a contractual partnership between industry and government, it sought to establish "fair wages and working conditions for the employed, fair prices for consumers," fair profits for businessmen, and a secure foundation for continuous prosperity. By giving businessmen everything they had always wanted vis-à-vis trade associationism, it was also trying to "show that the competitive system which requires heaped-up corporate surpluses and an overconcentration of wealth is not the life of trade, but the death of trade." Instead of the traditional laissez-faire philosophy, which emphasized conflict, scarcity, and self-interest, the NRA promulgated cooperation, abundance, and the public interest. Prices, wages, and profits would be brought into proportion not by the operations of the market but by the codes of fair competition and by industry's enforcement of those codes. The government's role in the process, moreover, would be just as important as industry's.[6]

Instead of the "policeman doctrine" of Progressive days, Tugwell argued that the government's role in the NRA was "to coordinate and control private enterprise" in order to "eliminate the anarchy of the competitive system [and] to ameliorate the recurrence of our spirals of inflation and deflation." Neither dictatorial nor all-imposing, it was the senior partner in the NRA, making certain that the codes were fairly written, enforced properly, and designed to serve the public interest. Tugwell argued that only the government could lead and guide industry and the country generally toward the planned economy that both the NRA and the AAA were designed to achieve.[7]

Seeing the NRA as a planning mechanism, Tugwell was emphatic in pointing out that it (and for that matter the AAA) was only the first step toward the planned economy. In seeking to bring about "a balance between production and purchasing power as will maintain the freest interchangeability" between industry and agriculture, it did not regiment industry, create a government dictatorship, or resort to any socialistic devices outside the realm of American democracy. Instead, the NRA fostered cooperation and experimentalism, as well as expertise and coordination.[8] For Tugwell, the experimental aspect of the NRA was especially important because it was the key to planning. In a speech entitled "The Responsibilities of Partnership," he developed this theme in even more detail.

In his opening remarks, Tugwell argued that "planning" was a rather confused word, meaning many different things to many different people. Some, for example, believed it implied a blueprint "laid out for a long time in advance upon some theory of what ought to happen in the future." Used in this sense, it demanded that the government direct the nation's activity "toward making the blue-print a reality." Rigid and theoretical, it took no account "of the creative possibilities of the human mind."

Others, however, believed that planning was a loosely defined concept which assumed that society evolved, that human events were fluid and flexible, and that human creativeness was vitally important. To these people, planning, or social management, involved the democratic process itself—"a living and changing thing, built up out of our own characteristic materials, not borrowed, not preconceived, highly practical and constantly revised." In direct contrast with Marxism, this conception of planning looked to the future and recognized that, for the United States, the future looms bright with the possibility of achieving an economy of abundance. Tugwell emphasized that the NRA and the AAA were the product of this idea of planning and of no other. In no way involving planning in the "forced sense," the NRA and the AAA

provide the opportunity for it in the democratic sense. Both are voluntary; but both provide certain compulsions for minorities when cooperation is withheld. Both take advantage of our own institutions; and both compel recognition of the need for widely social as against individual and group action. Both will result in considerable change; and both ought to raise the level of ordinary living. They represent, therefore, social management. They are, in that sense, planning.[9]

As a social machinery, moreover, Tugwell felt the NRA was a forum where "producing groups can cooperate and work out their differences," where industrialists could learn that "the interests of all can be the interests of each," and where government, industry, and labor could approach the problems of the economy with an open, experimental attitude.[10] In adopting this experimental approach, the NRA was simply following the general direction the New Deal itself was taking. Having rejected the tenets of laissez-faire and the principles on which the New Era in the 1920s had been based, it was breaking new ground, challenging old institutions, and offering the United States an alternative, through planning, to what had gone on before. In light of this, Tugwell believed, it was not surprising that the New Deal did not "lay down too specifically the structure of new things," and why the NRA in particular was experimental in its approach and policy. Relying on industrial cooperation, it would eventually "restore a workable exchangeability among the separate parts of our economic machine," provide the balancing mechanism for the economy "which the market itself use [sic] to do a century ago," sustain the economic process once the crisis of the depression had passed, and create a "Third Economy" for the unemployed and displaced worker.[11] In Tugwell's mind, the NRA assured the economic survival of the United States as long as industry cooperated with it and as long as it was given time to develop and adjust to the realities of American life.

Although Tugwell was consistent in publicly expressing his confidence in the future of the NRA, he was privately concerned about the way the program was being administered. Instead of the government supervising the operation of the NRA, he believed, the administrators of the program were relegating the government to an innocuous position and allowing business to dominate the code-making process. This was most clearly seen in big business's domination of the codes, the price-fixing provisions incorporated into the codes themselves, and the almost complete refusal by industry generally to consider the rights of the consumer, thereby undermining the basic principles of planning and government-industry cooperation. Not only were such policies dangerous for the effects they would have on the economy but, Tugwell believed, they also would alienate those groups, such as small businessmen and labor, on whom the NRA depended for its success and survival. In criticizing these policies, however, Tugwell did not argue that all the administrators were responsible for what was happening. As far as he was concerned, there was only one man who was culpable: Hugh Johnson.[12]

In much the way he had supported the initial appointment of Peek to the AAA, Tugwell had approved of Johnson's appointment as administrator of the NRA in June 1933. Having worked closely with him during the drafting of the NRA, Tugwell had come to feel that Johnson, despite his intimate relationship with Bernard Baruch, was a sincere, honest, and strong-minded individual who not only believed in social change but was determined to make the program a success.

Tugwell was convinced that Johnson believed in the necessity for and the feasibility of planning. Although he had a "tendency to be gruff in personal relations," and had a habit of "occasional drunken sprees," Tugwell still felt that Johnson would "do a good job." However, no sooner had Johnson begun to implement his interpretation of the NRA than Tugwell began to oppose him.[13]

Between July 1933 and September 1934, Tugwell argued with and criticized Johnson for attempting to codify all of industry with the Blue Eagle campaign, for interpreting section 7(a) in such a way that industry was allowed to openly disregard labor's rights with impunity, and for allowing and encouraging business to fix prices through the codes. By April 1934, Tugwell felt that Johnson's policies had created such a chaotic situation that the NRA had to reorient its position or face total disaster. Specifically, he recommended that the NRA crack down hard on industries that were fixing prices and, at the same time, "perfecting a series of industry boards which can . . . have a council among themselves for creating policy." Unless these things were done, Tugwell feared, the NRA would become the primary medium through which "a closed, restrictive industrial system" would be created, one in which "businesses maintain high prices, manipulate their production to maintain them, and in which taxes are imposed to take care of the unemployment" caused by industry itself. The choice was clear: either the NRA coerced business into acting in the public interest or it would be coerced by business into serving its interest.[14] Although preferring the former, Tugwell gradually concluded that Johnson was implementing the latter course of action. By the fall of 1934, he joined the chorus of New Dealers who sought to salvage the NRA by having Johnson resign.

Unlike his activities in the Peek resignation, Tugwell did not initiate or lead those who opposed Johnson's remaining as administrator of the NRA. Instead, he acted more as an errand boy for the president than as a leading character in the unfolding plot. In August 1934, Roosevelt asked him to consult with leading officials in the administration in order to determine what they thought should be done about Johnson and the NRA in general. Following the president's directions, Tugwell talked to Frances Perkins, Donald Richberg, Henry Wallace, Harold Ickes, and Harry Hopkins. What he found, and what he reported to Roosevelt in September, was that all agreed that Johnson had to be relieved, that his resignation should be accepted in such a way as not to create any subsequent problems with him, and that a National Industrial Recovery Board (NIRB) should be created to direct the NRA. As for membership of the board, Tugwell found and reported that all agreed on having Clay Williams, Averell Harriman, Leon Marshall, Sidney Hillman, Donald Richberg, W. H. Hamilton, W. H. Davis, and Leon Henderson serve, and, out of those, either Marshall, Hamilton, or Davis should be appointed chairman.[15] Tugwell added that he agreed with these recommendations and that they would have to be put into effect immediately, before Johnson created any more trouble. The president agreed, and by the end of September, he had decided to ask for Johnson's resignation. Realizing how much his position had deteriorated in the NRA, Johnson resigned.

Although Tugwell interpreted the Johnson resignation as a presidential endorsement of planning, and although he was pleased with the president's decision to establish the NIRB, he was unhappy with Roosevelt's selection of Donald Richberg as chairman of the NIRB. In Tugwell's opinion, Richberg was just as bad as Johnson—"muddleheaded in his economics, shifty in practice, and indecisive in action." Although Richberg was an advocate of planning, Tugwell felt he should not have been appointed chairman. Tugwell wanted Robert Hutchins, his friend and colleague, appointed because he believed Hutchins was more qualified and had the support of Ickes and Hopkins. What Tugwell was really saying, and what he really wanted, was to have his man appointed so that he could exert some influence over policy. Richberg realized what Tugwell was trying to do and, as a result, threatened to resign should Hutchins be appointed. In the end, Roosevelt, desirous of keeping Richberg in the NRA, did not appoint Hutchins as chairman.[16]

Between Richberg's appointment to the NIRB and the *Schechter* decision in May 1935, Tugwell's role in formulating policy and administering the NRA was minimal. He continued to publicly support the program while privately offering his ideas on how to make the NRA more effective. In late November 1934 and January 1935, for example, he recommended that the NRA be kept flexible; that the labor provisions in the program be separated from the NRA and placed within the Department of Labor; that special legislation be enacted to deal with price fixing, monopolies, and unfair trade practices; and that "government ownership in power and similar industries" be extended.[17]

Having entered a new stage of development, Tugwell believed, the NRA had to restrict some of its activities in certain areas while solidifying its authority in others. Although NRA officials like Richberg agreed with some of Tugwell's proposals, they were more concerned with renewing the NRA legislation after January 1935 and did not pay much attention to what Tugwell was advising. All of this changed drastically, however, when the Supreme Court declared the NRA unconstitutional in May. After the *Schechter* decision, NRA officials were concerned with protecting and preserving the principles on which the program had been based, and since Tugwell sought to do the same thing, they enlisted him in their campaign to convince Roosevelt of the need to re-create the NRA.

In Tugwell's opinion, the Supreme Court's decision in the *Schechter* case was politically motivated. The justices were more influenced by their own opposition to Roosevelt and the New Deal than by any concern for separation of powers and constitutional limitations. By declaring the NRA unconstitutional, he believed, the Court had clearly demonstrated its refusal to accept and adjust to the economic realities of the twentieth century. He strongly recommended that the president "clip the wings" of the Court by having a constitutional amendment passed that would increase the government's power over the economy, and that he immediately re-create the NRA so as to protect and preserve the principles on which it had been enacted.

Specifically, Tugwell suggested that Roosevelt ask the Congress to pass an Industrial Adjustment Act as a corollary to the AAA. Designed to place a "premium on the expansion of production on large volume and low price and at the same time [to protect] competition where it is appropriate," the bill would levy a tax on all industry in such a way that the revenues from the tax could be returned to all those industries "which would sign voluntary adjustment contracts" specifying "certain conditions of type and volume as well as conditions of labor and hours and the like." Since the program would be voluntary and since the government already had the right to tax, Tugwell believed that the Supreme Court would be unable to challenge it in any way. In reality, however, that might not be the case, and for that reason, Tugwell was not surprised when Roosevelt rejected the proposal.[18] Nevertheless, he continued to advise the president on reviving the NRA, even suggesting that the name "NRA" be dropped from any program and that the staff and personnel of the original NRA be transferred to the Federal Trade Commission. In this way, he hoped, the principles of planning would be maintained and the New Deal could gain some time to work out the details of its new policy.

In offering these suggestions, Tugwell was saying that business had failed to fulfill its obligations, and now the federal government had to act more decisively. But this did not imply that Tugwell felt the government had to take over the planning process without any regard to business. Instead, he believed that the government had to exert more compulsory influence over industry and the economy so that the public interest would be served. Business would still play a role in the planning process, but one that would be neither as free nor as co-operative as had been the case in the NRA. Regimentation through government planning was not the goal of Tugwell's suggestions, and he hoped a situation like that would never develop.[19]

Although nothing materialized in regard to his suggestions for the Industrial Adjustment Act and a constitutional amendment, Tugwell continued to advise the president on giving planning another chance, albeit in a different way. Instead of offering his own ideas, he began, by 1936, to endorse and support the recommendations being made by Mordecai Ezekiel and others in the Department of Agriculture, especially their Industrial Expansion Plan. According to this proposal, written and formulated by Ezekiel and Louis Bean between 1934 and 1936, industrial authorities, similar to the NRA codes, would be established and would act as the primary planning agencies for individual cooperating industries. Consisting of representatives from labor, industry, consumers, and the government, these authorities would be responsible for working out a program of expansion for each cooperating industry on an annual basis.

Once the plans were drawn up, they would be forwarded to an interindustrial planning board that would coordinate the plan with the rest of industry. After that was done and the plan was put into operation, the government would contract with industry to buy all surplus production at reduced prices. This surplus would be placed in a warehouse and would be considered in the production planning for the following year. The entire program would be paid for by a processing tax, the proceeds of which would be placed in a reserve fund for benefit payments to those who cooperated with the plan. To make certain that industry would cooperate, the government would establish minimum and maximum price levels and production quotas.[20]

Essentially a re-creation of the AAA in a different form, the Ezekiel program was designed to stimulate American recovery by scientifically calculating production and consumption needs. Although voluntary, it assumed that if the program worked, all industry would eventually be forced into expanding simultaneously and in balance, "so that the market for one product would be provided by the increased output of the others."[21] Full prosperity would follow, the United States would eventually be able to sustain an economy of abundance, and a new system of government-industry relations would be established. Even Tugwell believed that this would happen, that the theoretical possibilities of the plan would be realized because it was based on the primary ingredients of any planning program. Like Tugwell's Industrial Integration Board and Industrial Adjustment Act proposal, the Ezekiel program depended on cooperation, coordination, and balance within the economic system as well as on the willingness of the federal government to make certain that industry acted in the public interest. What Tugwell did not recognize, however, was that the plan was so complicated and so bureaucratic that it would probably create more problems in administration than the original NRA.

Tugwell bemoaned Roosevelt's refusal to re-create the NRA. An opportunity had been lost and might not come again. To Tugwell, Roosevelt had been overly cautious.[22] Nevertheless, from Tugwell's perspective, the NRA went a long way toward explaining how he perceived planning. By 1936, Tugwell had defined planning by its characteristics. Prior to and during the New Deal, he believed that planning implied cooperation among business, labor, and government; that coordination between industry and agriculture was necessary; that experts had to be used in policy making; and that an experimental approach and method were essential.

Seeing it as a constitutionally feasible idea, Tugwell felt that planning was the only means to assure the survival of the United States in the twentieth century. However, he distinguished between agricultural and industrial planning, recognized and emphasized an active, supervisory role for the government, and was inclined to accept consolidation with all its implications for the farmer and the small businessman. Although he placed primary responsibility for implementing planning on business, he was not averse to coercing businessmen to act in the public interest. Similarly, he believed that the government might have to coerce farmers into recognizing the public interest by controlling their production (preferably in a voluntary way) and by implementing a long-range land-use program. In many ways, Tugwell's planning represented a new value system for the United States, one that would prove fruitful in the long run if it was accepted and adhered to.

In light of this, it is not surprising that Tugwell believed the NRA and AAA were the first steps toward a planned economy. Together, they would not only resolve the depression, but also establish the foundation for planning by their emphasis on cooperation, coordination, expertise, the service ideal, and experimentalism. Much more, of course, would have to be done before planning became a reality, but at least some progress would have been made. And, as a New Deal administrator, Tugwell did everything he could to make certain that this would happen, that planning would materialize in the American economic system.

Although Tugwell had been actively involved in the NRA and the AAA, these activities did not limit his purview. Officially, he held three positions within the New Deal, all in the USDA. Using it as a base, he acted in a variety of capacities. Between March 1933 and December 1936, Tugwell was assistant secretary of agriculture (1933-1934), under secretary of agriculture (1934-1936), and director of the Resettlement Administration (1935-1936).

As assistant and under secretary of agriculture, Tugwell was responsible for filling in for Wallace when the secretary was unavailable, for administering the old-line bureaus of the USDA, for handling the daily operations of the department, and for serving on numerous boards and committees either connected with or established by the department. In every case, Tugwell worked hard. He fought with Lew Douglas to preserve the USDA's budgets, especially for research, and tried to reorganize and streamline the department's administrative bureaucracy. In August-September 1933, he visited ten western states, meeting personnel and getting a firsthand account of the USDA.[23] The trip helped him not only in understanding the department but also in establishing a better rapport with his civil servant subordinates. As for reorganization of the USDA, it was a good idea but one that Tugwell could do very little with, especially since Wallace was not fully in favor of it.

Throughout his tenure in USDA, Tugwell was given special assignments by the president and by Wallace. He played a role, for example, in setting up the Civilian Conservation Corps while serving on the Surplus Relief Corporation. The latter had been set up to provide surplus food, purchased with relief funds, for those in need. It was a task Tugwell was particularly satisfied with.[24] He also contributed to the founding of the Soil and Conservation Service. It was Tugwell who had Hugh Bennett work on the soil erosion problem. Although it initially was placed within Ickes' jurisdiction, Tugwell eventually had the Soil and Conservation Service placed permanently within the USDA. Similarly, he was responsible for having Ferdinand Silcox, an old friend, appointed head of the Forest Service. With Silcox in charge, the Forest Service moved into an active role in such programs as the shelterbelt. Finally, Tugwell was involved in the allocation of sugar production quotas among the United States, its insular possessions, and Cuba. He went to Puerto Rico in 1934, thereby starting a lifelong relationship with that American territory.[25]

Tugwell did all of these things, and more, while contributing his efforts to NRA and AAA. Politically, he assisted the president by serving as a liaison with the congressional Progressives, particularly Robert LaFollette, Robert Wagner, Hiram Johnson, Bronson Cutting, Burton Wheeler, George Norris, and others. This latter role was particularly pleasing to Tugwell, since he tended to associate himself with these Progressives' ideas and programs. There was also a 1934 trip to Rome, where he spoke at the International Agricultural conference and met Mussolini. In that year he also underwent promotion hearings in Congress.[26] When all this was combined with his role as public apologist for the New Deal, Tugwell was quite busy.[27]

Although each of these activities provided Tugwell with an opportunity to offer his own ideas on policy, there were two areas where he actually formulated and implemented his own decisions. In his fight for Pure Food and Drug legislation and in his direction of the Resettlement Administration, it was Tugwell the New Deal administrator who established priorities, defined objectives, and recruited a staff to carry out his decisions. It was primarily in these two areas that Tugwell had a chance to apply his own ideas on planning, consumer protection, and promoting the general welfare.

As assistant secretary of agriculture, Tugwell had the responsibility of supervising the old-line bureaus in the USDA, such as the Food and Drug Administration (FDA). Although new to government administration, he soon discovered that the agency was not as effective in enforcing the law as everyone believed. In fact, the 1906 Food and Drug Law was not very stringent. Not only had the secretaries of agriculture ignored it, but even the public seemed to be apathetic. In Tugwell's thinking, the only possible explanation was that the 1906 law was outdated and incomplete. Technically, the old bill said nothing about advertising, completely ignored the cosmetic industry, and provided loopholes for businessmen to exploit. This was especially true of the provisions that placed responsibility on the government for proving fraud in the manufacture of drug products. By 1933, businessmen had devised so many legal ways to avoid the law that they were abusive and callous toward the public, selling worthless and even harmful products and mechanical devices to cure all ills. In Tugwell's opinion, these abuses had to be stopped at all costs, and he decided that the best way to do it was to have Congress revise the 1906 law as soon as possible.

To accomplish this, Tugwell first talked to Walter G. Campbell, chief of the FDA, about what had to be done legislatively and within the USDA.[28] The issue of poisonous sprays on apples, something that appalled Tugwell, served as the initial stimulus. Much to Tugwell's chagrin, not even Wallace supported his desire to force the stoppage of such sprayings. Tugwell soon realized just how political Wallace was and just how powerful farmers and trade groups could be.

Having discussed the possibility of a new law with Campbell, Tugwell proceeded to get the president's approval for new legislation. Playing on the continuity with Theodore Roosevelt, Tugwell received Roosevelt's permission to go ahead, but the president did not give his former Brains Truster any indication that he would publicly endorse his efforts or support him if any opposition developed.[29] This lukewarm endorsement would go a long way in explaining the problems the new bill faced in Congress and the eventual watering down of the original Tugwell bill. Nevertheless, Tugwell continued his campaign.

His next step was to order the lowering of poisonous spray residue on all fruits and vegetables examined by the USDA, and then to have Professors Milton Handler of Columbia and David F. Cavers of Duke draft a bill revising the 1906 law.[30] Senator Royal S. Copeland, chairman of the Commerce Committee, took the bill and introduced it in the Senate.[31]

S.1944, the Copeland bill (better known as the Tugwell bill), was not only an updated version of the 1906 law but also a stringent corrective for all the harmful manufacturing practices of the drug industry. Essentially, it prevented the manufacture, shipment, and sale of all "adulterated, misbranded food, drugs, and cosmetics." It also outlawed false advertising; required that labels list all ingredients, especially alcohol and/or other habit-forming ingredients; and empowered the secretary of agriculture to establish standards of identity and quality for all products except fruits and vegetables. The bill further provided for a voluntary inspection service that, if it proved ineffective, would be replaced by federal licensing. While the voluntary service was in operation, the Federal Trade Commission was authorized to conduct investigations into all alleged malpractices and to use injunctions if necessary.[32]

For Tugwell, the basic purpose of the bill was to protect the consumer from the chiseling fakes in the drug industry. By strengthening the old Food and Drug Acts and by extending their authority to advertising, cosmetics, mechanical health devices, and standards of quality, the bill was protecting the honest drug manufacturer from these unscrupulous competitors. The bill in no way, at least in Tugwell's opinion, endangered the principle of self-medication or the operation of the free-enterprise system. Rather, it sought to give the people confidence in the drug industry's advertising and in its products. It was a beneficial corrective to what had been going on since 1906. If the industry accepted the bill and supported it, Tugwell was certain that everyone, from the consumer to the drug manufacturer, would benefit immensely.[33]

Although Tugwell was convinced of the bill's benefits and although he worked to get congressional and industrial support for it, opposition sprang up almost instantly after its introduction in the Senate.[34] Using the traditional arguments that the bill infringed on their rights, trade groups viciously attacked Tugwell as a Communist and Bolshevik who was trying to overthrow the American system. Assisted by the newspapers and reporters such as Frank Kent and Mark Sullivan, who made their life's goal the discrediting of Tugwell, this attack was so successful that they not only discredited the original Copeland (Tugwell) bill but also seriously damaged Tugwell's effectiveness in the drug campaign and, eventually, as a New Dealer.

By 1936, the stereotype of Tugwell had become so ingrained that it would contribute to his resignation. In immediate terms, it forced the Copeland (Tugwell) bill to be revised. S.1944 became, over the years, S.2800, S.2000, S.5, and S.3073, each time diluted more and more to suit the demands of the trade groups and members of Congress. All of this watering down took place in spite of Tugwell's, and eventually Campbell's, vigorous campaign showing, in the Chamber of Horrors poster exhibit, just how dangerous some of these drugs and mechanical devices were. In June 1938, a Food, Drug and Cosmetic Act was passed, but it was not satisfactory to Tugwell and other New Dealers, who wanted more stringent legislation.

Although failing in his efforts to have S.1944 passed, Tugwell's actions on behalf of the Copeland bill were still quite significant. First of all, they demonstrated that he believed planning affected every aspect of American life and every facet of American economic activity. By demanding that the drug industry maintain standards of quality in their products, Tugwell was saying that business had to act in the public interest and accept the service ideal. Also, by establishing a voluntary inspection service, he was telling businessmen that cooperation, not competition, was the key to prosperity. If all businessmen, as in the drug industry, cooperated to maintain standards of quality, then the dishonest businessman would not be able to undercut or undersell his competitors as he had been doing since 1906. And, finally, by providing for federal licensing should the drug manufacturers refuse to maintain standards of decent behavior, Tugwell was telling business that if it could not act in the public interest, then the government would force it to. As in the case of the NRA, industry had a choice in Pure Food and Drug. If it chose to cooperate in maintaining standards of quality in and for the public interest, there would be no need for the government to play more than a supervisory role. But if business refused to cooperate and failed to consider the rights of the consumer, Tugwell believed the government would have no choice but to compel businessmen to act in the way they should.

There is one other point illustrated by the Pure Food and Drug bill. Tugwell's role after the introduction of S.1944 was not as extensive as Copeland's or Campbell's. He did serve an important role as a liaison with Roosevelt, thereby keeping the prospects of a bill's passage alive but, given Roosevelt's lukewarm attitude toward consumerism and his dislike of Copeland, Tugwell could do only so much. In the end, the trade groups were able to force enough congressional compromises to get the bill they could live with. For Tugwell, the price was high. The press attacks would take their toll. Even his promotion would be clouded by them. Nevertheless, Tugwell was not completely innocent. As he himself readily admitted in *Roosevelt's Revolution*, he never went out of his way to explain himself. Or, to put it another way, if he "was harassed, it was partly [his] own fault."[35] He could have kept quiet (definitely a new experience for him).

The Resettlement Administration was just as important to Tugwell, if not more so. In retrospect, there is little doubt that it was the primary example of Tugwell's thinking on the use of planning in agriculture and the modernizing of the American system of agriculture. The basic inelasticity of agriculture; the relationships among technical efficiency, farm surplus, and shrinking markets; and the disequilibrium between industry and agriculture all demonstrated to Tugwell that something had to be done to modernize American agriculture before it went bankrupt.

By the time the New Deal started, he was convinced that land erosion was reaching phenomenal proportions, that many farmers were being doomed to a life of poverty, and that the farm-to-city migrations were hurting instead of helping the American economy. Unless something was done soon to help the poor farmer and to conserve the land, the United States would face serious economic problems in the future.[36] To make matters worse, the New Deal was doing nothing to relieve the plight of the poor farmers, especially tenants and farm laborers. Although the AAA had been established to resolve the farm crisis caused by the depression, it tended to sustain the large farmers of staple crops without considering those in more desperate straits.[37] For Tugwell, it was the farmers living on poor land or forced to migrate to the city who needed help, and he suggested that the only way to help them was to retire their lands and relocate them. If that were done, if a system of land-use planning were implemented, the United States not only would be conserving its natural resources but also would be making the fullest use of its human resources.[38] In an effort to facilitate the implementation of such a program, he worked and fought for the creation of the Resettlement Administration (RA) in his official capacity as a New Deal administrator.

Although the RA was not established until 1935, groundwork for the agency was being laid throughout 1934. Between February and July, several programs were set up in the USDA, the Federal Emergency Relief Administration (FERA), and the Department of the Interior, which sought to deal with the problem of land conservation and personal rehabilitation. The Submarginal Land Committee (USDA), the state Rural Rehabilitation Corporations (FERA), and FERA's land programs all were designed to help the poor farmers by having the government purchase their worn-out lands and then relocate them on better farms. The primary problem with these programs, however, was that they cut across several federal agencies' jurisdictions with no one agency consolidating their efforts. Also, they tended to duplicate one another to such an extent that they were becoming almost self-defeating.[39]

Instead of trying to resolve the jurisdictional disputes that erupted because of overlapping, Tugwell in early 1935 suggested to Secretary Wallace that an agency be created that would consolidate them and coordinate the overall government effort in land use. Wallace agreed, and together they approached Roosevelt with the idea. On May 1, 1935, the president gave his approval by issuing Executive Order 7027, creating the Resettlement Administration. In addition to appointing Tugwell as the director, the order stated that the RA would receive all its appropriations from the president under the authority given to him by the Emergency Relief Act of 1935.[40]

Almost from the beginning, Tugwell made it clear that the RA would serve three fundamental purposes. First, it would strive to conserve America's land by retiring poor land from crop cultivation and putting it to more beneficial use, such as forestry and/or recreation;

second, the RA would strive to help the farmers living on submarginal land to find new, better land to work on and earn a living; third, it would seek to aid people who were living on good land but who, "because of financial distress or because of inexpert farm management, are in need of help."[41] While concentrating on the short-term objective of helping these farmers in the depression crisis, the RA was also trying to achieve the long-term objective of land-use conservation.

In addition, Tugwell made it clear that retirement and resettlement were only part of an even larger problem confronting the United States—the migration of farmers to urban centers. To resolve this and to prevent the migrations from having a disastrous effect on the economy as a whole, he announced that the RA would construct suburban towns or garden cities to facilitate the changing and adjustment of rural America to twentieth-century economic life. Although Tugwell believed the RA could achieve these objectives in time, he soon learned that announcing policy and implementing it were two different things. No sooner had he taken direction of the RA than he confronted the administrative problems inherent in the creation of the agency.[42]

For all practical purposes, the RA was "a repository for a multitude of New Deal programs." Technically, it had the task of "carrying on rural relief and rehabilitation, of continuing the whole land-utilization program, and of extending the New Deal community-building program through both rural and urban resettlement." More important, whether he liked it or not, Tugwell inherited parts of other federal agencies when the RA was established, such as the Division of Subsistence Homesteads (Interior Department), three sections of the FERA, the state Rural Rehabilitation Corporations, the Land Policy Section of the AAA, and small sections of several other agencies. A hodgepodge of federal bureaucracy, the RA was supposed to consolidate all these programs into one agency under the direction of one administrator.[43] It was a monstrous administrative task and one that Tugwell tried to handle by himself.

Although Tugwell wanted the RA to deal primarily with suburban resettlement and land utilization, he reluctantly agreed to administer the rural resettlement (subsistence homesteads) and rural rehabilitation programs inherited by the RA for two reasons. First, he felt that both programs were in some respects necessary in the emergency caused by the depression; second, in light of the president's predilection for the "back-to-the-farm" movement, he felt that he had no choice in the matter. If the RA were to accomplish anything, it would have to have the support of Roosevelt, and it seemed that the only way it could get that support was to administer all the programs the president wanted it to, in spite of the problems that would cause in administration and objectives.[44] It was in the way he handled those problems that Tugwell proved himself a good administrator.

To help him fulfill the tasks assigned to the RA, Tugwell appointed highly qualified and capable individuals to assist him: Will Alexander, Calvin Baldwin, John Lansill, Joseph Dailey, Lewis Gray, Carl Taylor, Eugene Agger, and Lee Pressman.[45] Although they were subordinate to the administrator, Tugwell gave them enough authority so that they could, and did, effectively handle their responsibilities. Tugwell also demonstrated his administrative capacities by the skillful way he usually resolved the jurisdictional disputes his agency had with Secretary of Interior Ickes and with Harry Hopkins, the FERA administrator; by the adept way he got appropriations from the president; and by the cordial relationship he maintained with Secretary Wallace, who, technically, remained his boss.[46] Of all these activities, none better demonstrated his capability than the way he set up the RA structurally and organizationally. Here, Tugwell the New Deal administrator came into his own.

In light of the diverse and varied tasks assigned the RA, Tugwell decided that the only way it could be effective was to decentralize its administration. To accomplish that, he divided the country into 11 regions and established 4 main divisions within the RA. The Suburban Resettlement, Rural Rehabilitation, Land Utilization, and Rural Resettlement divisions were designed to coordinate all of the RA's activities; 12 subordinate divisions and numerous subsections would deal with all specialized functions and tasks, including management, planning, procedure, information, investigation, personnel, labor relations, business management, finance, and construction.[47] As administrator, Tugwell supervised all of the agency's activities, while his subordinates in the main divisions handled all matters relating to their particular responsibilities. Tugwell decided that all community programs would be handled, where possible, primarily by the regional offices, and that only the suburban resettlement projects would be controlled and administered from Washington.

Although the RA was eventually criticized for the complexity of its organization, the structural framework that Tugwell created proved to be beneficial. Each of the main divisions coordinated its activities and handled its responsibilities efficiently. The Rural Rehabilitation Division, for example, carried on the bulk of the RA's work, providing financial and educational assistance to farmers in the form of loans, grants, debt adjustment, and demonstration projects. In 1936 it provided extensive relief to drought-stricken farmers. The Land Utilization Division was primarily concerned with "completing the land-use program" inaugurated by the New Deal and promoted by Tugwell. It was responsible for retiring over 9 million acres of submarginal land from agricultural use and for studying the nation's overall land problems.[48] The other two divisions, Rural Resettlement and Suburban Resettlement, received the most attention and caused the most controversy while Tugwell was administrator.

The Rural Resettlement Division "initiated and planned all rural communities," including the subsistence homestead projects the RA inherited from the FERA. Although Tugwell disliked and disapproved of the idea of subsistence homesteads, since he believed that industry did not follow people, he did have the RA complete most of the projects begun by the FERA. In addition, he had the RA start more than 100 rural projects of its own. Most of these projects were all-farming communities located in the South and usually segregated. Each community contained one or more cooperative enterprises run by cooperative associations and sponsored by the government. For the most part, the projects were experiments in cooperative farming with land ownership residing with the government.[49] The Suburban Resettlement Division dealt with the greenbelt towns.

Of all the RA's programs, none received as much attention and/or criticism as these towns. Tugwell believed the greenbelt towns would be garden cities for full-time industrial workers. In light of the farm-to-city migrations, the impossibility of resettling thousands of slum dwellers in semiagricultural communities, and the unwillingness of industry to relocate, Tugwell felt there was no other way to deal with the problems of urban life. The greenbelt towns, capable of housing 500 to 800 families, would provide useful work for men on unemployment relief, low-rent housing for low-income families, and healthful surroundings for the urban poor. Tugwell felt that the towns would demonstrate the "soundness of planning and operating towns according to certain garden-city principles."[50]

At first, Tugwell had planned to build 25 greenbelt communities, but because of financial and legal problems, he completed only three. Those three towns (Greenbelt, Maryland; Greenhills, Ohio; and Greendale, Wisconsin) caused more controversy than any other project Tugwell had originated or implemented. Critics of the towns argued that they were too expensive, that they were alien to American traditions, and that they were incapable of solving the problems of urban life.

These critics began to identify all of RA's activities in terms of the towns. Instead of differentiating between greenbelt and other RA projects, they lumped everything together and attacked the agency as a whole, and Tugwell as director.[51] By the middle of 1936, their attack on Tugwell was so vehement that it, like the press attacks at the time of the Pure Food and Drug bill, contributed to his resignation from the RA. Despite his defense of the RA and the greenbelt towns, and despite everything he had accomplished while serving as administrator, the stereotype of Tugwell as a Communist and Bolshevik was too difficult to challenge and disprove. In the end, Tugwell had to leave not only RA but the New Deal as well.[52]

In retrospect, Tugwell's experience as administrator of the RA points to two important conclusions. First, the RA demonstrated Tugwell's administrative capabilities. Taking an organization with a variety of tasks and getting it to work is a feat in itself. Second, Tugwell's RA experience showed that he tried to implement his ideas on agricultural planning. In every activity that the RA was concerned with, the fundamentals of his planning were present. Whether it was in rural rehabilitation, where he tried to help the farmers get on their feet and adjust to the technological conditions of twentieth-century agriculture, or in rural resettlement, where he tried to demonstrate the advantages of consolidated, cooperative farms over traditional ownership, or in land utilization, where he sought to institute expert, long-range land-use planning, or in suburban resettlement, where he tried to facilitate the acceptance of functional planning on a small scale, he was trying to implement planning as he understood it. Without reverting to government coercion, he sought to instill a sense of appreciation into the American farmer for the cooperative spirit and for the need to conserve America's most treasured resource—its land. Although in the end his policies were criticized and misunderstood, Tugwell did what he said he would, thereby showing that he was a man of his word.

Tugwell's resignation from the RA and the New Deal came as no surprise to anyone who had followed his career. His influence in policy making was consistently being eroded well before that time. This was clearly demonstrated by the role he played in the Second New Deal. Unlike the First New Deal, which attempted to solve the depression through some form of planning, the Second New Deal, inaugurated in 1935, was more concerned with socially oriented, long-term welfare legislation. Encompassing the Social Security Act, the National Labor Relations Act, and the "soak-the-rich" tax bill, it at-

tempted to revive the economy by helping those groups which had
been ignored in the First New Deal. Although it, too, failed to solve
the depression, it did indicate that Roosevelt was changing his policies
and that people like Tugwell, who had played prominent roles in 1933-
1934, were no longer exerting substantial influence over the president.

In the case of Tugwell, this was especially pronounced because he
had been so closely identified with the First New Deal. Although he
supported most of the programs sponsored by Roosevelt in the Second
New Deal, his role in formulating those policies was so passive and
ineffectual that, to many, it demonstrated his declining influence as
well as Roosevelt's refusal to continue planning.[53] At that time, and
in his later writings, Tugwell argued that the Brandeisians, such as
Tom Corcoran and Ben Cohen, were responsible for this, that they
were the ones who were telling Roosevelt to think in "horse and
buggy terms" even after the *Schechter* decision. Opposed to planning
in any form, they wanted to turn the clock back and revert to the
orthodox Progressive formulas of the turn of the century to solve the
economic crisis of the 1930s. In their minds, Tugwell was their principal enemy and would have to be defeated before their ideas prevailed.[54] Tugwell, then and later, was certain they were the ones who
opposed his post-*Schechter* ideas as well as the Ezekiel plan, and who
prevented them from getting a decent hearing and fair trial through
legislative implementation.

In some respects, what Tugwell was saying was true—the Brandeisians did oppose him and his ideas. But, in other respects, this was not
the complete reason behind Roosevelt's refusal to revive the NRA
through either Tugwell's or Ezekiel's plan. By 1936, planning in any
way one wanted to define it was not working to overcome the depression, nor was it capable of doing so in light of the vague suggestions
Tugwell was making or the detailed, complicated scheme that Ezekiel
proposed. More important, considering Roosevelt's personality and
his inclination to pragmatic approaches to policy, it was not surprising
that he refused to continue a program that had not shown any positive results. Experimentalism, in short, was just as much a part of
Roosevelt's philosophy as Tugwell's, and as such, it was an important
factor in what he would decide to do in the future.

In a similar vein, Tugwell's Brandeisian theory did not take into
consideration how much of a liability he had become by 1936.[55]
Some high-level officials, such as Jim Farley, were convinced that the
president could no longer afford to have Tugwell in the administration.
Not only did he represent a destabilizing influence in policy making,

but he was the subject of so much media criticism that he was hurting the New Deal. Since Tugwell no longer served as an effective shield or diversion for the president, Farley refused to have him actively participate in the 1936 reelection campaign. He made it clear what he thought Tugwell's future was. By September 1936, Tugwell realized this and decided that, in the interests of the president and of the RA, he should resign.[56]

Offering his resignation in November, Tugwell did not feel any bitterness or resentment either toward the president or toward those he felt had forced him out. Instead, he was happy at the prospect of returning to professional life and gratified at having taken part in the New Deal. Philosophically, then and later, he believed that the New Deal had not done enough in reforming the American system, but that it had accomplished as much as was politically feasible. More important, a revolution in method and objective, it provided the foundation for planning in the future.[57] For Tugwell, that made it worthwhile. Also, he had gained experience and knowledge in offering his ideas and programs. After the New Deal, he would continue to develop what he now had.

NOTES

1. Rexford Tugwell, diary, May 30, 1933, folder "Notes from a New Deal Diary," p. 26, Tugwell papers, FDR Library, box 30; Tugwell, diary, folder "The Hundred Days and Addendum to Hundred Days," pp. 2, 40, Tugwell papers, FDR Library, box 30; Tugwell, "Reminiscences," pp. 47-50, Oral History Research Office, Columbia University; Tugwell, *Roosevelt's Revolution* (New York: Macmillan, 1977), 81; Sternsher, *Tugwell and the New Deal* (New Brunswick, N.J.: Rutgers University Press, 1964), 157ff.

2. Rexford Tugwell, "The New Deal: The Contributions of Herbert Hoover," p. 16, Tugwell papers, FDR Library, box 70.

3. Tugwell, "Reminiscences," p. 48; Tugwell, *Roosevelt's Revolution*, p. 136; Sternsher, *Tugwell and the New Deal*, p. 158.

4. Tugwell, diary, May 30, 1933, folder "Notes from a New Deal Diary," pp. 26ff., Tugwell papers, FDR Library, box 30; Tugwell, diary, folder "Hundred Days and Addendum," pp. 2, 40, Tugwell papers, FDR Library, box 30.

5. Tugwell, *Roosevelt's Revolution*, pp. 134-35, 215.

6. Rexford Tugwell, "Codes and Agreements," Tugwell papers, FDR Library, box 55; Tugwell, "The Prospect for the Future," address to Chicago Forum (October 29, 1933), in his *Battle for Democracy*, (New York: Columbia University Press, 1935), 55-72; Tugwell, "The Senior Partner," in *Battle for Democracy*, pp. 17-20.

7. Rexford Tugwell, "Design for Government," address to the Eighth Annual Meeting of the Federation of Bar Associations of Western New York (June 24,

1933), and "Freedom and Business," both in his *Battle for Democracy*, pp. 3-16 and 43-47, respectively; Tugwell, interview with Mrs. Isabella Greenway, CBS (October 30, 1933), AAA press release, R 145 # 2, USDA, National Archives; Tugwell, "Paying the Recovery Debt," *American Magazine* (December 1933), Tugwell papers, FDR Library, box 55; Tugwell to John Thompson, September 30, 1954, Tugwell papers, folder "Th-To," FDR Library, box 26.

8. Rexford Tugwell, "Taking Stock," address to Business and Professional Men's Group (University of Cincinnati, January 26, 1934), p. 2, and "Shall We Consent to Idleness?" address to the Commonwealth Club of San Francisco (1934), p. 9, both in Tugwell papers, FDR Library, box 56; Tugwell, "The Road to Economic Recovery," *Extension Service Review* 5 (March 1934): 33-34; Tugwell, address to the American Society of Newspaper Editors (Washington, D.C., April 21, 1934), printed in *U.S. News and World Report* (April 23, 1934): 15; Tugwell, "The Social Responsibility of Technical Workers," address to the Organization of Government Employees (Washington, D.C., May 1, 1934), USDA press release, RG-16, National Archives, box 298.

9. Rexford Tugwell, "The Responsibilities of Partnership," address to the Iowa Bankers Association (Des Moines, June 27, 1934), Tugwell papers, FDR Library, box 31.

10. Ibid. See also Tugwell, "The Prospect for the Future," address at Grace Church Parish House (Brooklyn, N.Y., November 15, 1933), Tugwell papers, FDR Library, box 55.

11. Rexford Tugwell, "America Takes Hold of Its Destiny," *Today* 1 (April 28, 1934): 6-7, Tugwell papers, FDR Library, box 56; Tugwell, "Relief and Reconstruction," address to the National Conference of Social Work (Kansas City, Mo., May 21, 1934), in his *Battle for Democracy*, pp. 302-21; Tugwell, "A Third Economy," address to Rochester Teachers' Association (Rochester, N.Y., April 9, 1935), USDA press release, National Archives, box 310.

12. Rexford Tugwell to secretary of commerce, November 18, 1933, USDA, RG-16, National Archives, box 59; Tugwell, diary, folder "Diary 1934," March 28, 1934, p. 1, Tugwell papers, FDR Library, box 31; Sternsher, *Tugwell and the New Deal*, p. 162; Arthur M. Schlesinger, Jr., *The Politics of Upheaval* (Boston: Houghton Mifflin, 1960), 214ff.; J. Franklin Carter, *The New Dealers* (New York: Simon and Schuster, 1934), 89-90; Paul Conkin, *The New Deal* (New York: Thomas Y. Crowell, 1967), 37.

13. Tugwell, diary, folder "Notes from a New Deal Diary," May 30, 1933, Tugwell papers, FDR Library, box 30; Tugwell, "Reminiscences," pp. 62-63.

14. Rexford Tugwell to Hugh Johnson, November 14, 1933, USDA, RG-16, National Archives, box 59; Tugwell, diary, folder "Diary 1934," April 13 and 23, pp. 8-11ff., and May 19, 1934, p. 2, Tugwell papers, FDR Library, box 31; Sternsher, *Tugwell and the New Deal*, pp. 163, 308.

15. Rexford Tugwell to President Roosevelt, September 5 and 7, 1934, FDR papers, FDR Library, OF-466, box 3; Tugwell, "Reminiscences," pp. 60-61.

16. Tugwell, diary, folder "Diary 1934," November 22, 26, and 28, December 6 and 12, 1934, Tugwell papers, FDR Library, box 31; Tugwell, "Reminiscences," p. 61.

17. Tugwell, diary, folder "Diary 1934," November 29, 1934, box 31, and diary, folder "Diary 1935," January 29, 1935, Tugwell papers, FDR Library, box 32.

18. Tugwell, diary, folder "Diary 1935," May 30 and 31, 1935, pp. 97-104, Tugwell papers, FDR Library, box 32. Tugwell recognized that the IAA was vague and incomplete as well.

19. Rexford Tugwell to David Lawrence, April 10, 1953, Tugwell papers, folder "La," FDR Library, box 13. By the 1950s, Tugwell was periodically saying that government ownership or operating control of the national utilities, including oil, would have saved everyone in the New Deal "infinite trouble."

20. Mordecai Ezekiel, *$2500 a Year: From Scarcity to Abundance* (New York: Harcourt, Brace, 1936), 160-68; Hawley, *The New Deal and the Problem of Monopoly* (Princeton, N.J.: Princeton University Press, 1966), 179-81; Schlesinger, *Politics of Upheaval*, pp. 216-18. Ezekiel expanded and developed his plan in his *Jobs for All Through Industrial Expansion* (New York: Alfred Knopf, 1939). Tugwell's role in writing the Ezekiel plan was not as clear-cut as Hawley and Schlesinger imply. Circumstantial evidence indicates that he consulted with Ezekiel on the proposal and later endorsed it. He did not, however, write it, even though it was similar to his own IAA and plans in *The Industrial Discipline*. One of the authors of the plan, Louis Bean, indicated that Tugwell was more of an adviser than originator. See Louis Bean, "Reminiscences," pp. 103-104, Oral History Office, Columbia University.

21. Schlesinger, *Politics of Upheaval*, p. 217.

22. Rexford Tugwell to David Lawrence, April 10, 1953, Tugwell papers, FDR Library, box 13.

23. Rexford Tugwell, "Log of Trip Through 10 Western States," August 17-September 20, 1933, Tugwell papers, FDR Library, box 55; Tugwell, *Roosevelt's Revolution*, pp. 26, 42, 153, 262-63; Sternsher, *Tugwell and the New Deal*, pp. 210, 216ff.

24. Tugwell, *Roosevelt's Revolution*, pp. 7, 78-79, 166, 217; Sternsher, *Tugwell and the New Deal*, pp. 210, 214.

25. Tugwell, *Roosevelt's Revolution*, pp. 246-47; Sternsher, *Tugwell and the New Deal*, p. 211.

26. Tugwell, *Roosevelt's Revolution*, pp. 102, 124-25, 140-43.

27. Tugwell, diary, folder "Notes from a New Deal Diary," January 13, 1933, Tugwell papers, FDR Library, box 30, and diary, folder "Diary 1934," November 23, 1934, Tugwell papers, FDR Library, box 31; Tugwell, diary, folder "Diary 1935," September 10, 1935, pp. 16-26, Tugwell papers, FDR Library, box 32; Franklin D. Roosevelt to Homer Cummings, memo, November 20, 1933, with attached Cummings to Roosevelt, November 24, 1933, with attached Cummings to Roosevelt, December 13, 1933, with attached Cummings to Roosevelt, January 26, 1934, all in FDR papers, FDR Library, OF-10; Sternsher, *Tugwell and the New Deal*, pp. 208-22, 307-09.

28. Tugwell, diary, folder "Notes from a New Deal Diary," February 26, 1933, Tugwell papers, FDR Library, box 30; Rexford Tugwell to Skipper (FDR), March 17, 1933, FDR papers, FDR Library, OF-1; Charles Jackson, *Food and Drug*

Legislation in the New Deal (Princeton, N.J.: Princeton University Press, 1970), 4-5ff.

29. Tugwell, diary, folder "Notes from a New Deal Diary," April 26, 1933, Tugwell papers, FDR Library, box 30; Rexford Tugwell, "The Preparation of a President," *Western Political Quarterly* (June 1948): 133ff.; Tugwell, "Recollections of '33 and Later: The Genesis of the Food, Drug and Cosmetic Act as Seen by Its Architect," *FDA Papers* 2 (June 1968): 4-8, Tugwell papers, folder "Food and Drug Administration," FDR Library, box 8.

30. Tugwell, diary, folder "Notes from a New Deal Diary," April 26, 1933, Tugwell papers, FDR Library, box 30; Jackson, *Food and Drug Legislation*, pp. 84ff.

31. Rexford Tugwell, interview by Charles Jackson, June 7, 1968, Tugwell papers, FDR Library, box 76; Sternsher, *Tugwell and the New Deal*, p. 225.

32. Tugwell, diary, folder "Notes from a New Deal Diary," April 26, 1933, Tugwell papers, FDR Library, box 30. Tugwell was not happy with the FTC's role in Pure Food and Drug. He believed it tended to protect one business against another without in any way protecting the consumer. See Franklin D. Roosevelt, memorandum to Rexford Tugwell, January 22, 1934, with attached Tugwell to Roosevelt, January 26, 1934, FDR papers, FDR Library, OF-375; Roosevelt, "Memo for Mac," February 9, 1935, with attached Donald Richberg to the president, memorandum, January 28, 1935, with attached Tugwell to Richberg, January 24, 1935, all in FDR papers, FDR Library, OF-375.

33. Rexford Tugwell, "The Copeland Bill and the Food Industries," *Grocery Trade News* (October 24, 1933), p. 9, USDA papers, RG-16, National Archives, box 289; Tugwell, "A New Deal for the Consumer," address at Columbia Alumni Luncheon (New York, February 12, 1934), pp. 3-5, Tugwell papers, FDR Library, box 56; Tugwell, "The Great American Fraud," *American Scholar* (Winter 1934): 85-95; Tugwell, "Freedom from Fakes," in his *Battle for Democracy*, pp. 97-104.

34. Tugwell, diary, folder "Notes from a New Deal Diary," April 26, 1933, p. 16, Tugwell papers, FDR Library, box 30; Rexford Tugwell to Franklin D. Roosevelt, June 1, 1933, FDR papers, FDR Library, OF-375. Tugwell's strategy was to get businessmen to think that the bill was theirs. However, he soon discovered that this did not work and that members of Congress, especially Senator Copeland, were willing to compromise freely with the drug manufacturers. See Rexford Tugwell to Franklin D. Roosevelt, February 21, 1934, attached to memo for McIntyre (February 28, 1934), FDR papers, FDR Library, OF-375; Tugwell, diary, folder "Diary 1935," January 16, 1935, p. 2, Tugwell papers, FDR Library, box 32.

35. Rexford Tugwell, "The Tugwell Bill Becomes Un-American," Tugwell papers, FDR Library, box 71; Arthur M. Schlesinger, Jr., *The Coming of the New Deal* (Boston: Houghton Mifflin, 1958), 360-61; Sternsher, *Tugwell and the New Deal*, pp. 231-38, 249. For a detailed discussion of the drug manufacturers' and press's attack on Tugwell, see Sternsher, *Tugwell and the New Deal*, ch. 18. In Tugwell's opinion, the 1938 drug law was not stringent enough. See also Jack-

son, *Food and Drug Legislation*, pp. 201ff.; Tugwell, *Roosevelt's Revolution*, pp. 225-32, 263.

36. Rexford Tugwell, "The Place of Government in a National Land Program," USDA press release (December 29, 1933), n.p., Tugwell papers, FDR Library, box 55; Tugwell, "Planned Use of the Land," *Today* 1 (January 20, 1934): 6-7, 23-24; Tugwell, "The Outlines of a Permanent Agriculture" (1934), pp. 53-63, Tugwell papers, FDR Library, box 69. See also Tugwell, "National Significance of Recent Trends in Farm Population," *Social Forces* 14 (October 1935): 1-7.

37. Tugwell, diary, folder "Diary 1935," January 23, 1935, pp. 5-6, Tugwell papers, FDR Library, box 32.

38. Tugwell, diary, folder "Diary 1935," August 20, 1935, pp. 117-18; Tugwell papers, FDR Library, box 32.

39. Tugwell, diary, folder "Diary 1935," January 16, 1935, p. 3, Tugwell papers, FDR Library, box 32; Tugwell, "Intimations of Resettlement," n.p., Tugwell papers, FDR Library, box 71.

40. Paul Conkin, *Tomorrow a New World: The New Deal Community Building Program* (Ithaca, N.Y.: Cornell University Press, 1959), 143; Sternsher, *Tugwell and the New Deal*, p. 264.

41. Rexford Tugwell "Why Resettlement?" *Labor Information Bulletin* 3 (May 1936): 1; Tugwell, "Down to Earth," *Current History* 44 (July 1936): 33-38; Tugwell, "The Reason for Resettlement," address on NBC Radio (December 2, 1935), n.p., Tugwell papers, FDR Library, box 57.

42. Tugwell, diary, folder "Diary 1935," March 3, 1935, p. 58, and April 14, 1935, p. 66, Tugwell papers, FDR Library, box 32; Tugwell, "Conservation Redefined," address on the fiftieth anniversary of the founding of New York's forest reserve (Albany, May 15, 1935), pp. 8ff., USDA press release, RG-16, National Archives, box 311; Tugwell, "A Closer Integration of Rural and Urban Life Is a Definite Part of the Future Pattern," n.d., pp. 16-17, Tugwell papers, FDR Library, box 70.

43. Conkin, *Tomorrow a New World*, pp. 153-54.

44. Sternsher, *Tugwell and the New Deal*, pp. 266-68.

45. Tugwell, diary, folder "Diary 1935," May 2, 1935, pp. 74-85, and May 19, 1935, p. 93, both in Tugwell papers, FDR Library, box 32.

46. Tugwell, diary, folder "Diary 1935," March 3, 1935, p. 58, May 7, 1935, p. 85, and May 9, 1935, p. 88, all in Tugwell papers, FDR Library, box 32; Franklin D. Roosevelt to Rexford Tugwell, June 13, 1935, Tugwell to Roosevelt, July 15, 1935, Harold Ickes to Roosevelt, July 13, 1935, with attached Roosevelt, memo to Tugwell, July 16, 1935, D. W. Bell to Roosevelt, memorandum, August 8, 1935, Roosevelt to Tugwell, telegram, October 1, 1935, with attached Tugwell to Roosevelt, telegram, September 28, 1935, all in FDR papers, FDR Library, OF-1568; Will Alexander, "The Reminiscences of Will Alexander," pp. 395-400, Oral History Research Office, Columbia University. For a different opinion of Tugwell as RA administrator, see Chester Davis, "Reminiscences," pp. 363ff., and Samuel Bledsoe, "Reminiscences," p. 346, both Oral History Research Office, Columbia University.

47. Rexford Tugwell to L. C. Gray, November 14, 1935, Resettlement Administration papers, Record Group 96, National Archives; Conkin, *Tomorrow a New World*, p. 155; Sternsher, *Tugwell and the New Deal*, p. 269.

48. Rexford Tugwell to division directors and section chiefs, June 11, 1935, Resettlement Administration papers, RG 96, National Archives; Conkin, *Tomorrow a New World*, pp. 156ff.; Sternsher, *Tugwell and the New Deal*, p. 273.

49. Sternsher, *Tugwell and the New Deal*, pp. 274-75; Conkin, *Tomorrow a New World*, p. 159.

50. Rexford Tugwell to Elizabeth Allen, January 31, 1974, with attachment, Tugwell papers, folder "Ab-Al," FDR Library, box 1; Sternsher, *Tugwell and the New Deal*, p. 270; Mark Gelfand, *A Nation of Cities: The Federal Government and Urban America, 1933-1965* (New York: Oxford University Press, 1975), 134.

51. For a detailed discussion of the attack on the greenbelt towns and on the RA, see Sternsher, *Tugwell and the New Deal*, ch. 22; Conkin, *Tomorrow a New World*, pp. 177ff.; and Joseph Arnold, *The New Deal in the Suburbs: A History of the Greenbelt Town Program, 1935-1954* (Columbus: Ohio State University Press, 1971), 196-209. See also Will Alexander, "Reminiscences," pp. 408ff.

52. Tugwell publicly defended the RA and the greenbelt towns in a series of articles. See Rexford Tugwell, "Changing Acres," *Current History* 44 (September 1936): 57-63; "Co-operation and Resettlement," *Current History* 45 (February 1937): 71-76; and "The Meaning of the Greenbelt Towns," *New Republic* 90 (February 17, 1937): 42-43. Years later, Tugwell reevaluated his tenure in the RA and explained why the RA failed in the long run. See Tugwell, "The Resettlement Idea," *Agricultural History* 33 (October 1959): 159-64. For a good overview of Tugwell's term in the RA, see Interim Report of the Resettlement Administration and Annual Report of the Resettlement Administration, both in RA papers, RG 96, National Archives. These last two documents, although written by the agency and its personnel, still give good overviews of what happened in 1935-1936.

53. Tugwell, diary, folder "Diary 1934," June 6, 1934, Tugwell papers, FDR Library, box 31; diary, folder "Introduction," pp. 11-16, Tugwell papers, FDR Library, box 30; Tugwell, "Reminiscences," pp. 53-54; Rexford Tugwell to Franklin D. Roosevelt, February 24, 1934, FDR papers, FDR Library, PSF: RT, 1934-1936, box 58; Tugwell, "The Problem of Social Insecurity," *Bulletin of the Chicago Dental Society* (March 7, 14, 21, 1935), Tugwell papers, FDR Library, box 57; Tugwell, "Commitments for Tomorrow," column, *New York Herald Tribune*, August 1934; Sternsher, *Tugwell and the New Deal*, pp. 122-33, 139, 308-13. Later, Tugwell consistently argued that the Second New Deal had started in late 1934 and became pronounced in early 1935.

54. Tugwell, diary, folder "Introduction," pp. 11-12, 14, 16, Tugwell papers, FDR Library, box 30; Rexford Tugwell to Harry Barnard, April 30, 1976, Tugwell papers, folder "Ba," FDR Library, box 1; Tugwell, *Roosevelt's Revolution*, p. 145.

55. Even Tugwell's promotion to under secretary caused problems in 1934. See 73rd Congress, 2nd Session, Senate Committee on Agriculture and Forestry, *Hearings, June 11, 1934, on the Confirmation of Rexford Guy Tugwell for the Position of Undersecretary of Agriculture* (Washington, D.C.: Superintendent of Documents, 1934).

56. Tugwell, "Reminiscences," p. 69; Franklin D. Roosevelt to Rexford Tugwell, November 17, 1936, Tugwell papers, FDR Library, box 23; Louis Bean, "Reminiscences," p. 160; Sternsher, *Tugwell and the New Deal*, pp. 321-28. Throughout his tenure as a New Dealer, Tugwell confided to his diary his feelings about his position in the New Deal. See, for example, diary, March 24, 1934, September 10, 1935, and May 19, 1935, in Tugwell papers, FDR Library, boxes 31 and 32.

57. The theme that the New Deal was a revolution was consistently expressed by Tugwell in the 1930s and subsequent years. See, for example, Tugwell, diary, folder "Diary 1935," August 15, 20, 21, 23, 1935, and September 1, 1935, Tugwell papers, FDR Library, box 32; Tugwell, "The Social Philosophy of the New Deal," Tugwell papers, FDR Library, box 69; Tugwell, *The Brains Trust* (New York: Viking Press, 1968), 520-22.

6

New York/Puerto Rico: 1937–1946

I was enamored of that great city where I had spent so many years
and part of whose body and spirit I had come to be. I felt defeated
in my efforts to contribute something to her well-being and for a long
time I was bothered by my obvious ineffectiveness in work I liked
and for a purpose I believed in.

> Rexford G. Tugwell, *The Municipal Gestalt*, cited in
> Salvador Padilla, ed., *Tugwell's Thoughts on Planning*
> (Puerto Rico: University of Puerto Rico Press, 1975), 236.

The government in Puerto Rico was pretty well dilapidated. It was
out of date. That gave me a chance to overhaul it. Of course, I had
the support pretty much of the progressive group that was just coming into power. Up until that time, a group of reactionaries had control of the government. They had looted it and managed it to their
own benefit. We stopped all that. We installed a budgetary system, a
personnel system, and a planning system. Generally we reorganized
things.

> Rexford Tugwell, "Reflections," *Center Magazine* 11
> (Sept./Oct. 1978): 69

If there was nothing else outstanding about his personality, Tugwell
was honest and outspoken about what he believed and, more significantly, about himself. He did not hold back at all. He simply stated
what he thought he had accomplished and what he had failed to do.
Oftentimes, though, he tended to be harsher on himself than he should
have been or he shared credit with others more freely than others
would have shared with him. Both statements cited above were made
toward the end of his life. Both also reflected these personality traits.

In assessing his performance in New York, Tugwell made it clear
how much the city meant to him, how much he wanted to help it, and
how much he felt he failed. What he didn't say was that there were
many more factors involved in what happened in New York than

Rexford Tugwell alone. Similarly, his analysis of his governorship
shows his willingness to share the credit with others in Puerto Rico,
especially Luis Muñoz Marín. What Tugwell doesn't say was that it
was he who championed many of those changes and that, without his
initiative, there is no certainty that what was accomplished would
have happened. If nothing else, what both statements ultimately indicate is that Rexford G. Tugwell did not return to academe in 1937
and fade away. In more respects than he could have realized, his post-
New Deal years were productive.

In December 1936, just a couple of weeks before his resignation as
director of the Resettlement Administration took effect, Tugwell
published his "swan song" article as a New Dealer. In it, he unfolded
his hopes and fears for the United States by addressing the issue of
planning's future. Succinctly and strongly arguing that the "immediate
problem" confronting the United States was how to develop and implement planning, he made it clear that the doctrinaire, "economic
council" type of planning proposed by many inside and outside of
administration circles was a naive approach to a major public policy.
Not only would a central economic council form of planning prove
fruitless, but it also would betray "a lack of familiarity with the American spirit," a spirit Tugwell believed might lack discipline and logic
but "makes up for that by vigor and forthrightness." He was convinced
that such a program demanded the "suppression of dissent" and the
"abandonment of democracy" because, like all doctrinaire systems,
"it seems to operate better [when] there is no criticism."[1]

Instead of monstrous, dictatorial economic councils, Tugwell proposed that any program seeking to implement planning within the
American system rely exclusively on cooperation and experimentation. In the industrial sector of the economy, for example, this meant
that American businessmen had to bear the primary responsibility
for planning. They had to recognize that interindustrial planning is
more important than intraindustrial planning, that the consumer must
be considered in all their programs, and that the public welfare, and
not private profit, is the goal for which they must be striving. Businessmen also had to recognize that only by cooperating with the government could they be successful in implementing a planning program.
If they did recognize this, if they agreed to cooperate with each other
and with the government, then, Tugwell believed, "everything will be
easy." But if business continued to refuse to fulfill its public responsibilities and obligations, trouble would follow. In light of Roosevelt's
reelection mandate, business had no choice—either it implemented

planning in the way it should or the federal government would extend its powers in a way never before known or considered.[2]

Similarly, Tugwell emphasized that agricultural planning had to be implemented by both the farmer and the government. Since the AAA and the Resettlement Administration had started the process, he recommended that this approach be continued. He argued that the government had to play a more active role by transforming the unprofitable lands into reserves, by resettling farmers on more productive lands, and by helping the tenants and sharecroppers in every possible way. If industrial planning were to succeed, Tugwell concluded, agricultural planning would have to complement and balance it, and his recommendations were one way of doing that.[3]

In retrospect, what Tugwell was saying in this last statement as a New Dealer was pretty much what he had been saying prior to and during the New Deal. He still defined planning in terms of cooperation, experimentalism, and industrial-agricultural equilibrium. Also, he still considered planning applicable to the American democratic system, since its implementation depended upon business and government in the industrial sector of the economy and farmers and government in the agricultural. Although he preferred having the government play a supervisory role in both cases, he was not averse to extending the government's authority if necessary, especially in regard to business. As far as Tugwell was concerned, planning was very much alive in 1936 and still dependent on business, labor, farmers, and the government for its successful implementation. Cooperation and experimentalism were the keys to success, and he was hopeful that they would eventually prevail in effecting planning in the United States, and thereby assuring America's future.

In many ways, this optimistic attitude explained why Tugwell proposed his Industrial Adjustment Act immediately after the *Schechter* decision, why he supported the Ezekiel Plan for Industrial Expansion in 1936, and why he worked so vigorously to have the Resettlement Administration transferred to the Department of Agriculture before his resignation took effect.[4] It also explained why Tugwell worked so hard throughout the latter part of 1935 and into 1936 to convince Roosevelt of the need for a constitutional amendment that would extend the federal government's power over interstate commerce, "clip" the wings of the Supreme Court, and clearly define the executive-congressional relationship in terms more favorable to the president.[5]

In his thinking, the foundations for a planned economy had already been laid in the First New Deal, and all that was needed now was for

Roosevelt to build on them. With his own experimental plans at the president's disposal and in view of the tremendous reelection mandate he received, Tugwell was certain that the American people would follow and support Roosevelt in his efforts to sustain and develop planning. Despite Roosevelt's refusal to follow his or anyone else's suggestions for planning, and despite the influence being exerted on the president by the "Frankfurter-Cohen-Corcoran" group, Tugwell did not give up his optimistic anticipation that eventually planning would prevail.[6] And even after his resignation took effect in December 1936, Tugwell still supported the man he believed would be responsible for it—Franklin D. Roosevelt.

Although confident and expectant that the New Deal would ultimately succeed in implementing planning, Tugwell returned to private life determined to help the president in this task. When Tugwell announced his resignation, he also made it known that once it took effect on December 31, 1936, he would assume the position of traveling consultant and executive vice-president of the American Molasses Company. No New Dealer could have made a more shocking announcement. "Rex the Red," "Tugwell, Rex," "Rex, the Sweetheart of the Regimenters," as he had been known, was about to accept the gray suits, plush offices, and all the other paraphernalia of the big businessman.

Superficially, it appeared that Tugwell, like many academics, usually said one thing while doing something else. On closer examination, however, such was not the case. The primary reason why Tugwell became an executive vice-president of American Molasses is that he had nowhere else to go. In view of his stormy career as a New Dealer and of the vicious attacks the press made on him, Columbia University, his academic home in the 1920s, no longer considered Tugwell a welcome addition to its faculty. More important, since no other university was willing to offer him a position, it was not surprising that he accepted the benevolent offer of his close friend, Charles Taussig, who owned the American Molasses Company.[7] At least for the time being, he was going to sell Grandma's molasses instead of his somewhat unorthodox economic programs.

While a vice-president in the business world, Tugwell continued his efforts to influence Roosevelt on economic policy. In the latter part of 1937, for example, he, along with Adolph Berle and Charles Taussig, arranged several meetings between the leaders of organized labor and big business for the purpose of seeing whether they could agree on a program to stimulate the economy. If such a program could be devised, Tugwell wanted to arrange a conference between these people and President Roosevelt. In light of the recurrent unemployment problem and the deepening recession that was beginning to plague the economy in 1937, it seemed to Tugwell that the president could use all the cooperation and help he could get, especially from the business world.

For all practical purposes, the meetings proved to be successful. The conferees, including John L. Lewis, Philip Murray, Lee Pressman, Thomas Lamont, Owen D. Young, Berle, Taussig, and Tugwell, all agreed that the president should institute policies that would provide relief for the unemployed, ease the credit situation for business, help to restore confidence by modifying the tax burdens on business and labor, and relax the antitrust laws. They also agreed that the railroads should be encouraged to consolidate with other public utilities being expanded and that a large housing program be implemented. If taken together, such a program would stimulate the economy immediately and in a most satisfactory manner.[8]

After agreeing on the essentials of the program, Tugwell arranged a meeting between Roosevelt and the labor and business leaders. On January 14, 1938, the president met with Tugwell and the others. Despite all their anticipation and hopes, nothing significant resulted. Roosevelt listened to their suggestions without making any commitments. More important, Roosevelt subsequently announced his basic agreement with the advocates of antitrustism.[9] No longer in sympathy with Tugwell's cooperative approach, Roosevelt decided to endorse the Thurman Arnold movement and the Temporary National Economic Committee (TNEC) investigations. In doing so, the president disappointed many of his former supporters. For Tugwell, Roosevelt's antitrust policy, although disappointing, was not disillusioning. He still believed that the president was at heart a planner and that eventually he would return to that approach. In the meantime, Tugwell would continue to advise him on the policies he believed were essential to America's well-being.

In retrospect, Tugwell's activity in arranging a conference between Roosevelt and the leaders of labor and business was significant because it demonstrated that he was still committed to a cooperative approach in resolving the depression and in implementing planning. It also demonstrated how much Tugwell had "fallen from grace" vis-à-vis Roosevelt and policy making. By early 1938, Tugwell was not exerting any influence whatsoever on the president. In a sense, this was a disappointing and frustrating experience for the former Brains Truster.

Yet, in another sense, it demonstrated that he still believed in the president and his potential. In spite of his disagreement with Roosevelt on policy then and later, he always remained a staunch supporter of Roosevelt and his New Deal.

While Tugwell was on the sidelines, helplessly watching the New Deal revive the old Progressive approach to industry-government relations, he faced personal problems. In 1938, he and Florence Arnold divorced, and in November of that year Tugwell married a former Resettlement Administration co-worker, Grace Falke. Ten months before his remarriage, he also had to face the prospect of either remaining in the business world or possibly returning to public service. Out of place at American Molasses and yearning to do more constructive things with his life, Tugwell unhesitatingly agreed to Mayor Fiorello La Guardia's offer to be chairman of the recently established New York City Planning Commission. (NYCPC).[10]

As a planning agency, the NYCPC was unique. In 1936, New York adopted a new municipal charter that, among other things, established an independent planning commission. Consisting of a full-time chairman and six members appointed by the mayor, with the chief engineer of the Board of Estimate also serving, the NYCPC was to provide for the improvement of the city and for its future growth and development. Its primary duty was to prepare and "from time to time modify a master plan of the city" in terms of its physical and aesthetic growth. It also had the responsibility of completing and maintaining the city map (zoning) and preparing an annual capital budget and a five-year capital program. Although broadly based in its responsibilities, the decisions of the NYCPC were considered final unless a three-fourths majority of the Board of Estimate overturned them. Combining some of the activities and powers of the legislative, executive, and judicial branches of government in one agency whose members supposedly were expert and nonpolitical, it was hoped that the NYCPC would promote and protect the public interest in a more satisfactory way than the borough presidents or Board of Estimate and other political institutions had done in the past.[11]

From the perspective of Rexford Tugwell, the two most interesting issues about the NYCPC were why Mayor Fiorello La Guardia chose him for the chairmanship and, more significantly, why he accepted. Described by Tugwell as "temperamental, a showman, and unpredictable," La Guardia found the City Charter provision on the NYCPC distasteful, yet politically popular.[12] Setting his sights on the 1940 presidential election and recognizing the popular support this particular reform had, he accepted the commission on his terms. In a typically La Guardian fashion, he not only decided to leave one seat on the commission vacant for "money-saving reasons," but he also waited almost to the last minute before announcing the appointments of Arthur V. Sheridan, Edwin A. Salmon, Cleveland Rodgers, and Lawrence Orton as commission members and Adolph A. Berle as commission chairman. Berle's appointment, however, was only temporary because, as was expected, he moved on to become assistant secretary of state.

It was at this point that La Guardia turned to Tugwell. From the Little Flower's point of view, the former Brains Truster and New Dealer could help him by maintaining contact with Roosevelt and congressional Progressives and, in so doing, help La Guardia in the 1940 presidential election.[13] For Tugwell, on the other hand, the NYCPC offered him an opportunity to exit American Molasses and the business world gracefully, to test and reformulate his economic ideas, especially on planning, and to serve in the public interest again. In April 1938, when he took the new job, Tugwell had the best of intentions and the highest hopes for New York, the NYCPC, planning, and himself.[14]

Tugwell faced a number of problems that eventually undermined not only what he wanted to do but the NYCPC as well. First and foremost, there was La Guardia, who jealously protected his mayoral position and tolerated the commission at best, while most of the time harassing Tugwell as chairman and providing only lukewarm support on controversial issues.[15] Next, there were the real estate, banking, and other vested interests in the city who, at the very best, would support the commission only when and if it promoted their interests.[16] And, finally, there was Robert Moses, New York's empire builder, who had refused La Guardia's offer of the NYCPC chairmanship because it would have been too confining.[17] This is not to say that Tugwell was an innocent lamb being led to slaughter. Committed to his evolving planning principles and to what he thought New York needed, he often acted in a typical Tugwellian manner—taking stands that were not only unpopular but also politically impossible. On three issues involving housing, zoning, and the Master Plan, Tugwell found out just how difficult his job was and how tenuous the NYCPC's existence could be.

In the area of public housing, the New York City Housing Authority sought to take advantage of the 1937 Wagner Act, which provided for a federal-local partnership in building housing for lower-income families. It initially sought to purchase land in the outlying boroughs because it was cheaper and the sites were unoccupied. Tugwell and the commission disagreed, however. They convinced the Housing Authority to locate public housing in the decaying areas of New York because, in the long run, such building would be cheaper because fewer city services would be needed. The city, moreover, would benefit by having more public housing units. Even business groups endorsed the commission's proposal, because it entailed less municipal spending while providing for slum clearance.

The problem arose when the Federal Housing Agency objected to the higher prices for land in the decaying areas. A compromise was eventually reached whereby the federal government funded the purchase of slum property sites and the city agreed to build more houses on each site. The compromise was contrary to the better judgment of the NYCPC, since higher population densities followed instead of open spaces and fewer people. Tugwell, nevertheless, had no choice but to agree—even though he realized that many of the projects his commission approved were not going to help the city in the long run.[18] It was a political compromise that eventually helped to erode the purpose of the NYCPC.

Similarly, Tugwell faced a difficult time in the area of zoning. He felt strongly that New York City needed to restructure its zoning ordinances and strike out nonconforming uses. Neighborhoods originally designed as residential had advertising signs, gasoline stations, and other unattractive, nonconforming activities within them. In the spring of 1939, Tugwell and the commission proposed a retroactive nonconformity use ordinance, held hearings, and officially adopted it in 1940. Despite the commission's hopes, the Board of Estimate overturned the ordinance. The reason for the reversal was quite simple— real estate, business groups, and other vested interests felt they had too much to lose. A defeat for Tugwell, the zoning affair lined up the opposition even more strongly.[19]

The final battle came with the Master Plan. For Tugwell, the Master Plan was "the function of its assumptions, the direct . . . representation of estimates concerning the future." Making the future effective in the present, Tugwell believed the Master Plan

. . . is more like the architect's rough sketches than the finished working drawings of the house, but like those sketches it is perhaps the most important influence, determining the nature of the city structure that is to be built.[20]

In the fall of 1940, the rough sketch was released—the proposed Master Plan of Land Use. Taking a 50-year view of New York's future, it recommended that Manhattan, commercial and financial heart of the city, be provided with better access to the city's port facilities. Residential neighborhoods were given priority in the city's future. And, finally and most controversially, by 1990 the plan would transform one-third of the city's land surface into open spaces.[21] All of this was projected in a report of five pages and three maps. To say that the proposed plan caused people's eyebrows to be raised understates its impact. In the hearings that followed, the NYCPC listened to numerous speakers representing numerous groups attack the plan. Yet, as the leading student of urban municipal planning has said, only one man was really heard—Robert Moses.

Described by Tugwell as "temperamental, violent, unfair, and unpredictable," Robert Moses was New York's towering force. A representative of "the well-to-do citizens," he built bridges, parks, hospitals, and everything else he set his mind to. Invariably successful, no one, not even LaGuardia, could stand up to him. In the December 1940 hearings, Moses so resolutely attacked the Master Plan as unwise, impractical, and useless that he effectively destroyed any chance it had of being adopted and put into practice. With Moses' frontal assault dealing such a tragic blow to the Master Plan, Tugwell's effectiveness and tenure as chairman of NYCPC were over.[22]

With the defeat of the Master Plan, Tugwell realized the time had come to move on. By 1940, in fact, he believed that the NYCPC was not working well, in that it lacked a sufficient staff to perform its duties; it depended too much on the mayor and the Board of Estimate; and it was operating in an inherently hostile environment, especially in light of the real estate and business interests, and individuals like Robert Moses. Assessing his own performance, as the opening quote demonstrates, Tugwell felt he had failed.[23] Having tried his best to implement planning for everyone, he concluded that not everyone wanted planning. But was Tugwell's failure as complete as he intimated? Although Robert Moses was eventually appointed to the NYCPC, thereby assuring the dismissal of master plans, the idea of municipal planning lived on. Also, given the obstacles he faced from the very start, Tugwell did quite well in restraining himself from attacking his opponents in his determination to give the NYCPC his best shot. True, municipal planning was hurt by the failure of the NYCPC, but Tugwell cannot be blamed for all of that. While he was indeed important, he was not the only one responsible for planning in New York.

For Tugwell personally, serving as chairman of the NYCPC was especially significant for at least two reasons. First, it provided him with an opportunity to see and think about planning in microcosm. Whereas in the 1920s and 1930s he had developed his planning programs for the national level, he now had a chance to develop his programs for the local level. Instead of interindustrial councils, Industrial Integration Boards, and Industrial Plans for Expansion, he now had to concentrate on zoning regulations, budgets for each year as well as a projected five-year plan, and master plans. Second, by serving as chairman, he was given the opportunity to modify, expand, and correct his theories of planning by actually implementing them. Whether he was dealing with the problems of developing suburbs, rezoning land in the interior of the city, or differentiating budgets, he could see what problems were involved in implementing planning and, in so doing, he could adjust his own thinking to the realities of political and social life.[24]

Tugwell recognized this, and he argued that city planning was important because it provided a small test area for a broader, comprehensive national planning program. Without national planning, he felt, city planning would not be too important, but at the same time, he believed that city planning was leading to national planning and, therefore, was "useful."[25] Throughout his chairmanship, then, it is not surprising that he tried to implement his planning ideas and programs in New York as best he could.[26] More important, it was while he was in New York that he wrote his most significant works on planning. Between 1938 and 1941, he wrote a series of articles that demonstrated his evolutionary progress toward understanding planning on the national level in its theoretical and practical aspects. Of those writings, the one that stands out is "The Fourth Power."

In many respects, "The Fourth Power" was a watershed in Tugwell's thinking. While culminating much of what he had been saying throughout the 1920s and 1930s, it also represented a significant transformation and new direction in his planning philosophy. Not only did he introduce new concepts and utilize a different terminology in discussing planning, but he also suggested new ways of making certain that planning could and would be implemented.

Specifically, Tugwell argued that as civilization advanced, societal problems became more and more difficult and complex, with fewer and fewer people capable of understanding and/or resolving them. In the United States, for example, technology was causing so many changes in industry and government that the old ideals of competition and conflict were tearing the republic apart with internal struggles. Instead of achieving an economy of abundance, the nation was continually witnessing depressions, economic dislocations, and poverty. In Tugwell's thinking, the only explanation for this was that the United States was not recognizing the inevitable need to cooperate, adopt collective customs, and institute planning. Although it was susceptible of use by autarkies, Tugwell emphasized that, in the United States, "planning [could] preserve a useful kind of democracy" by sustaining and modernizing it so as to adjust to the technically sophisticated form of societal life.[27]

Despite what its opponents had said, Tugwell argued that planning was "not direction when it is at the service of special interests in society; it becomes direction only when it can affect economic divisiveness, becoming a unifying, cohesive, constructive, and truly general force." In practical terms, this meant that business, which had consistently used planning in its operations, had failed to use it in the general interest, thereby making planning a tool of private profit and all its concomitant activities. Production, for example,

... assisted by special planning has increased until it has caused successively unemployment, malapportionment of income, and stoppage of production—a cycle which has been amazingly shortened in the last four decades. Planning of this sort helped to create surpluses without doing anything to add proportionate income-receivers (or increasing the incomes of existing workers) who might use the product.[28]

Tugwell also felt that this special-interest form of planning operated "by sacrificing other interests, and eventually, though they may not realize it, at a sacrifice to themselves." This form of planning not only lacked direction but also endangered the very existence of the whole society. For obvious reasons, it had to be stopped, and replaced by a system of planning that was both directive and holistic.

To implement such a directional, holistic planning system would not be easy. In view of the dangerous directions that planning had taken in Italy (Fascism), Germany (Nazism), and Russia (Communism), Tugwell believed that an evolutionary method of implementing planning in the United States would have to be adopted. Such a method would have to emphasize the whole, not the parts; experimentalism, not rigid blueprints; and expertise, not selfish individual interests.[29] Such a method would also have to devise a "conjunctural mechanism" capable of overseeing and implementing planning. In view of the inadequacy and ineffectiveness of America's tripartite form of government, Tugwell recommended that a "Fourth Power" be created to carry out this responsibility.

Unlike the president, who is hemmed in by the Senate and dependent upon special-interest-oriented administrative agencies, and unlike the Congress, which is incapable of providing direction for the whole of society, and unlike the judiciary, which is hampered by legal precedents, Tugwell believed the Fourth Power would be independent, scientific, and holistically oriented.[30] Its members would be chosen on the basis of highly selective qualifications, and they would be given terms of office longer than any other government officials, except the judiciary. Although it would serve as a directional agency, Tugwell did not believe that the Fourth Power would evolve into a national planning board right away (or at all). Instead, he felt that it would function and grow gradually under a "rigorously fixed procedure of expert preparation, public hearings, agreed findings, and careful translation into law—which are in turn subject to legislative ratification."

The public would have the right at the beginning and end of the process to accept or reject the Fourth Power's findings. Since the Fourth Power would be staffed with experts, it would not concern itself with determining social aims; rather, it would concentrate on devising ways of managing the economy in order to achieve the general aims the people indicated they wanted.[31] And, in so doing, it would assure the people that the planning being done was in *their* interests and not for the benefit of special-interest groups and/or political leaders.

In a similar vein, Tugwell, in other writings, tried to show that it would only be through the Fourth Power that planning could be successfully implemented. In "The Superpolitical," for example, he argued that politicians and business leaders, by the very nature of their success and the system in which they operated, were incapable of effectively running the economic system. Like the individualist who is willing to sacrifice the interests of others so as to obtain his own objectives, the businessman and political leader in the United States could not envision or understand the "whole" or the need to develop a holistic, conjunctural mechanism to protect and promote all of society's interests.[32] Even on the municipal level this was true, because no one, whether a politician or a businessman, could recognize the city as "an emergent" that could be understood only in terms of its behavior.[33] "The whole configuration—the gestalt—[had] to be accepted as unique and its behavior as fundamental"—and in Tugwell's thinking, that was not yet being done.[34]

On the national level, on the other hand, Tugwell felt that Roosevelt and the New Deal, especially in the NRA, had tried to do that.

Although it suffered from many weaknesses as well as from the old Progressives' yearning for business liberty, it was still a step in the right direction because it recognized that "the ideological concomitant of the machine process" centered "in operational wholeness." More important, Tugwell argued that Roosevelt recognized the need to collectivize, coordinate, and cooperate through planning, but political considerations and obsolete American values prevented him from going any further.[35] The foundations for planning, in short, had been laid, and Tugwell hoped that Roosevelt would eventually build some more, perhaps in the direction of a Fourth Power program. In view of the circumstances confronting the United States in the twentieth century, he believed there was no alternative.

In retrospect, there is no doubt that what Tugwell said in "The Fourth Power" and his related writings was of the utmost importance in his thinking on planning. First of all, those writings demonstrated clearly that he was still evolving in his understanding of planning both theoretically and practically. Although the themes of cooperation, experimentalism, expertise, and coordination still permeated his thinking, they were now being presented in a different terminology and framework. The concepts of the emergent, conjuncture, and institutional lag replaced the simpler explanations that he had used in the pre-1939 period. Also, in addition to his new conceptualization of planning, Tugwell presented a new dimension in the practical sense. Where he had consistently argued that planning would be effected within the political system prior to 1939, he now recommended that planning be implemented outside the traditional American political realm. The Fourth Power or fourth branch of government was to be independent and separate from the other branches of the American government, and its personnel would be recruited from the nonpolitical, professional classes of American society. Here, it seems apparent that Tugwell had learned quite a bit from his experiences as a New Dealer and chairman of the NYCPC.

Finally, his writings on the Fourth Power indicated that Tugwell expected fundamental changes in America's value system to take place before planning could be successfully effected. Although he had always indicated that some changes would be necessary—for example, in America's adherence to laissez-faire—he now made it explicit just how fundamental such changes would be. Not only would laissez-faire and individual ideals be replaced by cooperation and collective values, but even the people's view of the government would have to change to one that accepted and respected the role the "experts" would play in facilitating America's achievement of its goals. In Tug-

well's opinion, this did not imply creating an aristocracy of expertise
or an elite of professionals; it meant placing more trust in those who
knew what to do, because the people told them, as well as how to do
it, because that is what they were trained for. In light of the sophis-
cated industrial system the United States had developed, there was
no other way. As far as Tugwell was concerned, his "Fourth Power"
program was much more readily adaptable to American democracy
than either the compulsory planning system of Communist Russia or
the autocratic dictatorial regimes of Fascist Italy and Nazi Germany.
It was America's choice, and Tugwell felt that, in time, the American
people would make the right one.

By 1940, his career as chairman of the NYCPC in trouble and sensing that the time was right for moving on, Tugwell welcomed the suggestion of Secretary of the Interior Harold Ickes that he investigate
land law in Puerto Rico. In many ways Ickes' decision to involve Tugwell in Puerto Rican affairs was not unusual. He knew, for example,
that Tugwell had been either directly or indirectly involved with
Puerto Rico since 1934, when he traveled there to survey the sugar
situation. Afterward, Roosevelt consulted the former Brains Truster
on many different aspects of Puerto Rico's economy. More significant
was the fact that Ickes, although he disagreed with Tugwell on many
things, liked him personally and felt that he was a good administrator.
In Ickes' opinion, Tugwell had been unfairly treated by the press
while he was in the New Deal and should, for that reason, be given
another chance. And, in light of his own dislike for dealing with ter-
ritorial affairs, Ickes thought this would be a good way to do that.[36]

Essentially, Ickes asked Tugwell to investigate the 500-acre law of
land ownership in Puerto Rico. Although the law expressly forbade
anyone to acquire more than 500 acres, many American corporations
continued to violate it with impunity, owning substantially larger
amounts of land. Tugwell's task was, therefore, to determine how
much the law was violated and to recommend a specific program to
prevent violation in the future. After an exhaustive study and investigation, Tugwell submitted a report with a list of 11 points and specific recommendations, all of which suggested a more stringent enforcement of the law and a wider diffusion and distribution of the
land among the people of Puerto Rico.[37]

At approximately the time Tugwell submitted his report, the governor of Puerto Rico, Guy Swope, announced that he was going to
resign, thereby leaving the governorship vacant. According to the
Organic Act, such a vacancy was to be filled by the president of the

United States, and since both Roosevelt and Ickes thought Tugwell would be a good choice, they decided to offer him the position. Before the appointment was finalized, however, Tugwell had also been offered the position of chancellor of the University of Puerto Rico. In August 1941, he formally accepted the latter offer while simultaneously agreeing to become governor, asking the university for leave without pay. By the fall of 1941, then, Tugwell was both chancellor and governor, a situation so outrageous, and illegal in a strict sense, that he eventually was forced to resign the chancellorship.

Here, it is important to understand why Tugwell accepted both positions. From his point of view, World War II was a major crisis that the United States was involved in, and he wanted some part to play. Ideally, he would have preferred working with Roosevelt again. Yet he was realistic enough to accept that this was not possible. In his thinking, then, the governorship was a wartime task he would undertake as a temporary duty. Once the war was over, he would assume his responsibilities as chancellor. This perception was clearly illustrated when Tugwell originally agreed to be chancellor. In addition to demanding that the Board of Trustees allow him to establish a junior college system and a master plan for Puerto Rican higher education, he also made it clear to the board that he wanted a ten-year contract and a two-year leave of absence without pay so that he could serve in a wartime capacity as governor.

What made the opposition's success in preventing him from doing this so hard for Tugwell to swallow was that he felt university leaders on the mainland were serving in government while remaining within their university systems. What he wanted, therefore, did not, *in his mind*, seem unreasonable at all. Nevertheless, in hindsight, it is easy to criticize Tugwell for accepting both positions. If nothing else, it demonstrated his naiveté in thinking that, given his reputation and his background, he could do and act like everyone else, especially in wartime. In the end, he resigned the chancellorship, but he was still governor, and he was determined to implement ideas designed to reform the territory's relationship with the federal government.[38]

On taking office, Tugwell was confronted with a unique situation. By 1941, the Populares party, led by Luis Muñoz Marín, had successfully launched a political revolution against the landholding classes in Puerto Rico. Desiring to implement broad political, social, and cultural changes, Muñoz Marín built up a large enough following in the legislature to get whatever he wanted. However, like most Puerto Rican leaders, he was not certain about how to go about implementing change and, as a result, gradually allied himself with Tugwell. In fact, throughout his gubernatorial term, Tugwell and Muñoz Marín administered many of the changes the Populares party wanted. Tugwell, moreover, appointed a group of young Puerto Ricans to help him accomplish these changes, including Jaime Benítez (University of Puerto Rico), Rafael de J. Cordero (auditor), Sol Luis Descartes (Office of Statistics), Roberto de Jesús Toro (Finance Division), Teodoro Moscoso (Operation Bootstrap), Guillermo Nigaglioni (Civil Service and Budget), Rafael Pico (Planning), and Roberto Sánchez Villella (Transportation). Tugwell let these men develop their ideas and administrative skills, and set policy without interference. In so doing, he was preparing them for leadership positions once Puerto Rico was on its own.

For Tugwell and Muñoz Marín, the accomplishments were impressive. In civil service, land reform, public financing, and legislature-Congress relations, Tugwell helped Muñoz Marín to get the changes through in an orderly and efficient manner. What made this feat more impressive was that, as they were conducting and implementing the political transformation, World War II was in full progress.

As a wartime governor, Tugwell had to face a variety of problems quickly and resolutely. He had, for example, to maintain law and order among the people, provide air raid shelters, and protect water and other necessities. Fire services also had to be developed in case the island was attacked by enemy planes. There was no doubt in Tugwell's mind that, given Puerto Rico's strategic position, it could become a strongly held enemy position relatively easily. Events of 1942 and 1943 seemed to prove that point.

Throughout 1942 and 1943, the military situation in Puerto Rico was quite tenuous, with severe problems developing in food and fuel supplies, and military defense against the freely roaming Axis submarines. It was to Tugwell's credit, along with others, like the Anglo-American Commission, that Puerto Rico and Latin America survived the war intact and, in Puerto Rico's case, even made significant headway in advancing the general standard of living of the people.[39] More important, much of the legislation enacted during the war years is still in effect today.[40]

Tugwell signed into law a long list of impressive bills, many of which were in line with his thinking on planning, particularly as manifested in "The Fourth Power." Legislation, for example, was passed that transferred the municipal water systems to the Water Resources Authority; a more efficient fire service and park management system under insular control were established; the university was purged of much of its political orientation; a transportation and communications authority was created; the sugar mills were placed under government regulation; a Puerto Rican state guard was set up; a modern budget bureau was devised; and the Puerto Rico Development Company and the Development Bank of Puerto Rico were established. He also established the Institute of Tropical Agriculture and the Agricultural Company.[41] Of all these accomplishments, the one that was the most significant for Tugwell was the Planning Act of 1942.

The draft planning bill was written by Alfred Bettmann, a member of the National Resources Planning Board in Washington, D.C. In the Bettmann draft, planning boards for all of Puerto Rico's municipalities were set up and given the authority to regulate land use. The boards, however, were not allowed to prepare fiscal plans, nor were their decisions to be considered final, since legislative ratification would be necessary before their proposals were put into effect. A fairly conventional planning bill, the Bettmann draft seemed to be the best Puerto Rico could hope for, at least in the opinion of those who wrote it. In Tugwell's thinking, however, nothing could have been further from the truth.[42]

When Tugwell received the Bettmann bill, he rejected it, on the grounds that it was too dependent on the municipalities, that it lacked authority to deal with long-range budgetary planning, and that it was too closely affiliated with the political government. He demanded a bill creating a stronger, more independent planning agency and, for that reason, he decided to write his own. Working closely with his friend Frederick Bartlett, Tugwell drafted a bill calling for the creation of a central planning agency with total jurisdiction over the island. The agency was to have the authority to plan for and regulate the use of all land in Puerto Rico, the power and obligation to prepare annual and long-range budgets, and the right to be free from any legislative and/or executive interference.

To accomplish this latter objective, Tugwell devised a planning board consisting of three men who would serve staggered six-year terms and whose salaries and budgets would be immune from a gubernatorial veto. Also, to make certain that the board's decision would be carried out, he wrote a provision into the bill that the board's programs would be automatically implemented unless a majority of the insular legislature voted against them. All in all, the Tugwell planning bill, very much in line with "The Fourth Power" principles, was designed to create a "near-perfect" planning agency that was independent, holistically oriented, and filled with experts.[43]

Although the Tugwell draft was introduced in the insular legislature with Muñoz Marín's blessing, by the time the legislators were finished with it, it was quite different from the original. The Puerto Rican Planning Act of 1942, as passed, established a three-man Puerto Rico Planning, Urbanizing and Zoning Board with the power to prepare plans for land use as well as fiscal policy. However, unlike the Tugwell bill, the final law did not give the board complete jurisdiction over the island, nor did it dismiss the possibility of supplementing it with municipal planning agencies. Also, the final law did not contain Tugwell's "automatic provision" or immunity from either legislative or gubernatorial veto, especially in budgetary considerations. In effect, the Planning Board, although powerful, was not to be omnipotent and independent of the insular government.

When the final law was sent to the governor for his signature, Tugwell initially refused to sign it. However, after considering what the law did accomplish, he acquiesced and placed his name on it.[44] In the long run, Tugwell realized, the law was a beginning that could develop into the type of planning that he envisioned for the United States as a whole. Time and experience would determine whether the Planning Board would be successful, and if it was, it could serve as the model for others. In fact, everything he had done in Puerto Rico depended upon similar criteria. Once the legislation was passed, it would be up to the Puerto Rican people to make certain that these changes were successful. Tugwell thought they would be.

Despite everything that he and Muñoz Marín had done, Tugwell was still not finished. He worked hard, during his governorship and in subsequent years, to have the Organic Act revised so that Puerto Rico would be given self-government and would have its own governor. Changes in this area were of the utmost importance, and Tugwell was determined to get them. However, in fighting for those changes as well as for everything else he had done, Tugwell quickly encountered heavy opposition, especially from the Coalitionists and the landed classes. In 1943-1944, he was attacked so bitterly by the Coalition that two congressional committees, the Chávez and Bell subcommittees, were sent to the island to investigate.[45]

The Senate Insular Affairs Committee, headed by Sen. Dennis Chávez, and a subcommittee of the House of Insular Affairs Committee, headed by Rep. C. Jasper Bell, were sent to Puerto Rico to investigate the economic crisis that was supposedly taking place there. Extensive hearings were held, especially by the Chávez committee. In the end, the Chávez committee recommended that the federal government continue the Works Progress Administration (WPA) so as to provide jobs for the Puerto Rican people. The Bell committee, on the other hand, decided it would investigate not only economic conditions but social and political affairs as well. In June 1943, the committee arrived and started hearings. Tugwell appeared before the committee and discussed what he considered to be the major problems of the island: the cost of food, the people's desire for statehood, and problems with disease and housing. After his testimony and that of quite a few others, the Bell committee returned to Washington and recommended that the federal government continue WPA funding for Puerto Rico.

Although nothing detrimental or harmful was found, and although Tugwell himself was cleared eventually, the committee hearings had an impact on him. He was beginning to realize that the time had come to retire from public service.[46] After World War II ended, Tugwell submitted his resignation to President Truman in 1946, thereby ending a long, hard, and significant five years as governor of Puerto Rico.

In retrospect, there is little doubt that what Tugwell did in Puerto Rico was to demonstrate his abilities as an administrator and to apply his ideas, especially those of the Fourth Power, in a concrete way. Also, his tenure as governor was a success from whatever perspective one wanted to take. Not only did he bring the Puerto Rican people through the war, but he assisted in changing much of their political and economic situation. In many ways that were similar to his actions as an administrator in the New Deal, Tugwell translated his theories, especially on planning, into programs. Whether it was with the Planning Act of 1942, or the various developmental authorities, or the Budget Bureaus, it was Tugwell the practical economist and planner, and not simply the theoretician, who was attempting to demonstrate the feasibility of his ideas. And, in so doing, he explicitly demonstrated that he believed planning could work only if it was directional, holistic, and apolitical. For all practical purposes, Tugwell's resignation as governor ended his public service career. He returned to private life and remained there. However, this time he did not go into the business world. Instead, he returned to academe.

NOTES

1. Rexford Tugwell, "The Future of National Planning," *New Republic* 89 (December 9, 1936): 162-64.
2. Ibid.
3. Ibid.

4. Rexford Tugwell, diary, folder "Introduction," pp. 34-37, Tugwell papers, FDR Library, box 30. Before his resignation took effect, Tugwell had convinced Roosevelt and Wallace to transfer the RA into the Department of Agriculture. In light of the attacks on him and the RA throughout 1936, Tugwell believed this was the only way to make certain it would survive.

5. Tugwell, diary, folder "Diary 1935," May 19, 30, 31, 1935, and June 5, 1936, pp. 91, 97-98, 103-104, 106, all in Tugwell papers, FDR Library, box 32. Tugwell's ideas on Congress and the Supreme Court extended beyond 1936. See Rexford Tugwell to the president, July 21, 1937, Tugwell papers, folder "New Deal Materials, 1937," FDR Library, box 41.

6. Tugwell believed that, after the *Schechter* decision, the Cohen-Corcoran group, expressing the Brandeisian atomistic philosophy, were influencing the president. See, for example, Tugwell, diary, folder "Diary 1935," May 19, 1935, and diary, folder "Introduction," p. 16, both in Tugwell papers, FDR Library, boxes 32 and 30, respectively. See Chapter 5 for a more detailed discussion of this theme.

7. Tugwell, diary, folder "Introduction," pp. 34-37, Tugwell papers, FDR Library, box 30; Bernard Sternsher, *Rexford Tugwell and the New Deal* (New Brunswick, N.J.: Rutgers University Press, 1964), 322-23. An interesting point of information is that as early as January 1936, Raymond Moley was worried about Tugwell's future after he resigned from the New Deal. Despite his disagreement with him, Moley felt that Tugwell had something to offer economics and Columbia University. See Raymond Moley to H. Lee McBain, January 21, 1936, Felix Frankfurter papers, Library of Congress, box 84.

8. Rexford Tugwell, "Summary of Conference Meetings," December 24, 1937, and December 30, 1937, both in Charles Taussig papers, FDR Library, box 30.

9. Tugwell's attempts to influence policy, or at least to stay in touch, were also demonstrated by his keeping in touch with Mordecai Ezekiel. See Mordecai Ezekiel to Dr. Rexford Tugwell, April 11, 1939, Tugwell papers, folder "Ezekiel, M.," FDR Library, box 7; Ellis Hawley, *The New Deal and the Problem of Monopoly* (N.J.: Princeton University Press, 1966), 395-98.

10. Rexford Tugwell, "City Planning Commission," *New York Advancing: World's Fair Edition* (1939): 9; Will Alexander, "Reminiscences," p. 633, Oral History Research Office, Columbia University.

11. Tugwell, "City Planning Commission," pp. 6, 9; Tugwell, "Planning in New York City," *Planner's Journal* 6 (1940): 33-34; Tugwell, "Implementing the General Interest," *Public Administration Review* 1 (Autumn 1940): 32, 34-35; Mark Gelfand, "Rexford G. Tugwell and the Frustration of Planning in New York City," *Journal of the American Planning Association* 51 (Spring 1985): 152.

12. Rexford Tugwell to August Heckscher, February 9, 1977, Tugwell papers, folder "He-Hi," FDR Library, box 10; Tugwell, "LaGuardia: Good Government Can Be Mismanagement," in E. C. Banfield, ed., *Urban Government: A Reader*

in Politics and Administration (New York: Free Press of Glencoe, 1961), 284-91; Tugwell, *The Art of Politics* (Garden City, N.Y.: Doubleday, 1960), 27-33, 103-04.

13. Mark Gelfand, "Politics and the Public Interest: LaGuardia, Moses, Tugwell and Planning in New York City, 1936-1941," preliminary draft, Spring 1977, Boston College, pp. 18-19, 25-26, in Tugwell papers, FDR Library, box 79; Gelfand, "Tugwell and the Frustration of Planning," p. 153.

14. Gelfand, "Tugwell and the Frustration of Planning," p. 153.

15. Rexford Tugwell to Edward Banfield, March 17, 1971, Tugwell papers, folder "Banfield, Edward C.," FDR Library, box 2; Tugwell papers, folder "City Planning Commission," FDR Library, box 5; Tugwell to August Heckscher, February 9, 1977, Tugwell papers, FDR Library, box 10; Tugwell, diary, folder "11/17/39-12/30/40," December 16, 1939, Tugwell papers, FDR Library, box 32.

16. Tugwell, diary, folder "11/17/39-12/30/40," December 30, 1940, p. 74, Tugwell papers, FDR Library, box 32; Gelfand, "Politics and the Public Interest," pp. 36-37; Gelfand, "Tugwell and the Frustration of Planning," p. 154.

17. Tugwell, diary, folder "Nov. 1939-December 1941," April 17, 1940, pp. 141-42, Tugwell papers, FDR Library, box 32; Rexford Tugwell to Dear Bob, n.d., folder "Moses, Robert," Tugwell papers, FDR Library, box 15; Tugwell to Robert Moses, May 22, 1940, and Rexford Tugwell to R. Childs, July 14, 1942, both in Tugwell papers, FDR Library, box 5; Tugwell, "The Moses Effect," in Banfield, *Urban Government*, pp. 462-72. See also Robert Caro, *The Power Broker: Robert Moses and the Fall of New York* (New York: Alfred Knopf, 1974), p. 599.

18. Rexford Tugwell, "When the USHA Buys Land," *New Republic* 100 (October 25, 1939): 341-42; Fiorello LaGuardia to Rexford Tugwell, October 20, 1939, and Tugwell to mayor, memorandum, December 22, 1939, both in Tugwell papers, FDR Library, box 5; Gelfand, "Tugwell and the Frustration of Planning," pp. 154-55; Gelfand, "Politics and the Public Interest," pp. 41-45.

19. Rexford Tugwell to Fiorello LaGuardia, December 22, 1939, Tugwell papers, FDR Library, box 5; Gelfand, "Tugwell and the Frustration of Planning," pp. 155-56.

20. Tugwell, diary, folder "11/17/39-12/30/40," July 13, 1940, p. 42, Tugwell papers, FDR Library, box 32; Tugwell, "Remarks by R. G. Tugwell, Chairman, City Planning Commission," folder "Citizens Housing Council," Tugwell papers, FDR Library, box 5.

21. Rexford Tugwell to Aba Khoushy, January 8, 1952, folder "Ki-Kl," Tugwell papers, FDR Library, box 12; Tugwell, diary, folder "11/17/39-12/30/40," December 30, 1940, p. 74, Tugwell papers, FDR Library, box 32; Gelfand, "Tugwell and the Frustration of Planning," p. 156.

22. Tugwell, diary, folder "Nov. 1939-Dec. 1941," April 17, 1941, Tugwell papers, FDR Library, box 32; Rexford Tugwell to Robert Moses, May 22, 1940, Tugwell papers, FDR Library, box 5; Tugwell to Dear Bob, n.d., Tugwell papers,

FDR Library, box 15; Gelfand, "Tugwell and the Frustration of Planning," p. 158; Gelfand, "Politics and the Public Interest," 61-71; Tugwell, "The Moses Effect," pp. 462-72.

23. Tugwell, "Implementing the General Interest," pp. 37, 39, 40-43, 45-48.

24. Tugwell, "When the USHA Buys Land," 341-42; Rexford Tugwell, "The Real Estate Dilemma," *Public Administration Review* 2 (Winter 1942): 27-29, 33-36, 38-39; Tugwell, "Implementing the General Interest," pp. 42-48.

25. Rexford Tugwell, "Notes on the Bankruptcy of Cities," n.d., pp. 40-46, 53-59, 65-87, Tugwell papers, FDR Library, box 70.

26. Cleveland Rodgers, "The Reminiscences of Cleveland Rodgers," pp. 193ff., Oral History Research Office, Columbia University.

27. Rexford Tugwell, "The Fourth Power," *Planning and Civic Comment* (April-June 1939): 2-7.

28. Ibid., p. 8.

29. Ibid., pp. 8-17.

30. Ibid., pp. 18-26.

31. Ibid., pp. 27-30.

32. Rexford Tugwell, "The Superpolitical," *Journal of Social Philosophy* 5 (January 1940): 97-114.

33. Tugwell, "Implementing the General Interest," pp. 34-35.

34. Rexford Tugwell, "The Directive," *Journal of Social Philosophy and Jurisprudence* (October 1941): 5-37. Quote is from p. 12.

35. Rexford Tugwell, "After the New Deal: 'We Have Bought Ourselves Time to Think,' " *New Republic* 99 (July 26, 1939): 323-25; Tugwell, "Must We Draft Roosevelt?" *New Republic* 102 (May 13, 1940): 630-633.

36. Rexford Tugwell, diary, folder "Diary—March/December 1934," March 6, 1934, Tugwell papers, FDR Library, box 31; Tugwell, diary, folder "1935," January 23, 1935, Tugwell papers, FDR Library, box 32; Tugwell, "Reminiscences," pp. 55-56, Oral History Research Office, Columbia University; Tugwell, *The Stricken Land* (Garden City, N.Y.: Doubleday, 1947), 62; Harold Ickes, *The Secret Diary of Harold Ickes: The Lowering Clouds, 1938-41* (New York: Simon and Schuster, 1954), 6.

37. Tugwell, *The Stricken Land*, pp. 94-107; Rexford Tugwell, ed., *Puerto Rican Public Papers of R. G. Tugwell, Governor* (San Juan: Service Office of the Government of Puerto Rico, Printing Division, 1945), 291-347; Enrique Lugo Silva, *The Tugwell Administration in Puerto Rico, 1941-1946* (Rio Piedras, P.R.: Editorial Cultura, T.G., S.A., 1955), 17-18.

38. Tugwell, diary, folder "Nov. 1939-Dec. 1941," June 4, 1941, p. 180, Tugwell papers, FDR Library, box 32; Harold Ickes to Franklin D. Roosevelt, July 28, 1941, and Franklin D. Roosevelt, "Memorandum for the Secretary of Interior," July 30, 1941, with attached letter, Franklin D. Roosevelt to Mr. Bolívar Pagán, August 7, 1941, all in FDR papers, FDR Library, OF-6-S; Tugwell, *The Stricken Land*, pp. 108-45. Tugwell was also considered for a job in the Department of the Interior in Forestry and Insular Possessions. See Tugwell papers, folder "Ickes, Harold, 1937-1965," FDR Library, box 11, especially September

18, 1939, letter. See also Tugwell, diary, folder 11/17/39-12/30/40," July 30, 1940, PM entry, p. 51, and November 17, 1940, Tugwell papers, FDR Library, box 32.

39. While Tugwell did much to help solve the immediate wartime problems of Puerto Rico, he wasn't alone. On March 9, 1942, the United States and England established the Anglo-American Caribbean Commission, cochaired by Charles Taussig and Sir Guy Stockdale. Although concerned with the immediate food supply and other problems caused by war, the commission went beyond that to deal with the long-term problems of the Caribbean. Tugwell, as governor of Puerto Rico and a friend of Taussig, was involved from the early days, although he and Taussig eventually split over the commission. See Tugwell papers, folder "Anglo-American Commission," FDR Library, box 44; Rexford Tugwell, "The Caribbean Commission: Notes on Its Beginnings," in A. Curtis Wilgus, ed., *The Caribbean: British, Dutch, French, United States* (Gainesville: University of Florida Press, 1958), 262-75.

40. Tugwell, diary, folder "Diary 1942," Tugwell papers, FDR Library, box 32; Tugwell, *The Stricken Land*, pp. 148-54, 170-82, 194-220, 228-55; Charles Goodsell, *Administration of a Revolution: Executive Reform in Puerto Rico Under Governor Tugwell, 1941-1946* (Cambridge, Mass.: Harvard University Press, 1965), 2, 19-23; Silva, *Tugwell Administration in Puerto Rico*, pp. 43-45.

41. Tugwell, *The Stricken Land*, pp. 262-63, 346-52; Rexford Tugwell, "Puerto Rico also Serves," *New Republic* 107 (July 13, 1942): 51-52; Tugwell, "Little Brother's Growing Up!" *World Week*, n.d., 8-9, in Tugwell papers, FDR Library, box 63; Goodsell, *Administration of Revolution*, pp. 21-23, 90-139; Lugo-Silva, *Tugwell Administration*, pp. 126-31.

42. See Tugwell papers, folder "Bettmann, Alfred," FDR Library, box 3, for detailed correspondence on the Bettmann draft as well as a final draft copy of the bill. Alfred Bettmann was sent by the National Resources Planning Board, at Tugwell's request, to help in drafting the planning law. Tugwell thought the NRPB was a step in the right direction for planning, but that it was serving primarily as a research tool. See Tugwell, diary, folder "11/17/39-12/30/40," July 12, 1940, p. 41, Tugwell papers, FDR Library, box 32. Tugwell disliked the TVA because he felt it was piecemeal planning, a surrender to the states, and, under David E. Lilienthal's direction, a supplier of electrical power. See Rexford Tugwell to Oscar Chapman, February 17, 1949, Tugwell papers, folder "Chapman, Oscar," FDR Library, box 5, and Rexford Tugwell to California Power Users Association, Att: Walter Packard, June 21, 1965, Tugwell papers, folder "Packard, Walter E.," FDR Library, box 18.

43. Tugwell, *The Stricken Land*, pp. 256-61; Rexford Tugwell, *The Place of Planning in Society* (San Juan, P.R.: Government Service Offices, Printing Division, 1954), 7-14; Goodsell, *Administration of Revolution*, pp. 144-47.

44. Tugwell, *The Place of Planning*, pp. 14-16; Goodsell, *Administration of Revolution*, pp. 147-49.

45. See Tugwell papers, folder "Insular Affairs: Bell Commission, 1941-1945," FDR Library, box 11; Tugwell, diary, folder "March-June, 1944," May 30, 1944,

May 31, 1944, June 3, 1944, June 4, 1944, all in Tugwell papers, FDR Library, box 33; Tugwell, diary, folder "January-June 1943," Tugwell papers, FDR Library, box 33, on Chávez hearings.

46. Tugwell papers, folder "Truman, Harry S.," FDR Library, box 26; Tugwell, *The Stricken Land*, pp. 426-70, 512-35, 547-60; Lugo-Silva, *Tugwell Administration*, pp. 96-104; Rexford Tugwell, "In Defense of Puerto Rico," *New Republic* 114 (April 15, 1946): 509-12. Tugwell, in subsequent years, kept close watch on Puerto Rico. See, for example, "The View from Puerto Rico," *Nation* 192 (June 10, 1961): 496-97.

7

Return to Academe: 1946–1979

I am an incorrigible optimist . . . I anticipate survival. . . . Penetration
of the inner and outer worlds of matter, changes in the control of
life and health, discovery of new sources of energy—all these and
other advances are happening rapidly. . . . [I] must have been part of
what went on—and most of it has been progress.

Rexford G. Tugwell to George Haessler, August 10, 1977,
Tugwell papers, FDR Library, box 10

Written less than two years before his death, the above statement is
an excellent commentary on the inner dynamics of Rexford Tugwell.
Looking back over his life and how far mankind and the world had
changed in his 85 years, Tugwell could conclude that he was an optimist, anticipating survival even though he had experienced moments of
despair after the dropping of the atomic bomb. The world had changed,
was changing, new sources of life and energy were being uncovered,
and Tugwell was excited at such prospects. Assessing what had occurred in his lifetime and his contribution to it, he was certain that
progress had indeed been made and that he had played some role in
it. After 1946, upon leaving the governorship of Puerto Rico, he returned to where it had all begun: academe.

From 1946 until his death in 1979, Tugwell remained within academic life, making only a brief foray into the political world in 1948.
As a public servant, Tugwell's career was over. In the early 1960s, he
would serve as a consultant on Latin American affairs and write a
weekly column on world events, but it was all done within the con-
fines of academe. In many respects, Tugwell's permanent transition
from public service to the university proved quite beneficial. His post-
1946 years were, from a publishing viewpoint, comparable with the
1920s, even surpassing that prolific part of his career. In his last 33
years, Tugwell published 15 books, wrote over 100 articles and book
reviews, and gave quite a few speeches. His contributions to scholar-

ship, public service, and professional life were noted on a number of occasions with prestigious awards, including the Woodrow Wilson Foundation Award (1958), the silver medal of the American Association of Planning (1967), the Bancroft Award for *The Brains Trust* (1969), an honorary degree from the University of Pennsylvania (1971), and the Veblen-Commons Award (1978). After so many years, his worth had been recognized publicly and officially, something Tugwell must have relished.[1]

In all these activities after 1946, two significant characteristics stand out. First of all, Tugwell returned to academe not as a professor of economics but as a professor of political science. His disillusionment with economics as a profession that failed to confront the realities of the world and concentrated instead on classical theories, selfish profit maximization, and promotion of a business ethic he had fought so long against explained, to a large degree, why Tugwell now saw himself as a political scientist. Also, this transformation was caused by Tugwell's background. By 1946, his career as a public servant had been impressive: member of the Brains Trust, assistant and under secretary of agriculture, director of the Resettlement Administration, chairman of the New York City Planning Commission, and governor of Puerto Rico. From whatever perspective one took, Tugwell spoke on issues that he not only thought about but also had extensively experienced. Not surprisingly, his writings reflected this in their concentration on such topics as the presidency, the American Constitution, and planning.

Second, Tugwell's post-1946 academic career was more diverse than previously. Unlike the 1920s, when he had served on the faculty of Columbia University, Tugwell moved around regularly after 1946. Unlike his 1937 experience, when he resigned from the New Deal and found Columbia University and other academic institutions not wanting his services, he was in demand after his resignation as governor of Puerto Rico. A chronicle of his professional appointments clearly illustrates this.[2] He served as a professor of political science at the University of Chicago (1946-1957), director of the Planning Program at the University of Chicago (1946-1952), visiting professor at the London School of Economics (1949-1950), Hillman lecturer at Howard University (1959), consultant to the chancellor of the University of Puerto Rico (1961-1964), professor at Columbia University summer session (1962), visiting fellow at the Center for the Study of Democratic Institutions (1964-1965), research professor of political science at Southern Illinois University (1965-1966), and senior fellow,

Center for the Study of Democratic Institutions (1966-1979). It was an impressive academic career, even more so coming on the heels of an eventful life in the New Deal, New York, and Puerto Rico.

While Tugwell made his mark at all the institutions where he worked after 1946, his appointments at Chicago, Howard, Puerto Rico, and the Center for the Study of Democratic Institutions stand out. At the University of Chicago, for example, he was able to implement his ideas on planning in a practical fashion. Tugwell's contribution here was developing a graduate program for the teaching and training of planners. Involved in developing the curriculum and recruiting the full-time faculty to teach in the program, Tugwell worked hard to make planning a professional discipline with all the academic appurtenances. His success in this endeavor was clearly demonstrated by the University of Chicago's coming to be known not only as a pioneer in the professionalization of planning but also as one of the most renowned institutions for students of planning.[3] Not everything at Chicago, of course, was easily accomplished. Budgets, administration policy, and departmental differences all introduced Tugwell to university life again. Nevertheless, like many professors, he took it in stride, completing more of his program than he may have thought at the time.

In a similar vein, Tugwell's presentation of the Hillman Lectures at Howard University in 1959 was significant. Discussing the development of the democratic process, Tugwell analyzed the development of the democratic idea in the United States by tracing it from the framers of the Constitution through the succession of American presidents to the problems of the nation in the 1950s. His thinking on the presidency, Franklin D. Roosevelt, the American Constitution, and the U.S. position in the Cold War world of the 1950s had replaced his earlier concentration on classical economics, laissez-faire, and the American business system. He was moving beyond his earlier thinking. The Hillman Lectures, coinciding with his publications, were a perfect illustration of Tugwell's development.[4]

In Puerto Rico in the 1960s, Tugwell's activities included serving as a consultant to Chancellor Jaime Benítez of the University of Puerto Rico on developing a program "of instruction and research relative to the economics of development in Latin America."[5] Tugwell applied himself enthusiastically to this task, presenting ideas on how the University of Puerto Rico might establish its own criteria for admission of students, developing graduate programs, and working with junior colleges.[6] In line with this, he accepted William O. Douglas' offer in

1962 to serve as a Parvin Foundation visitor to Venezuela, studying education there and elsewhere in Latin America.[7] Tugwell's activities in both capacities and as a columnist for the *San Juan Star* demonstrated his commitment to the people of Puerto Rico and Latin America as well as his attempt to do all he could to help, even as an professional consultant and guest commentator.

If Tugwell's work at Chicago and Puerto Rico showed that he was still active, it was his tenure at the Center for the Study of Democratic Institutions in Santa Barbara, California, that was the ultimate ideal for him. The Center provided him with the perfect environment for what he had been and what he always was. Tugwell did not simply "cerebrate." Rather, he thought, read, discussed, relied on his experience to constantly probe deeper into issues, events, personalities, problems, and whatever else occupied his attention. In doing so, he was persistently evolving in his thinking and perceptions. From 1964 until his death in 1979, he was at a place where he did all of this every day. Through working papers, conferences with the leading experts on the issue under study, seminars, and discussions, Tugwell probed to the depths of the topics he was so concerned with—the American constitutional system, the presidency, planning, and the world's survival. And, in all of it, there was no doubt in his mind that the Center and its members were making their "contribution to the world by studying what is and what can be."[8] Much of what Tugwell wrote at the Center was published, showing even more convincingly how much he evolved in his thinking, especially on the above issues.

Chicago, Howard, Puerto Rico, Center—in all his activities at these places Tugwell as an academic was still trying to serve mankind actively. From 1946 to 1979, he did what academics normally do: teaching, research, and service. Only once in that 33-year period did he venture back into the political realm. In 1948, Tugwell joined Henry Wallace's campaign for the presidency.

Tugwell's support of Wallace's Progressive party bid for the presidency stemmed from his disillusionment with Harry Truman as well as his own activist personality. In Tugwell's opinion, by 1948 Truman's record was so bad, and the future of the world in so much jeopardy, in light of the atomic bomb, that something had to be done. Feeling that he "belonged in it," Tugwell joined the ranks of Wallace's supporters and served on the platform committee. Then and later, Tugwell believed that the 1948 Progressives "were starting a true Progressive movement, worthy to succeed that of LaFollette and his co-workers" and hoping to purify "American political life."[9] That didn't happen.

Upset with the evasive actions and unrealistic demands of the Americans for Democratic Action, Tugwell thought Wallace's bid for the presidency was designed to restore all that was good in the New Deal as well as to preserve personal liberty, but that it was seriously hurt by Communist infiltration of the party. He—and Wallace, as far as Tugwell knew—always considered the Communists to be "dangerous, inimical to democracy, and interested only in subversion."[10] Tugwell refused to work with them and objected to Wallace about their infiltration of the Progressive party, but it was to no avail. Without broad-based support, Wallace's defeat was inevitable. Afterward, Tugwell quietly acquiesced in Truman's victory, only to find that his participation in 1948, when added to his well-established reputation, caused him some problems.[11]

Given his reputation as a New Deal radical along with his 1948 Progressive party participation, it is not surprising that, as McCarthyism started to grow, Tugwell would be considered suspect. While teaching at the University of Chicago, Tugwell was summoned to appear before the Broyles Committee on Un-American Activities of the Legislature of Illinois. Like many other individuals at that time, Tugwell had to defend himself, something he did quite calmly and persuasively.[12] It was the last time he publicly "suffered" for his beliefs and opinions.

Academics do research and are expected to publish the results of their efforts. Tugwell did just that after 1946. From the time he left Puerto Rico as governor until a few months before his death, he wrote prolifically on everything from American foreign policy in the Cold War to the failure of the American political system to the passing of America's simple life. He also wrote about himself and his experience in public service In all of his writings Tugwell concentrated on four major topics and themes: the atomic bomb, the need for national and global planning, Franklin D. Roosevelt and the evolution of the American presidency, and the American constitutional system. He believed that all of America's history and its future could be understood by examining these subjects. Of the four, the one that truly gripped him emotionally and permeated much of his post-1946 writings was the atomic bomb.

No other event in American or world history affected Tugwell as profoundly as did the dropping of atomic bombs on Hiroshima and Nagasaki in August 1945. It filled him with anger, disgust, and occasionally, despair. In his opinion, the bomb represented a tragic failure on the part of mankind, the United States, and his own generation to use its creative powers in constructive ways. Instead of technology helping to ease man's life, instead of facilitating the realization of an abundant life for all people and especially Americans, it was used to destroy life. He believed that the bomb only led to other bombs that were more powerful and more deadly. Mankind could now destroy itself a hundred times over anytime it wanted to and, in view of the tensions of the Cold War, there seemed more of a chance that it might happen. Tugwell even felt a personal responsibility for the bomb because he had always promulgated the importance of developing newer and more efficient technology. At all costs, he felt, this use of technology had to be stopped. Perhaps the only way to do it would be to create a world government as soon as possible.[13]

As a practical matter, Tugwell consistently recognized that establishing a world government might be impossible. In order for it to happen, nations would have to give up some, if not all, of their sovereignty; the people of the world would have to think in collective, world terms and not in nationalistic ones; and international diplomacy would have to change radically. Nevertheless, in spite of these difficulties and in view of the ever-growing possibility of world nuclear war, an effort in this direction had to be made before mankind destroyed itself. In personal terms, Tugwell believed this meant joining the Committee to Frame a World Constitution.[14]

Organized in November 1945, the Committee consisted of Robert Hutchins, Richard McKeon, Giuseppe Borgese, Mortimer J. Adler, William E. Hocking, Wilber Katz, James Landis, Charles McIlwain, Reinhold Niebuhr, Robert Redfield, Beardsley Ruml, and Rexford Tugwell. Concerned with the growing tensions existing in the world and the possibility of a nuclear war, its purpose was to devise a tentative constitution for a world government that would attempt to preserve peace and harmony. Meeting frequently throughout the years 1945-1947, it completed its task in March 1948, when it published its "Preliminary Draft of a World Constitution." As its name implies, the draft was only a proposal, a working document that was supposed to serve as a basis for discussion and consideration.[15] Essentially, the draft called for the creation of a federated world government composed of the Federal Convention, the president, the Council, and three special bodies (a House of Nationalities and States, a Syndical (functional) Senate, and an Institute of Science, Education and Culture), the Grand Tribunal, the Supreme Court, the Tribune of the People, and the Chamber of Guardians. Each branch and leader of the government, moreover, had its powers and authority defined, its term of office determined, and the relationships to the others delineated.

More important, as far as Tugwell was concerned, was the creation of a Planning Agency, whose purpose was to estimate the needs of the world and to bring world society into accord with its possibilities. It was to consist of 21 members who were to be appointed by the president for terms of 12 years. Their duties, although only briefly sketched, were to envisage income, prepare budgets for expenditure, and approve or reject all plans "for the improvement of the world's physical facilities" and plans for the productive exploitation of resources and inventions.[16] Through the Planning Agency, it was hoped, especially by Tugwell, not only would the world's needs be calculated and met, but the people of the world would attain a higher standard of living.

Although in retrospect the draft seemed utopian and unworkable, it was still a significant document as far as Tugwell was concerned. First of all, it demonstrated how much the bomb affected him, how much he worried about the world's survival, and how far he would go to assure the continuation of the human race. Also, it demonstrated clearly that he now considered planning feasible on a global scale. Only through a global, "Fourth Power" type of agency could the economic problems of the world be resolved quickly and efficiently. And, finally, by signing his name to the document, Tugwell demonstrated again that he was still evolving in his understanding of planning in the theoretical and practical senses. In committing himself to world planning, however, he did not deny the importance of national planning. In fact, while working on the world constitution, he also wrote quite a bit on planning in the United States.

In all of his writings on planning in the United States after 1946, Tugwell consistently expressed a new sense of urgency and immediacy about what had to be done. Instead of talking about how "wonderful" planning is, he told American planners to get down to the details of a planning program and work out an implementation procedure. Although theory was important, practice was essential. In fact, Tugwell felt, in the late 1940s and 1950s, that few planners did not know what planning really meant. Most now agreed that

Planning is no more than scientific appraisal of resources and energies and evolvement of a one-best-way which is embodied in a development plan and budget, together with an outline of ways to proceed.[17]

Most also agreed that planning was simply a way of "trying to bring about a state of nature, a balance between man and his physical world," and that the way this would be accomplished would be through voluntarism, not compulsion.[18] The problem, however, was how to accomplish all this quickly and efficiently. Although he never doubted that it would be resolved, Tugwell was worried about how long it would take, and for that reason he suggested some of his own answers.

In his thinking, the answer lay in the theory of planning itself. Before planning could be implemented, the planner had to recognize that planning was simply a way of devising means for direction, that it dealt with the "whole organism" in a spatial and temporal sense, and that it relied on scientific and behavioral-psychological techniques.[19] It had to conceive of society as a human being with a collective mind that was trying to survive. In this sense, planning and the Planning Agency was, and is

a coagulator, a putter-together, a conjoiner which brings hopes into focus and promises into possibility, a protector of reason among competing imaginative conceptions, a reducer of vague expectations to measured charts, tables, and maps, a filler-out of strategies with the stuff of tactical reality. It is sometimes a kill-joy; but sometimes also a fulfiller of dreams.[20]

Precision was and is its trademark; independence, its means to survive; and expertness, its vital center. Tugwell also argued that planning and the Planning Agency, by their very nature, were opposed to the way the American government operated. Instead of promoting conflict and special interests, they relied on cooperation and coordination for the general interest of the people.[21] And, in so doing, they naturally fostered the enmity of the legislative branch of the American government. In Tugwell's thinking, all this had to change—the government had to accept planning and its agencies as well as its philosophy. The American people, too, would have to accept the collective philosophy with its emphasis on cooperation, coordination, and balance. If it did, if the government and the people endorsed planning, then, Tugwell believed, the United States would achieve its phenomenal economic potential. But if it did not, he feared for its survival.

Tugwell was so emphatic about the need for planning within the United States, as well as so certain that it could be done, that, less than a year before his death, he wrote an article entitled "Planning and Democracy." In many ways a superb summary of everything he had been saying for so many years, it boiled everything down to four basic rules. Recognizing that planning and democracy could coexist, he suggested that planning not be wholly entrusted to either the president or Congress, that government economic planning must involve all vital areas of public welfare in its designs, that planning must be separated from other activities associated with it, such as research, and that there must be a development plan encompassing the nation's aspirations.[22]

In evaluating America's history, Tugwell consistently felt there was some hope that all of this would happen. The NRA, the National Resources Planning Board, the NYCPC, the Puerto Rican Planning Board, and the Employment Act of 1946, which established the Presidential Council of Economic Advisers, were all steps in the right direction, steps that now had to be expanded upon and developed by American planners.[23] However, at the same time that he saw hope, Tugwell also was worried by what was going on in the United States. Not only were business, labor, and government getting too big in power and responsibility, but American political leaders seemed incapable of leading the country effectively. Presidents Truman, Eisenhower, Kennedy, Johnson, and Nixon all had basic weaknesses in their leadership potential and suffered failures in their domestic and foreign policies. Instead of directing the country toward planning and survival, they seemed to be moving the nation toward socialism, nuclear war, and annihilation. At all costs, this had to be stopped, and Tugwell felt the only way to do it was to elect another Franklin D. Roosevelt as president and to revise the basic structure of government by rewriting the Constitution.[24]

Tugwell, of course, did not reach these conclusions overnight. In fact, his call for another Franklin D. Roosevelt, as well as his recommending a new Constitution, were the natural consequences of his evolutionary thinking on American politics, the American economy, planning, and his own institutionalism. Similarly, in the post-1946 period Tugwell analyzed the development of the American political system, especially regarding the presidency, before reaching these conclusions.

Whether in the Hillman Lectures (1959), *The Enlargement of the Presidency* (1960), *How They Became President* (1964), *Grover Cleveland* (1968), or *The Presidency Reappraised* (1977), along with review articles on the Kennedy and Johnson presidencies, the same themes continually surfaced in Tugwell's writings.[25] In assessing American presidents, Tugwell argued that a majority of America's chief executives sought the office; some were not qualified to be president (Buchanan, Harding, and Coolidge); and only a few, such as Franklin D. Roosevelt, Woodrow Wilson, Abraham Lincoln, James Polk, Andrew Jackson, John F. Kennedy, and Lyndon Johnson, were exceptional. Others—Thomas Jefferson, George Washington, John Quincy Adams, Theodore Roosevelt, James Madison, and James Monroe—

exhibited qualities of strong leadership.[26] Tugwell singled out a few as particularly inept or as presidents who offended him in some way, such as Harry Truman and Dwight Eisenhower.[27] While not profound in its depth of analysis, Tugwell's assessments reinforced what he thought was needed: another FDR.

To explain Tugwell's concentration on Franklin D. Roosevelt after 1946 is not as difficult as it may seem. Perhaps the simplest explanation is that Tugwell truly loved the man he had served so faithfully from 1932 on. His love for Roosevelt, moreover, while deep, was not blind. More like the bond between a husband and wife, Tugwell might criticize Roosevelt for not doing what he wanted, but it was always done in a way that could explain the president's failure.

Although he continually argued that Roosevelt failed to resolve the depression, failed to implement planning, and failed to facilitate the acceptance of collectivism, Tugwell still believed that Roosevelt and the New Deal had accomplished quite a bit. Whether it was in the NRA, AAA, RA, or any other program, Roosevelt was trying to prepare the American people for what had to be done vis-à-vis the American economy and its need for planning. If Roosevelt failed— and Tugwell readily admitted that he did—it was not because of a personality or leadership defect, but because the opposition to him, especially among businessmen, was too strong or the American people were not ready for what he wanted. As a leader, moreover, Tugwell believed that Roosevelt was unique. He was experimental, pragmatic, democratic, compromising, and realistic. Capable of dealing with any crisis situation, he exuded confidence and strength of character to such an extent that the American people elected him four times. In the post-World War II world, no American president could equal him in ability or understanding. For that reason, Tugwell believed, the United States had much to worry about. Until a "new Roosevelt" came along, the people would have to work alone and try their best to compel their leaders to act in their interest.[28]

Even if another Roosevelt appeared, Tugwell was no longer certain he could do enough. Since he would be constrained by politics and restrained by Congress and the Supreme Court, Tugwell concluded that a restructuring of the Constitution was necessary.

After 1946, Tugwell consistently and persistently argued that the Constitution had to be updated to coincide with the realities of twentieth-century American life. A product of the eighteenth century, it had little or no relevance for the twentieth century. More important, Tugwell believed that the Constitution, by establishing the tripartite form of government with all its checks and balances, had continually served as a major obstacle to the implementation of a "planned economic system." The Constitution sustained the American value system of laissez-faire, blocked Roosevelt in his efforts to implement planning, and prevented a national planning agency from being created. In what it had done and continued to do, Tugwell believed, it kept the American people from achieving their economic potential. For that reason, it had to be changed and made more flexible.[29]

In the preamble to Tugwell's new Constitution, the purpose of this new government was to "welcome the future and create an adequate and self-repairing government." Following this introductory statement, Tugwell delineated the rights and responsibilities of the nation's citizens. Very much like the Bill of Rights of the 1789 Constitution, Tugwell's Bill of Rights was built into the original document, telling people what they could and should do. From there, Tugwell got down to the details of the government.

He recommended that the new Constitution create the "Newstates of America." Each Newstate, numbering "no less than 5 percent of the whole people," would have a constitution, a governor-general, a legislature, and planning, administrative, and judicial systems. Each Newstate, moreover, would have its own "electoral Overseers," who would supervise and organize the elections. They would have the right to charter subsidiary governments and to levy taxes, and would be responsible for administering all public services not reserved to the government of the Newstates of America. They would not, however, have the right to coin money, provide for the payment of debts in anything but legal tender, or tax exports and/or quarantine imports from other Newstates. If they should in any way violate the Constitution, the Senate of the Newstates would have the right to suspend them from their duties.[30]

For the government of the Newstates, the new Constitution would establish six branches of government: electoral, planning, presidential, legislative, regulatory, and judicial. Each branch would have its own powers and responsibilities. The electoral branch, headed by an overseer, would be concerned with the election of officials and the identification of all national parties, while the planning branch, headed by a Planning Board of 11 members appointed by the president, would be concerned with preparing 6- and 12-year development plans, the annual budget, and any program designed to "advance . . . the excellence of national life." The presidential branch, headed by a president serving a term of nine years, would be concerned with executing the laws of the Newstates. The president would serve as the "head of their government, shaper of its commitments, expositor of its policies, and supreme commander of its protective forces." Working with the legislature, he would be assisted by two vice-presidents; chancellors of external, financial, legal, and military affairs; the Planning Board; the watchkeeper; and the National Regulatory Board.

The legislative branch would be concerned with formulating the laws of the Newstates of America. It would consist of two bodies, the Senate and the House of Representatives. The members of the former body, who would serve for life, would be distinguished citizens of the nation, such as former presidents and vice-presidents. Its responsibilities would be to elect a convener to preside over the Senate, to consider all measures approved by the House except the budget, to advise the president on matters of public interest, to declare a national emergency, and to elect a watchkeeper, who would "gather and organize information concerning the adequacy, competence, and integrity of governmental agencies and their personnel." The House of Representatives would consist of members elected by the people and would be "the original law-making body" in the Newstates of America. Everything from the levying of taxes to the expenditure of revenues to the operation and maintenance of publicly owned industries would come under the jurisdiction of the House.[31] The Senate and the House would work with the president in conducting the domestic and foreign policies of the nation.

The last two branches of the new government, the regulatory and the judicial, would have certain powers and responsibilities. The former, for example, would be headed by a national regulator and a National Regulatory Board; its primary purpose would be to regulate and control all industry and corporations. The judicial branch would consist of a principal justice of the Newstates of America, a Judicial Council, a Judicial Assembly, a High Court of Appeals, a High Court of the Constitution, and lower court systems. Essentially, the judicial branch would review the laws of the Newstates, the constitutions of the individual Newstates, and the Constitution. But its decisions, unlike the decisions of the Supreme Court of today, would not be final, since its primary purpose would not be to interpret the law but to review it. If the High Court of the Constitution, in attempting to decide whether a law is in accordance with the Constitution, cannot decide on the basis of the Constitution, it must return the law to the House for clarification. If the House fails to act in 90 days, then the Court is allowed to interpret. All in all, the judicial, like the other branches, would carry out the powers and responsibilities assigned to it by the Constitution and would be obliged to work with and coordinate its actions with those of the government itself.[32]

In assessing Tugwell's Constitution, there are two different perspectives one can take. The first is relatively easy. The Constitution can be viewed objectively and its author judged accordingly. From this point of view, one can criticize Tugwell for being a "wild-eyed academic" calling for the complete overhaul of the foundation of American society. Tugwell can be portrayed as being out of touch with reality, living in an ivory tower, and completely out of tune with American values, traditions, beliefs, and customs, and with the American people. The Constitution, in this regard, can be attacked from as many angles as one wants.

On the other hand, Tugwell's Constitution can be seen in light of who Tugwell was, where he came from, what he strove for, and what he wanted for the United States and its people. In evaluating the Constitution from this perspective, it is apparent that what Tugwell had done was to apply everything he had been thinking about, saying, and writing on planning, American politics, and American institutions for quite a number of years. Strongly believing in the absolute need for a coordinated, powerful, and holistic national government, he tried to create one without completely eliminating the good aspects of America's traditional democracy, especially its pluralism and theory of separation of powers.[33] This is, for example, why his Constitution replaced the states with Newstates; why the national government had six branches instead of three; and why the powers of each are clearly and explicitly defined.

In the Newstates of America, the national government was a coordinated structure, each branch working with the others. There would be no failure to precisely define the relationships among the three branches of government, as with the original Constitution. More important, instead of having the national government represent special-interest groups, it would represent the national interest. The electoral branch would supervise and organize the national elections and the national parties; the president, no longer a party chief, would execute the national laws in the national interest without worrying about re-election, since his term would be nine years; the legislative branch, both the Senate and the House, would make the national laws in the interests of general welfare; the judicial branch would review the national laws and not interpret them according to the individual justices' predilections; and the regulatory branch would regulate and control industry for the people's sake and not the individual businessman's. The planning branch would work on its own and with the other branches to develop the necessary expert plans that would assure the American people as a whole the high standard of living they deserve. All in all, Tugwell's Newstates government was not only to assure America's survival in the twentieth century, it was also to guarantee that the nation would reach ever higher levels of economic growth through planning. In Tugwell's thinking, this would happen, given the time and opportunity.

Not surprisingly, Tugwell's Constitution was criticized as an artificial, laboratory experiment having nothing to do with reality and not having much constructive to offer. It was a sad commentary that this perspective was taken instead of the other alternative, which saw the Newstates of America in terms of Tugwell himself.

What made the criticisms even more biting was that they came at the end of Tugwell's life. There was no doubt that the proposed Constitution was his last contribution to improving American life.[34] With his health declining and age having its effect, Tugwell entered Santa Barbara Cottage Hospital on June 19, 1979. Diagnosed as having cancer, he died less than a month later, on July 21, 1979. He was 88 years old. His long life, filled with controversy, public service, and academic achievement, was over.[35]

NOTES

1. Rexford G. Tugwell to Dennis O'Harrow, April 24, 1967, Tugwell papers, folder "O," FDR Library, box 17; Tugwell papers, folder "Bancroft Award," FDR Library, box 2; Martin Meyerson to Rex, February 12, 1971, and Tugwell to Martin, February 17, 1971, Tugwell papers, folder "Meyerson, Martin," FDR Library, box 15; Tugwell, "The Well-Ordered Economy: Remarks upon Receipt of the Veblen-Commons Award," *Journal of Economic Issues* 12 (June 1978): 243-49.

2. Rexford Tugwell, diary, folder "July-December, 1945," July 28, 1945, and August 3, 1945, Tugwell papers, FDR Library, box 34; "Professor R. G. Tugwell's Program for Session 1949-1950," Tugwell papers, folder "London School of Economics," FDR Library, box 14; Williston H. Lofton to Rexford G. Tugwell, October 22, 1959, and October 26, 1959, Tugwell papers, folder "Howard University, 1959," FDR Library, box 11; Tugwell to Norman F. Cantor, November 7, 1961, Tugwell papers, folder "Columbia University, 1940-1963," FDR Library, box 6; Jaime Benítez to Tugwell, April 18, 1961, Tugwell papers, folder "Benítez, Jaime," FDR Library, box 2; Tugwell to William O. Douglas, December 18, 1962, with memorandum to Parvin Foundation, Tugwell papers, folder "Albert Parvin Foundation," FDR Library, box 1; Tugwell to Jaime Bení-

tez and Jaime Benítez to Tugwell, October 19, 1964, Tugwell papers, folder "Benítez, Jaime," FDR Library, box 2.

3. Tugwell, diary, folder "July-December 1945," July 28 and August 3, 1945, Tugwell papers, FDR Library, box 34; Tugwell, journal, 1946, all handwritten, Tugwell papers, FDR Library, box 35; Tugwell, diary, folder "July-December, 1945," "Proposed University of Chicago Planning Center," Tugwell papers, FDR Library, box 34; Tugwell papers, subject file "University of Chicago," FDR Library, box 45; Harvey S. Perloff, *Education for Planning: City, State, and Regional* (repr. Greenwich, Conn.: Greenwood Press, 1977), 138-139, 153.

4. Rexford G. Tugwell, "The Hillman Lectures—Howard University, 1959," Tugwell papers, FDR Library, box 11.

5. Jaime Benítez to Rexford Tugwell, April 18, 1961, Tugwell papers, folder "Benítez, Jaime," FDR Library, box 2.

6. Rexford Tugwell, "Argument Preliminary to an Education Plan, 1961," Tugwell papers, FDR Library, box 77.

7. Rexford Tugwell to William O. Douglas, December 18, 1962, with memorandum, Tugwell papers, folder "The Albert Parvin Foundation," FDR Library, box 1.

8. Rexford G. Tugwell to Dr. Alexander Comfort, June 29, 1969, Tugwell papers, folder "Com-Cow," FDR Library, box 6. To cite all the working papers Tugwell wrote from 1964 to 1979 would be a small bibliography in itself. The reader is, therefore, referred to the following: Rexford G. Tugwell, senior fellow, memorandum to Chairman Moos, July 10, 1974, Tugwell papers, folder "Moos, Malcolm," FDR Library, box 15. See also Tugwell papers, folder "Center for the Study of Democratic Institutions," FDR Library, box 4, and boxes 77, 78, and 98.

9. Tugwell, Journal 1948, 1/19 entry, handwritten, Tugwell papers, FDR Library, box 35; Rexford G. Tugwell to Ernest C. Fackler, April 29, 1964, Tugwell papers, folder "Fa-Fe," FDR Library, box 8. See also Tugwell papers, folder "Progressive Party 1948," FDR Library, box 36.

10. Rexford Tugwell to Leon Henderson, chairman, ADA, January 29, 1948, Tugwell papers, folder "He-Hi," FDR Library, box 10; Tugwell to Fackler, April 29, 1964, Tugwell papers, FDR Library, box 8; Rexford G. Tugwell to John H. Thompson, September 30, 1954, Tugwell papers, folder "Th-To," FDR Library, box 26.

11. Rexford Tugwell, "Progressives and the Presidency," *The Progressive* (April 1949): 5-6.

12. Tugwell, Journal: Jan.-June 1949, 5/22/49 entry, handwritten, Tugwell papers, FDR Library, box 36; Rexford Tugwell to Sen. Paul W. Broyles, May 13, 1949, Tugwell papers, folder "Be," FDR Library, box 2; Tugwell, "Statement of R. G. Tugwell Before the Committee on Un-American Activities of the Legislature of Illinois," Tugwell papers, folder "Broyles Investigation," FDR Library, box 24.

13. Rexford Tugwell, "Consolation in Time of Jeopardy," Santa Barbara Unitarian Church, 1970, Tugwell papers, FDR Library, box 77; Tugwell, *A Chronicle of Jeopardy, 1945-1955* (Chicago: University of Chicago Press, 1955), 1, 4-5, 9-10, 24, 37-45, 62-63; Tugwell, *The Light of Other Days* (Garden City, N.Y.: Doubleday, 1962), 12, 111, 192, 230; Tugwell, *Off-Course: From Truman to Nixon* (New York: Praeger, 1971), 189.

14. Rexford Tugwell, *The Stricken Land* (Garden City, N.Y.: Doubleday, 1947), xv, and *A Chronicle of Jeopardy*, p. 64; Tugwell, "Notes on Some Implications of Oneness in the World," *Common Cause* 1 (November 1947): 165-72.

15. Tugwell, *A Chronicle of Jeopardy*, pp. 64-65; Tugwell et al., "Preliminary Draft of a World Constitution," *Common Cause* 1 (March 1948): 326-27. During the drafting stages, Tugwell and the other committee members argued fairly extensively over the world constitution. See, for example, Tugwell, diary, folder "Jan.-June 1946," March 22, 1946, and March 31, 1946, Tugwell papers, FDR Library, box 34; Tugwell, diary, folder "July-Dec. 1946," "Committee to Frame a World Constitution," and "Memorandum Concerning the Place of Planning in the Proposed World Constitution," Tugwell papers, FDR Library, boxes 34 and 35 respectively.

16. Tugwell, *A Chronicle of Jeopardy*, pp. 68, 134, 141; "Preliminary Draft of a World Constitution," pp. 329-45.

17. Rexford Tugwell, "The Utility of the Future in the Present," *Public Administration Review* 8 (Winter 1948): 49, 56.

18. Rexford Tugwell, "Earthbound: The Problem of Planning and Survival," *Antioch Review* 9 (December 1949): 485.

19. Rexford Tugwell, "The Study of Planning as a Scientific Endeavor," Michigan Academy of Science, Arts and Letters (1948), pp. 34-38, Tugwell papers, FDR Library, box 63; Tugwell, "Wonders May not Cease," address to Agricultural Economics Society (July 1950), pp. 11-13, Tugwell papers, FDR Library, box 67.

20. Tugwell, *The Place of Planning in Society* (San Juan: Government Service Office 1954), 22-38; Rexford Tugwell to Mel, January 19, 1979, Tugwell papers, folder "Branch, Melville," FDR Library, box 4.

21. Tugwell, *Place of Planning*, pp. 48-55; Rexford Tugwell to William F. Larsen, February 1, 1954, Tugwell papers, folder "La," FDR Library, box 13; Tugwell, "Planners, Lawyers, and Scientists Cannot Control Use of Their Work," in American Institute of Planners, *The Planner in Emerging Urban Society* (1965), 60-61, Tugwell papers, FDR Library, box 107.

22. Rexford Tugwell, "Planning and Democracy," *Center Magazine* 11, no. 5 (September/October 1978): 59-67.

23. Tugwell, "The Utility of the Future in the Present," pp. 57-58; Tugwell, *The Democratic Roosevelt* (Garden City, N.Y.: Doubleday, 1957), 348, 415, 612.

24. After 1945 Tugwell wrote prolifically on the failure of American leadership at home and abroad. See, for example, Tugwell, *A Chronicle of Jeopardy*,

pp. 81-87, 113-23, 160-63; Tugwell, *Off-Course*, chs. 5-6; Tugwell, "Letters from Latter-Day Britain," 15-article series, *Common Cause* (March 1950-June 1951); Tugwell, "The Consequences of Korea," *Bulletin of the Atomic Scientists* (May 1951): 133-38; "Two Top F.D.R. Aides Hit Trend to Socialism," *Chicago Daily Tribune*, October 4, 1954, Donald Richberg papers, Library of Congress, box 15.

25. Rexford Tugwell, Hillman Lectures, 1959, Tugwell papers, FDR Library, box 11; Tugwell, *The Enlargement of the Presidency* (Garden City, N.Y.: Doubleday, 1960); Tugwell, *How They Became President: Thirty-five Ways to the White House* (New York: Simon and Schuster, 1964); Tugwell, *Grover Cleveland* (New York: Macmillan, 1968); Tugwell, "On Bringing Presidents to Heel," in *The Presidency Reappraised*, ed. by Thomas E. Cronin and Rexford Tugwell (New York: Praeger, 1974), 302-320; Tugwell, "The President and His Helpers: A Review Article," *Political Science Quarterly* 82 (June 1967): 253-67; Tugwell, "The Historian and the Presidency: An Essay Review," *Political Science Quarterly* (June 1971): 183-205.

26. Tugwell papers, folder "Harry S. Truman," FDR Library, box 26; Tugwell, diary, folder "July-December 1946," 6/30, handwritten, FDR Library, box 35; Tugwell, *Enlargement of the Presidency*, *Grover Cleveland*, etc. Same as books cited in note 25.

27. Tugwell papers, folder "Harry S. Truman," FDR Library, box 26; Tugwell, *Off-Course*, chapters 8, 9, and 10.

28. Rexford Tugwell, "The Preparation of a President," *Western Political Quarterly* 1 (June 1948): 131-53, and "The New Deal in Retrospect," *Western Political Quarterly* 1 (December 1948): 373-85; Tugwell, "The New Deal: The Progressive Tradition," *Western Political Quarterly* 3 (September 1950): 390-427; Tugwell and E. C. Banfield, "Grass Roots Democracy: Myth or Reality?" *Public Administration Review* 10 (Winter 1950): 47, 49, 53-54; Tugwell, "The New Deal: The Decline of Government, Parts I and II," *Western Political Quarterly* 4 (June and September 1951): 295-312, 469-86; Tugwell, "The New Deal: The Rise of Business, Parts I and II," *Western Political Quarterly* 5 (June and September 1952): 274-89, 483-503; Tugwell, *A Chronicle of Jeopardy*, pp. 18ff., and *The Stricken Land*, pp. 442, 679-82; Tugwell, *The Democratic Roosevelt*, pp. 270-474; Tugwell, *The Light of Other Days*, pp. 240-41; Tugwell, *Enlargement of the Presidency* (Garden City, N.Y.: Doubleday, 1960), 390-456; Tugwell, *The Brains Trust* (New York: Viking Press, 1968), 520-22; Tugwell, *Off-Course*, pp. 3-166; Tugwell, *In Search of Roosevelt* (Cambridge, Mass.: Harvard University Press, 1972), chs. 3, 4, 6; Tugwell, *Roosevelt's Revolution* (New York: Macmillan, 1977), 40ff.; Tugwell, *FDR: Architect of an Era* (New York: Macmillan, 1967), 1-150.

29. Tugwell, "The Fourth Power," *Planning and Civic Comment*, pt. 2 (April-June 1939): 19-23; "The Directive," *Journal of Social Philosophy and Jurisprudence* (October 1941): 24; "The Decline of Government, Part I," pp. 470-79 and "The Rise of Business, Part II," pp. 484-86, 491-93. See also Rexford Tug-

well, *The Compromising of the Constitution* (South Bend, Ind.: University of Notre Dame Press, 1968), and *The Emerging Constitution* (New York: Harper's Magazine Press, 1974).

30. Rexford Tugwell et al., "Constitution for a United Republics of America: A Model for Discussion, Version 37," *The Center Magazine* 3, no. 5 (September 1970): 25-27; Tugwell, *The Emerging Constitution*, chs. 6-15.

31. Tugwell, *Emerging Constitution*, ch. 15.

32. Ibid.

33. Rexford Tugwell, "The Presidency and the Silences of the Constitution," *New Hampshire Bar Journal* 4 (July 1962): 169-93; Tugwell, "When the Constitution Is Silent, Bold Voices Speak," *Columbia University Forum* 6 (Spring 1963): 17-23.

34. See, for example, D. S. Broder, "Critique on Constitution Experiments," *Current* 123 (November 1970): 24-26.

35. There were a number of obituaries on Tugwell's death. Of these, the obituary in the *New York Times*, July 24, 1979, was particularly good.

Conclusion

I am strong
I am big and well-made
I am muscled and lean and nervous
I am frank and square and incisive;
I am wrought out of twisted fibers of racehood
Seasoned and fit.

I bend the forces untamable; I harness the powers irresistible
All this I do; but I shall do more.

I see the great plan already
And the keen joy of the work will be mine.
I shall be the creator;
I shall be God.
The materials are in my hands,
The vision in heart and head;
My vast work is just now beginning.

I am surpassingly glad to be young,
To have power to measure up my job.

I have dreamed my great dream . . .
I have gathered my tools and my charts;
My plans are fashioned and practical.
I shall roll up my sleeves—make
America over!

Rexford Tugwell, "A Young Man Looks Forward,"
in *Red Bud*, Tugwell papers, FDR Library, box 51.

In the literally millions of words that he wrote throughout his life, there must have been times when Tugwell regretted these. Written when he was a college student in 1915, he paid dearly in reputation for the exuberance of his youthful dreams as expressed by these verses in a poem he titled "A Young Man Looks Forward." Critics mercilessly attacked him, using these very words to prove just how dangerous he was. In reality, of course, Tugwell was as dangerous as they were and, in many ways, far less so.

What made the critics' attacks on Tugwell based on these verses so incomprehensible was that Tugwell was writing about America and democracy. Without a doubt, he could, and should, have been forgiven for saying what he did. He was young, energetic, and feeling he could do anything at age 24. The irony of it is that these verses, if analyzed from the standpoint of his long life, can become the basis for assessing him.

When Tugwell wrote this poem, he was indeed strong, muscled, lean, frank, and incisive. He was, moreover, studying to be an economist, a profession he believed very capable of finding ways to bend the forces untamable and harness the powers irresistible. As he grew older, the great plan, already perceived fragmentarily at a young age, took on more shape and form. His commitment to formulating and implementing it more and more became pronounced and an integral part of his very being. Slowly, gradually, over time, Tugwell came to see a society that he wanted in which everyone shared the abundant gifts of nature freely and openly. Throughout his life, he dreamed of this society, gathered his tools and charts to find ways to achieve it, and fashioned his plans more and more to fit it. While he did not make America over, Tugwell did try to make America better.

If these verses demonstrated anything, it was that Rexford G. Tugwell was a deeply compassionate, caring man who wanted to help people enjoy life and achieve their potential. Committed to service, from the time he entered Wharton to the end of his life, he worked hard as an economist, New Dealer, chairman of the New York City Planning Commission, governor of Puerto Rico, academic, and writer to do just that. Sometimes he failed, and he has to bear a good portion of the responsibility for those failures. His self-confidence often bordered on and became outright condescension and arrogance. Also, his frustration, whether in public service or academe, many times led him to say things he might have only been thinking about instead of being committed to. And, finally, he sometimes acted too rashly. He can, and should, be held accountable for all of these faults, but the motivation was still pure.

To speak of Tugwell as a revolutionary or a conservative is to miss who and what he was and was seeking to do. Always an institutionalist, he was constantly evolving his thinking in economics, politics, social issues, and basic ideas on life. Never committed to blueprint planning, he persistently emphasized the need to experiment, especially in the economic realm. Even his choice of words to explain his thoughts must be understood in the time and environment he wrote them. Since he "wrote out loud," his ideas need to be examined over his lifetime and not in a tunnel-vision fashion. As an economist in the 1920s and 1930s, for example, his understanding of "collective" often meant "cooperation," his ideas on coordination meant balance, and his emphasis on expertise was identified with service. Writing prolifically on America's economic problems, he offered tentative suggestions and ideas for those problems, not detailed, complete solutions.

To a large extent, his return to academe after 1946 as a political scientist was a result of the frustration he felt with the economics profession that stemmed from its refusal to see the economic system properly and to offer ideas on how to make it work better. Throughout his life, it was incomprehensible to him that the United States, so richly endowed in natural resources, was committed to a laissez-faire, profit-maximization philosophy and policy that promoted the individual businessman so much that the general welfare was ignored and usually harmed.

Similarly, to speak of Tugwell as "cerebrating" is misleading. He did think a lot, he read a lot, he learned by experience, and he was influenced by people. Nevertheless, Tugwell was never, nor could he be, an ivory tower academic with no relationship to the real world. The world was his place to be and to work. Thus, he was active throughout his long life. A simple listing of all his positions demonstrates this: professor at Columbia, member of the Brains Trust, assistant and under secretary of agriculture, director of the Resettlement Administration, chairman of the New York City Planning Commission, governor of Puerto Rico, academic, lecturer, and writer. Tugwell, in other words, was a doer.

Was he influential in what he did? To some extent. In the New Deal, Tugwell played an active role in the USDA and RA. He was also involved in a variety of activities ranging from introducing new Pure Food and Drug legislation to the NRA. Did FDR always listen to him? No, but neither did FDR always listen to anyone else. Tugwell's economic ideas of the 1930s, especially on planning, were designed to start the ball rolling, not end the game. Even Pure Food and Drug was designed to correct what existed and to redirect the Pure Food and Drug Administration toward the public interest. Tugwell learned from all of these activities. After 1939, he fully realized that planning not only involved America's values but also touched upon its political system. The Fourth Power and later his new Constitution were the culmination of all those years of thinking and experience from the 1930s on.

In New York, Tugwell learned even more about America's economic system and the role of planning in it. He studied and analyzed the details of everyday planning. The question that is apropos is whether anyone could have made planning work in New York in the late 1930s and early 1940s. Probably not, given Fiorello LaGuardia, Robert Moses, and the political-economic interests of the city. Tugwell tried and failed, but that failure was not totally his; it was as much New York's.

In Puerto Rico, Tugwell accomplished more. It was a situation in which he was in the right place at the right time. With Muñoz Marín and the young group of administrators he put together, Tugwell assisted in facilitating the revolution. It was a revolution under way when he arrived. He helped it throughout his governorship, but he did not cause it. This is not to deny what he did, but to place it in its proper perspective. Under constant congressional scrutiny and attacked consistently by the Coalitionist opposition on the island, he worked well and successfully with the Populares to make Puerto Rico a better place to live. And this was all done in the midst of World War II.

Finally, in academe after 1946, Tugwell wrote on a variety of topics and issues he deemed important to America's survival: the atomic bomb, FDR, planning, and the Constitution. To devote one's attention to seeing if he was consistent or inconsistent in his views on FDR or any of these issues is to miss the point of who Tugwell was and what he had done. Given his evolutionary way of development, there is no other way to understand him. In his treatment of FDR, in particular, one other point must be borne in mind. Tugwell's love for Roosevelt overshadowed all else. While he may have faulted FDR for not going far enough or for listening to the Cohen-Corcoran group, he always believed that FDR could only do so much. There were too many factors over which he had no control. Along these lines, Tugwell's call for a new American Constitution was not an academic exercise. It was the culmination of Tugwell's thinking on the American economy and the American political system. Given America's laissez-fairism, business's profit maximization, and the disappointing record of post-Roosevelt presidents in the United States, he concluded that fundamental change was absolutely necessary.

It was clear throughout his life that Tugwell did not care as much about who owned or controlled business as he did about how the general welfare was being promoted and served. If only businessmen and politicians could cooperate to promote society's welfare, all would be well. After 88 years of life and a good portion of them not seeing this happen, Tugwell concluded that changing the constitutional system was the only way left. It was a conclusion reached after many years of thought and after much practical experience in public service.

In concluding, it might be appropriate to assess Tugwell by a poem he wrote about life and his role in it:

I should like to be brave Enough to live a real life in the world. To love, to hope, to trust in the ultimate good, and yet to be a believer in things-as-they-are, to be a Prophet of the Ultimate—and to order my life with the proper perspective—in accord with the Universe not with the World . . . and in accord with All Time not today, nor a Century. To do all these things and live with Men—have their friendship and belief—not in the things I believe—but in me . . . to have the Open Heart to all humanity and all knowledge.[1]

Undoubtedly, looking back over his life and what he said and did, Tugwell did all of this.

NOTE

1. Tugwell papers, folder "Memorabilia," FDR Library, box 114.

Chronology

1891	Born July 10 in Sinclairville, New York
1914	Married Florence E. Arnold on June 7
1915	B.S., economics, University of Pennsylvania
1916	M.A., economics, University of Pennsylvania
1917-1918	Assistant professor of economics, University of Washington
1918	Manager, American University Union (Paris)
1919	Farming in Wilson
1920-1922	Instructor in economics, Columbia University
1922	Ph.D., economics, University of Pennsylvania
1922-1926	Assistant professor of economics, Columbia University
1926-1931	Associate professor of economics, Columbia University
1927	Delegation, trip to Soviet Union
1928	Al Smith campaign adviser
1931-1933	Professor of economics, Columbia University
1932	Brains Trust
1933-1934	Assistant secretary of agriculture
1934-1935	Under secretary of agriculture
1935-1936	Director, Resettlement Administration
1937	Vice-president, American Molasses Company
1938	Divorced Florence Arnold; married Grace Falke
1938-1941	Chairman, NYCPC
1941	Chancellor, University of Puerto Rico
1941-1946	Governor of Puerto Rico
1945-1948	Committee to Frame a World Constitution
1946-1952	Director, University of Chicago Planning Program
1946-1957	Professor of political science, University of Chicago
1948	Wallace for President Committee
1949	Broyles investigation

1949-1950	Visiting professor, London School of Economics
1957	Retires from University of Chicago
1958	Woodrow Wilson Foundation Award
1959	Hillman Lectures, Howard University
1961-1962	Columnist for *San Juan Star*
1961-1964	Consultant, University of Puerto Rico
1962	Parvin Foundation Fellow
1962	Professor, Columbia University, summer session
1964-1965	Center for the Study of Democratic Institutions
1965-1966	Research professor of political science, Southern Illinois University
1966	Senior fellow, Center for the Study of Democratic Institutions
1967	Silver medal, American Association of Planning
1969	Bancroft Prize (*Brains Trust*)
1971	Honorary degree, University of Pennsylvania
1978	Veblen-Commons Award
1979	Died July 21 in Santa Barbara, California

Bibliography

The purpose of this bibliography is not to list all the sources used in the biography, but to point out those materials that were particularly relevant. For a complete account of all the sources used, the reader is referred to the notes at the end of each chapter. The bibliography is divided into two parts: the first section is a listing of sources used in the book, and the second section is a selective list of Rexford G. Tugwell's published books, articles, and reviews.

REXFORD G. TUGWELL PAPERS

The personal papers of Rexford Tugwell are deposited at the Franklin D. Roosevelt Library in Hyde Park, New York. The collection consists of 114 boxes of materials plus 9 scrapbooks. It is divided into two parts: the original donation of papers made by Tugwell and an accretion added to the collection after his death and processed in the 1980s. All citations of the Tugwell papers used in this biography are based on the 1986 cataloging completed. All other primary sources cited used the cataloging systems in effect in 1975.

The Tugwell collection is complete with correspondence, diaries, subject files, speeches, writings, and memorabilia. It contains a very representative collection of his published writings as well, ranging from books to book reviews. Undoubtedly the most important source in the collection is the diary. Tugwell kept a diary for the years 1932-1960. Unfortunately, he was not always conscientious about making entries; the diaries for the 1930s are more complete than those for the later years. The diary is also available in the papers in an expanded form. Tugwell, probably in the 1950s, had thought of publishing the diary, with the result that he began an extensive editing of his notes. For the most part, though, the original remained intact. When combined with his correspondence and prolific writings, the Tugwell diaries offer a most important source of information.

In addition to the papers at Hyde Park, there are some Tugwell documents in Washington, D.C. also listed in this bibliography. Another important primary source for Tugwell is his oral history memoir at the Columbia Oral History Project. Although much of what he said in 1950 should be assessed in terms of the time at which he was interviewed, it is still a valuable addition to available information.

Another significant primary source used in this study was the personal correspondence I carried on with Tugwell. Although he tended to be very concise in answering my questions, the information he relayed was important. These letters are in my possession along with letters from Raymond Moley, Sam Rosenman, and two of Tugwell's former students, Richard L. Meier and John W. Dyckman.

Finally, Tugwell's published autobiographies proved to be invaluable. They helped fill in gaps, especially in the early years of Tugwell's life.

RELATED PERSONAL COLLECTIONS

In addition to the Tugwell papers, the collections of several prominent individuals who knew him were examined. These included the papers of Felix Frankfurter, Henry Wallace, Raymond Clapper, Harold Ickes, and George Norris, all of which are deposited at the Library of Congress. At the Franklin D. Roosevelt Library, the papers of Franklin D. Roosevelt, Harry Hopkins, Frances Perkins, Louis Howe, Samuel Rosenman, Charles Taussig, Mordecai Ezekiel, and Claude Wickard were examined.

GOVERNMENT AGENCIES

Probably the least helpful of all the sources were the records of government agencies with which Tugwell was connected. The papers of the USDA, the NRA, and the RA, all deposited in the National Archives, are voluminous and somewhat tedious for the researcher. However, the records of each of these agencies did provide some insights into how Tugwell did as an administrator.

ORAL MEMOIRS

An interesting source of information for this biography was the oral history collection at the Columbia Oral History Project. The memoirs of the following individuals were examined: Harry Mitchell, Oscar Stine, Arthur Krock, William Cumberland, Louis Bean, Rudolph Evans, Chester Davis, Will Alexander, Samuel Bledsoe, Charles Fahy, Jerome Frank, John Frey, Lindsey Rogers, Cleveland Rogers, and Rexford Tugwell.

PUBLISHED MEMOIRS

The last significant primary sources examined were the published memoirs of individuals who knew Tugwell. These included Harold Ickes, Hugh Johnson, David E. Lilienthal, Raymond Moley, Frances Perkins, Samuel Rosenman, and Adolph Berle.

SECONDARY MATERIALS

The reader is referred to the notes at the end of each chapter for a detailed listing of secondary sources used. Some works stood out as being particularly useful.

Very little work has been done that deals exclusively with Rexford Tugwell, yet what is available is usually good. The best study is Bernard Sternsher, *Rexford Tugwell and the New Deal* (New Brunswick, N.J.: Rutgers University Press, 1964). It is a thorough, detailed, and comprehensive study of Tugwell's New Deal years.

Another interesting study, dealing with Tugwell's chairmanship of the NYCPC, is Mark Gelfand, "Politics and the Public Interest: LaGuardia, Moses, Tugwell and Planning in New York City, 1936-1941," an unpublished manuscript available from the author and also in the Tugwell papers.

Two works on Tugwell's governorship of Puerto Rico are quite useful: Charles Goodsell, *Administration of a Revolution: Executive Reform in Puerto Rico under Governor Tugwell, 1941-1946* (Cambridge, Ma.: Harvard University Press, 1965); and Enrique Lugo-Silva, *The Tugwell Administration in Puerto Rico, 1941-1946* (Rio Piedras, P.R.: Editorial Cultura, T.G., S.A., 1955).

Among the general New Deal studies, the ones that were most helpful were Arthur M. Schlesinger, Jr., *The Age of Roosevelt*, vol. 1: *The Crisis of the Old Order*, vol. II: *The Coming of the New Deal*, and vol. III: *The Politics of Upheaval* (Boston: Houghton Mifflin, 1956-1960); James M. Burns, *Roosevelt: The Lion and the Fox* (New York: Harcourt, Brace, and World, 1956); Paul Conkin, *The New Deal* (New York: Thomas Y. Crowell Co., 1967); and William Leuchtenburg, *Franklin D. Roosevelt and the New Deal* (New York: Harper and Row, 1963).

Among the more specialized New Deal studies, the following were helpful: Irving Bernstein, *The New Deal Collective Bargaining Policy* (Berkeley: University of California Press, 1959); Sidney Fine, *The Automobile Under the Blue Eagle: Labor, Management, and the Automobile Manufacturing Code* (Ann Arbor: University of Michigan Press, 1963); Ellis Hawley, *The New Deal and the Problem of Monopoly* (Princeton, N.J.: Princeton University Press, 1966); Joseph Arnold, *The New Deal in the Suburbs: A History of the Greenbelt Town Program, 1935-1954* (Columbus, Oh.: Ohio State University Press, 1971); Paul Conkin, *Tomorrow A New World: The New Deal Community Building Program* (Ithaca, N.Y.: Cornell University Press, 1959); Barton J. Bernstein, "The New Deal: The Conservative Achievements of Liberal Reform," in *Towards A New Past: Dissenting Essays in American History*, ed. Barton J. Bernstein (New York: Vintage Books, 1967); Elliot Rosen, *Hoover, Roosevelt and the Brains Trust* (New York: Columbia University Press, 1977); and Charles Jackson, *Food and Drug Legislation in the New Deal* (Princeton, N.J.: Princeton University Press, 1970).

Among studies on economic theory and planning, the following were helpful: Allan G. Gruchy, *Modern Economic Thought: The American Contribution* (New York: Augustus M. Kelley, 1967); John K. Galbraith, *The New Industrial State* (New York: Signet Books, 1967); and George Soule, *A Planned Society* (New York: Macmillan, 1932).

REXFORD G. TUGWELL

The following is a very representative listing of all of Rexford Tugwell's published writings, including books, chapters in books, contributions, articles, and reviews.

Books/Chapters in Books/Contributions

The Economic Basis of Public Interest, Menasha, Wisconsin: George Banta, 1922. Repr. New York: Augustus M. Kelley, 1968.

American Economic Life and the Means of Its Improvement, 2nd ed., New York: Harcourt, Brace, 1924. Joint Author with Thomas Munro and Roy E. Stryker.

"Experimental Economics." In *The Trend of Economics*. Edited by Rexford Tugwell. New York: F.S. Crofts, 1924.

Essays in Economic Theory, by Simon N. Patten. Edited by Rexford Tugwell. New York: Knopf, 1924.

Industry's Coming of Age. New York: Harcourt, Brace, 1927.

"Russian Agriculture." In *Soviet Russia in the Second Decade*. Edited by Rexford Tugwell, Stuart Chase, and Robert Dunn. New York: John Day, 1928.

Teaching American Economic Life and a Manual of Questions, New York: Harcourt, Brace, 1928. Written with Thomas Munro, Roy E. Stryker, and Donald J. Henderson.

The American Year Book and Directory of The American-Russian Chamber of Commerce, 1928-29 (in Russian). Edited by Rexford Tugwell. Moscow, 1929.

Mr. Hoover's Economic Policy. New York: John Day, 1932.

The Industrial Discipline and the Governmental Arts. New York: Columbia University Press, 1933.

Our Economic Society and Its Problems, New York: Harcourt, Brace, 1934. Written with Howard C. Hill.

Essays upon Field Husbandry in New England, and Other Papers, 1748-1762, by Eliot Jared. Edited by Rexford Tugwell and Harry J. Carman. New York: Columbia University Press, 1934.

Redirecting Education. Edited by Rexford Tugwell and Leon Keyserling. 2 vols. New York: Columbia University Press, 1934-1935. Tugwell contributed "Social Objectives in Education," in vol. 1.

The Battle for Democracy. New York: Columbia University Press, 1935.

"Resettlement Administration." In *The Democratic National Convention, 1936*. Washington, D.C.: Democratic National Committee, 1936.

Review of *This Ugly Civilization*, by Ralph Barsodi. In *Designed for Reading: Anthology from the Saturday Review of Literature, 1924-1934*. New York: Macmillan, 1936.

"Economics." In *Roads to Knowledge*. Edited by W. A. Neilson. New York: Halcyon House, 1937.

Changing The Colonial Climate: The Story, from His Official Messages, of Governor Rexford Guy Tugwell's Efforts to Bring Democracy to an Island Possession Which Serves The United Nations as a Warbase. Selection and explanatory comments by J. Lear. San Juan: Bureau of Supplies, Printing, and Transportation, 1942.

Forty-fifth Annual Report of the Governor. San Juan: Government of Puerto Rico, 1945.

Puerto Rican Public Papers of R. G. Tugwell, Governor. San Juan: Service Office of The Government of Puerto Rico, Printing Division, 1945.

The Stricken Land: The Story of Puerto Rico. Garden City, New York: Doubleday, 1947.

"Caribbean Obligations." In *The Caribbean.* Edited by A. C. Wilgus, Gainesville, Florida: University of Florida Press, 1952.

"New York." In *Great Cities of the World.* Edited by William A. Robson. London: Allen and Urwin, 1954.

A Chronicle of Jeopardy, 1945-1955. Chicago: University of Chicago Press, 1955.

The Democratic Roosevelt: A Biography of Franklin D. Roosevelt. Garden City, New York: Doubleday, 1957.

The Art of Politics as Practiced by Three Great Americans: Franklin Delano Roosevelt, Luis Munoz Marin, and Fiorello H. LaGuardia. Garden City, New York: Doubleday, 1958.

The Place of Planning in Society: Seven Lectures on the Place of Planning in Society with Special Reference to Puerto Rico. San Juan: Government Service Office, Printing Division, 1954.

Early American Policy: Six Columbia Contributions. New York: Columbia University Press, 1960. Written with Joseph Dorfman.

The Enlargement of the Presidency. Garden City, New York: Doubleday, 1960.

The Light of Other Days. Garden City, New York: Doubleday, 1962.

How They Became President: Thirty-five Ways to the White House. New York: Simon and Schuster, 1964.

F.D.R.: Architect of an Era. New York: Macmillan, 1967.

The Brains Trust. New York: Viking Press, 1968.

Grover Cleveland. New York: Macmillan, 1968.

A Model Constitution for a United Republics of America. Santa Barbara, Ca.: Center for The Study of Democratic Institutions, 1970.

Off Course: From Truman to Nixon. New York: Praeger, 1971.

In Search of Roosevelt. Cambridge Ma.: Harvard University Press, 1972.

The Emerging Constitution. New York: Harper's Magazine Press, 1974.

The Presidency Reappraised. New York: Praeger, 1974. Edited with Thomas E. Cronin.

The Compromising of the Constitution: Early Departures. South Bend, In.: University of Notre Dame Press, 1976.

Roosevelt's Revolution: The First Year, A Personal Perspective. New York: Macmillan, 1977.

To the Lesser Heights of Morningside: A Memoir. Philadelphia: University of Pennsylvania Press, 1982.

Articles and Reviews

"Meaning and Making of Milk Strikes." *Pennsylvania Farmer* 42 (September 22, 1917): 1, 4ff. Written with Charles Reitel.

"The Marketing of Farm Products." *Pennsylvania Farmer* 42 (December 22, 1917): 12.

"The Casual of the Woods." *Survey* 44 (July 3, 1920): 472-74.

"The Outlaw." *The Survey* 44 (August 16, 1920), 641-42.

"The Philosophy of Despair: Outlawing the I.W.W." *New York Call*, magazine section, October 17, 1920.

"The Gipsey Strain." *Pacific Review* 2 (September 1921): 177-96.

"The Economic Basis for Business Regulation." *American Economic Review* 11 (December 1921): 643-58.

"Country Life in America." *Pacific Review* (March 1922), 566-86.

Review of *Guild Socialism and the Industrial Future*, by G. D. H. Cole. *The International Journal of Ethics* 32 (April 1922): 282-88.

"Human Nature in Economic Theory." *Journal of Political Economy* 30 (June 1922): 317-45.

"Economic Theory and Practice." *American Economic Review, Supplement* 13 (March 1923): 107-109.

"Some Formative Influences on the Life of Simon Nelson Patten." *American Economic Review, Supplement* 13 (March 1923): 273-85.

"Notes on the Life and Work of Simon Nelson Patten." *Journal of Political Economy* 31 (April 1923): 153-208.

"Bibliography of the Works of Simon Nelson Patten." *The Annals of The American Academy of Political and Social Science* 107 (May 1923): 358-67.

"The Distortion of Economic Incentive." *International Journal of Ethics* 34 (April 1924): 272-82.

"The Problem of Agriculture." *Political Science Quarterly* 39 (December 1924): 549-91.

"The Woman in the Sunbonnet." *Nation* 120 (January 21, 1925): 73-74.

"The Hired Man." *Nation* 121 (August 5, 1925): 164-66.

"An Economist Reads Dark Laughter." *New Republic* 45 (December 9, 1925): 87-88.

"Henry Ford in this World." *Saturday Review of Literature* 3 (August 7, 1926): 17-19.

"Chameleon Words." *New Republic* 48 (August 25, 1926): 16-17.

"The End of Laissez Faire." *New Republic* 48 (October 13, 1926): 222.

"America's Wartime Socialism." *Nation* 124 (April 6, 1927): 364-67.

"What Will Become of the Farmer?" *Nation* 124 (June 5, 1927): 664-66.

"Economics as the Science of Experience." *Journal of Philosophy* 25 (January 19, 1928): 29-40.

"High Wages and Prosperity: Discussion." *Bulletin of the Taylor Society* 3 (February 1928): 1-22.

"Paradox of Peace." *New Republic* 54 (April 18, 1928): 262-66.

"Hunger, Cold, and Candidates." *New Republic* 54 (May 2, 1928): 323-25.

"Governor or President?" *New Republic* 54 (May 16, 1928): 381-82.

"Communist Theory vs. Russian Fact." *New Republic* 54 (May 16, 1928): 367.

"Contemporary Economics." *New Republic* 54 (May 16, 1928): 397-98.

"Platforms and Candidates." *New Republic* 55 (May 30, 1928): 44-45.

"What Is a Scientific Tariff?" *New Republic* 55 (June 13, 1928): 92-93.

"That Living Constitution." *New Republic* 55 (June 20, 1928): 120-22.

"Experimental Control in Russian Industry." *Political Science Quarterly* 43 (June 1928): 161-87.

"A Plank for Agriculture." *New Republic* 55 (July 4, 1928): 161-63.

"Wage Pressure and Efficiency." *New Republic* 55 (July 11, 1928): 196-98.

"Governor Smith's Dilemma." *New Republic* 55 (August 1, 1928): 276-77.

"The Liberal Choice." *New Republic* 56 (September 5, 1928): 74-75.

"Banker's Banks." *New Republic* 57 (December 12, 1928): 95-96.

"Reflections on Farm Relief." *Political Science Quarterly* 43 (December 1928): 481-97.

"Farm Relief and a Permanent Agriculture." *The Annals of the American Academy of Political and Social Science* 142 (March 1929): 271-82.

"Agricultural Policy of France." *Political Science Quarterly* 45 (June-December 1930): 214-30, 405-28, 527-47.

"Human Nature and Social Economy." *Journal of Philosophy* 27 (August 14 and 28, 1930): 449-57, 477-92.

"Elements of a World Culture: Economics." *World Unity* 7 (November-December 1930): 95-105, 202-7.

"Occupational Obsolescence." *Journal of Adult Education* 3 (January 1931): 19-21.

"The Theory of Occupational Obsolescence." *Political Science Quarterly* 46 (June 1931): 171-227.

"The Reverend John McVickar: Christian Teacher and Economist." *Columbia University Quarterly* (December 1931). Written with Joseph Dorfman.

"Flaws in the Hoover Economic Plan." *Current History* 35 (January 1932): 525-31. Written with A. T. Cutler and G. S. Mitchell.

"What the World Economic Conference Can Do." *New York Herald Tribune* (April 12, 1933).

"The Role of the State in American Economic Life." *L'Esprit International* (April 1933).

"Government in a Changing World." *Review of Reviews* 88 (August 1933): 33-34.

"Tugwell Defends Food and Drug Bill." *Editor and Publisher* 66 (September 16, 1933): 1, 6, 46.

"The Copeland Bill and the Food Industries." *Grocery Trade News* (October 24, 1933).

"New Monetary Policy Regarded Logical Step." *Washington Star* (November 5, 1933).

"One Aim of the *Consumer's Guide* of the Agricultural Adjustment Administration." *Consumer's Guide* 1 (November 14, 1933): 2.

"Freedom from Fakes." *Today* (November 18, 1933): 6-7.

"Are the Increasing Powers of the President Improving the American Government?" *Congressional Digest* 12 (November 1933): 268ff.

"The Farm Price Level." *Fortune* 8 (November 1933).

" 'Grasping' Congressmen Feel Constituents' Need." *Washington Star* (December 10, 1933).

"Henry Vethake: A Chapter in the Development of Higher Learning in the United States." *Columbia University Quarterly* (December 1933): 335-64. Written with Joseph Dorfman.

"How Shall We Pay for All This?" *American Magazine* 116 (December 1933): 11-13.

"Planned Use of the Land." *Today* 1 (January 20, 1934): 6-7.

"The Price Also Rises." *Fortune* 9 (January 1934): 70-71, 107-8.

"The Road to Economic Recovery." *Extension Service Review* 5 (March 1934): 33-34.

"Should Congress Enact a New Pure Food and Drugs Law?" *Congressional Digest* 13 (March 1934): 72ff.

"America's International Policy: Tariff Revision Almost Certain to Come." *British Industries* 17 (March 1934): 57-59.

"New Deal as Brains Trust Sees It." *United States News and World Report* 2 (April 23, 1934): 15.

"America Takes Hold of Its Destiny." *Today* 1 (April 28, 1934): 6-7.

"The Great American Fraud." *American Scholar* 3 (Winter 1934): 85-95.

"Agriculture and the Consumer." Washington, D.C.: USDA, 1934.

"A Fireside Symposium." *Columbia University Quarterly* (March 1935): 20-36.

"The Progressive Tradition." *Atlantic Monthly* 155 (April 1935): 409-418.

"No More Frontiers." *Today* (June 22 and 29, 1935): 3-4, 8-9.

"William Beach Lawrence: Apostle of Ricardo." *Columbia University Quarterly* (September 1935): 195-242. Written with Joseph Dorfman.

"National Significance of Recent Trends in Farm Population." *Social Forces* 14 (October 1935): 1-7.

"Spain as a Colonizer." *Bulletin of the Pan American Union* 69 (October 1935): 768.

"New Deal Objective." *United States News and World Report* (November 18, 1935): 10-11.

"Our New National Domain." *Scribner's Magazine* 99 (March 1936): 165-68.

"New Frontier: The Story of Resettlement." *Chicago Sun-Times* (April 19, 1936).

"Should the Administrator's Housing Policy Be Continued?" *Congressional Digest* 15 (April 1936): 114-16.

"Why Resettlement?" *Labor Information Bulletin* 3 (May 1936), 1-4.

"Down to Earth." *Current History* 44 (July 1936): 33-38.

"Changing Acres." *Current History* 44 (September 1936): 57-63.

"Grass Did Not Grow." *Fortune* 14 (October 1936): 114-17.

"The Future of National Planning." *New Republic* 89 (December 9, 1936): 162-64.

"The Meaning of the Greenbelt Towns." *New Republic* 90 (February 17, 1937): 42-43.

"Co-operation and Resettlement." *Current History* 45 (February 1937): 71-76.

"Will Government Aid for Small Farm Purchasers Solve the Tenancy Problem?" *Congressional Digest* 16 (February 1937): 57-60.

"Is a Farmer-Labor Alliance Possible?" *Harper's Magazine* 174 (May 1937): 651-61.

"Wesley Mitchell: An Evaluation." *New Republic* 92 (October 6, 1937): 238-40.

"On the Troublesome 'X'." *Philosophy of Science* 4 (October 1937): 412-26.

"Land of Plenty." *Current History* 48 (February 1938): 18-21.

"Alexander Hamilton: Nation-Maker." *Columbia University Quarterly* (September and December 1938): 59-72. Written with Joseph Dorfman.

"Francis Lieber: German Scholar in America." *Columbia University Quarterly* (September and December 1938). Written with Joseph Dorfman.

Annual Report of the City Planning Commission of the Department of City Planning, The City of New York. New York: Julien Printing Corporation, 1938.

"Veblen and 'Business Enterprise.' " *New Republic* 98 (March 29, 1939): 215-19.

"Notes on the Uses of Exactitude in Politics." *Political Science Quarterly* 54 (March 1939): 15-28.

"Frightened Liberals." *New Republic* 98 (April 26, 1939): 328-29.

"The Fourth Power." *Planning and Civic Comment*, part 2 (April-June 1939): 1-31.

"It's Tough." *Radio Digest* (May 1939).

"After the New Deal: 'We Have Bought Ourselves Time to Think.' " *New Republic* 99 (July 26, 1939): 323-25.

"When the USHA Buys Land." *New Republic* 100 (October 25, 1939): 341-42.

"The Superpolitical." *Journal of Social Philosophy* 5 (January 1940), 97-114.

"The City Planning Commission." *New York Advancing*, World's Fair Edition (1939): 6-10.

Annual Report of the City Planning Commission of the Department of City Planning, The City of New York. New York: Julien Printing Corporation, 1939.

"Does Roosevelt Want a Third Term?" *Look Magazine* 4 (January 16, 1940): 10-19.

"What Should America Do for the Joads?" *Town Meeting Bulletin* (March 11, 1940).

"Parts of a New Civilization." *Saturday Review of Literature* 21 (April 13, 1940): 3-4.

"Planning in New York City." *Planner's Journal* 6 (April 1940): 33-34.

"The Sloping Walls of Casa Grande." *Atlantic Monthly* 165 (April 1940): 555-56.

"Must We Draft Roosevelt?" *New Republic* 102 (May 13, 1940): 630-33.

"Forester's Heart." *New Republic* 102 (March 4, 1940): 304-5.

"Roosevelt Will Not Run for a Third Term." *Look Magazine* 4 (June 18, 1940): 8-11.

"Planning for Living." *Child Study* 17 (Summer 1940): 102-3.

"Must We Socialize Business to Restore Prosperity?" *American Economic Foundation Bulletin* (November 18, 1940).

"Implementing the General Interest." *Public Administration Review* 1 (Autumn 1940): 32-49.

"Crisis of Freedom." *Common Sense* 10 (October 1941): 291-95.

"The Directive." *Journal of Social Philosophy and Jurisprudence* 7 (October 1941): 5-36.

"Investigation into the Administrative Responsibilities under the 500 Acre Limitation on Land Holding." *Report on the Five Hundred Acre Law*. San Juan: Service Office of the Government of Puerto Rico, Printing Division, December 1941.

"Puerto Rico Also Serves." *New Republic* 107 (July 13, 1942): 51-52.

"Puerto Rico and Its Housing Problem." *American City* 57 (July 1942): 43-45.

"The Real Estate Dilemma." *Public Administration Review* 2 (Winter 1942): 27-39.

"In Defense of Puerto Rico." *New Republic* 114 (April 15, 1946): 509-12.

"Puerto Rico's Bootstraps," *Harper's Magazine* 194 (February 1947): 160-69. Written with Grace F. Tugwell.

Review of *Welfare and Planning in the West Indies*, by T. S. Sidney. *Journal of Political Economy* 55 (October 1947): 473-74.

"Notes on Some Implications of Oneness in the World." *Common Cause* 1 (November 1947): 165-72.

Review of *The United States and the Caribbean*, by Dexter Perkins. *Saturday Review of Literature* 30 (December 27, 1947): 9-10.

Review of *Henry Wallace*, by Dwight MacDonald. *Chicago Sun-Times* (February 23, 1948).

"Preliminary Draft of a World Constitution." *Common Cause* 1 (March 1948): 325-46. Written with others.

"The Preparation of a President." *Western Political Quarterly* 1 (June 1948): 131-53.

"An Open Reply to Mr. Borgese." *Common Cause* 2 (October 1948): 81-84.

"The New Deal in Retrospect." *Western Political Quarterly* 1 (December 1948): 373-85.

"The Utility of the Future in the Present." *Public Administration Review* 8 (Winter 1948): 49-59.

"Can the United Nations Become a World Government?" *Common Cause* 2 (February 1949): 244-51. Written with E. C. Banfield.

"A Planner's View of Agriculture's Future." *Journal of Farm Economics* 31 (February 1949): 29-43.

"Progressives and the Presidency." *The Progressive* (April 1949): 5-9.

Review of *Property, Wealth, Land: Allocation, Planning and Development*, by M. S. McDougal and D. Habar. *Yale Law Journal* 58 (April 1949): 809-18.

"Beyond Malthus: Numbers and Resources." *Common Cause* 2 (May 1949): 375-77.

"Variation on a Theme by Cooley." *Ethics* 59 (July 1949): 233-43.

"Great Rehearsal or Great Compromise?" *Common Cause* 2 (July 1949): 449-56. Written with E. C. Banfield.

"Looking Outward of the Americans." *Antioch Review* 9 (September 1949): 340-53.

"Earthbound: The Problem of Planning and Survival." *Antioch Review* 9 (December 1949): 476-94.

"The New Deal: The Available Instruments of Governmental Power." *Western Political Quarterly* 2 (December 1949): 545-80.

"The New Deal: The Progressive Tradition." *Western Political Quarterly* 3 (September 1950): 390-427.

"Letters from Latter-Day Britain." *Common Cause* 3 and 4 (March 1950-June 1951). Fifteen articles.

"To Succor the Weak." *Common Cause* 3 (April 1950): 450-67.

"Welfare State." *Common Cause* 3 (July 1950). 639-49.

"The Experimental Roosevelt." *Political Quarterly* 21 (July 1950): 239-70.

"Wonders May Not Cease." *British Agricultural Economics Society Transactions* (Summer 1950): 1-14.

"One-World—One Wealth." *Ethics* 61 (April 1951): 173-94.

"The Consequences of Korea." *Bulletin of the Atomic Scientists* (May 1951): 133-38.

"Governmental Planning at Mid-Century." *Journal of Politics* 13 (May 1951): 133-63. Written with E. C. Banfield.

"The New Deal: The Decline of Government," Parts I and II. *Western Political Quarterly* 4 (June and September 1951): 295-312, 469-86.

"Beyond Nationalism." *Political Quarterly* 22 (October 1951): 346-58.

"The Two Great Roosevelts." *Western Political Quarterly* 5 (March 1952): 84-93.

"The New Deal: The Rise of Business," Parts I and II. *Western Political Quarterly* 5 (June and September 1952): 274-89, 483-503.

Review of *Roosevelt and Daniels*, by Carroll Kilpatrick. *Western Political Quarterly* 5 (December 1952): 718-20

"What Next for Puerto Rico?" *The Annals of the American Academy of Political and Social Science* 285 (January 1953): 145-52.

"L'Attitude Réticente des Etats Unis à L'Egard de la Planification." *Revue Economique* (March 1953).

"The Compromising Roosevelt." *Western Political Quarterly* 6 (June 1953): 320-41.

"The Progressive Orthodoxy of Franklin D. Roosevelt." *Ethics* 64 (October 1953): 1-23.

"The Protagonists: Roosevelt and Hoover." *Antioch Review* 13 (December 1953): 419-42.

"The Sources of New Deal Reformism." *Ethics* 64 (July 1954): 249-76.

"Roosevelt and Howe." *Antioch Review* 14 (September 1954): 367-73.

Review of *Transformation: The Story of Modern Puerto Rico*, by Earl P. Hanson. *Saturday Review* 38 (February 12, 1955): 16-17.

"Fuel of Magnificence: The Case of Puerto Rico." *Confluence* 4 (October 1955): 266-91.

"The Fallow Years of Franklin D. Roosevelt." *Ethics* 66 (January 1956): 98-116.

"Franklin D. Roosevelt on the Verge of the Presidency." *Antioch Review* 16 (March 1956): 46-79.

"F.D.R.: Living Memorials." *Nation* 182 (April 7, 1956): 272-76.

Review of *Roosevelt: The Lion and the Fox*, by James M. Burns. *Chicago Sun-Times* (August 12, 1956).

Review of *The Crisis of the Old Order*, by Arthur M. Schlesinger, Jr. *Chicago Sun-Times* (March 3, 1957).

Review of *Franklin D. Roosevelt and Conservation, 1911-1945*, comp. and ed. by Edgar B. Nixon. *American Historical Review* 63 (April 1958): 758.

"A Memorable Christmas." *The Evening Star* (Washington, D.C.), (December 9, 1958).

Review of *LaGuardia: A Fighter Against His Time, 1882-1933*, by Arthur Mann. *New York Times Book Review* 7 (November 15, 1959): 3.

Foreword to *Puerto Rican Politics and the New Deal*, by Thomas G. Mathews (Jersey City, N.J.: Da Capo Press, 1960).

"The View from Puerto Rico." *Nation* 192 (June 10, 1961): 496-97.

"The Farmer and the Commissar." *Nation* 193 (July 29, 1961). 57-59.

"The Presidency and the Silences of the Constitution." *New Hampshire Bar Journal* 4 (July 1962): 169-93.

"When the Constitution is Silent, Bold Voices Speak." *Columbia University Forum* 6 (Spring 1963): 17-23.

"Congressional Control of the Executive Branch." *Science* 144 (May 1, 1964): 524-25.

"The President and His Helpers: A Review Article." *Political Science Quarterly* 82 (June 1967): 253-67.

"Roosevelt and Frankfurter: An Essay Review." *Political Science Quarterly* 85 (March 1970): 99-114.

"Constitution for a United Republics of America." *Center Magazine* 3 (September 1970): 24-49.

"The Historian and the Presidency: An Essay Review." *Political Science Quarterly* 86 (June 1971): 183-205.

"Case Against a Six Year Term." *Current* 137 (February 1972): 30-36.

"Roosevelt and the Bonus Marchers." *Political Science Quarterly* 87 (September 1972): 363-76.

Review of *Organizing the Presidency*, by S. Hess. *New Republic* 176 (February 26, 1977): 26-28.

Review of *Conflict and Crisis. The Presidency of Harry S. Truman*, by R. J. Donovan. *New Republic* 177 (November 26, 1977): 39-40.

"Planning and Democracy." *Center Magazine* 11 (September/October 1978): 59-67.

"Reflections." *Center Magazine* 11 (September/October 1978): 68-74.

Index

ABOUT THE AUTHOR

MICHAEL V. NAMORATO is an associate professor of history at the University of Mississippi. He received his B.A. from Iona College (New York) and his M.A. and Ph.D. from Michigan State University. His areas of specialization include twentieth-century American history, American/Southern economic history, and American business history. He has edited *Have We Overcome? Race Relations Since Brown* and co-edited *The New Deal and the South*. He has also published in the *Journal of Economic History*, the *Journal of Mississippi History*, and the *Wall Street Review of Books*.